The
GOLDEN
SCREEN

The GOLDEN SCREEN

THE MOVIES THAT MADE
ASIAN AMERICA

JEFF YANG

BLACK DOG
& LEVENTHAL
PUBLISHERS
NEW YORK

Cover design by Katie Benezra
Front cover illustration by Toma Nguyen
Back cover photos: Frederic J. Brown (Bong Joon-ho), Everett Collection (Anna May Wong), Everett Collection (John Cho and Kal Penn)
Cover copyright © 2023 by Hachette Book Group, Inc.

Interior illustrations by Toma Nguyen, Jun Cen, Yu-Ming Huang, Ashraf Omar,
barbarian flower, Zi Xu, Cliff Chiang, Cryssy Cheung, Jiyeun Kang

Black Dog & Leventhal Publishers
Hachette Book Group
1290 Avenue of the Americas
New York, NY 10104

www.hachettebookgroup.com
www.blackdogandleventhal.com

First Edition: October 2023

More copyright/permissions information can be found on page 288.

Black Dog & Leventhal Publishers is an imprint of Perseus Books, LLC, a subsidiary of Hachette Book Group, Inc.
The Black Dog & Leventhal Publishers name and logo are trademarks of Hachette Book Group, Inc.

The publisher is not responsible for websites (or their content) that are not owned by the publisher.

The Hachette Speakers Bureau provides a wide range of authors for speaking events.
To find out more, go to www.HachetteSpeakersBureau.com or email HachetteSpeakers@hbgusa.com.

Black Dog & Leventhal books may be purchased in bulk for business, educational, or promotional use. For more information, please contact your local bookseller or the Hachette Book Group Special Markets Department at Special.Markets@hbgusa.com.

Print book interior design by Katie Benezra

Library of Congress Cataloging-in-Publication Data
Names: Yang, Jeff, author.
Title: The golden screen : the movies that made Asian America / Jeff Yang.
Description: First editions. | New York : Black Dog & Leventhal Publishers, 2023. | Includes index. | Summary: "Written by NYT bestselling author Jeff Yang, The Golden Screen is a first-of-its-kind history and celebration of Asian Americans on the big screen. Covering more than 130 films, spanning more than 100 years—from Cecil B. DeMille's 1915 film The Cheat to Wayne Wang's The Joy Luck Club to the Daniels' Everything Everywhere All at Once in 2022—this groundbreaking book explores how these iconic films have shaped how America sees Asians and how Asian Americans see themselves"—Provided by publisher.
Identifiers: LCCN 2022048925 (print) | LCCN 2022048926 (ebook) | ISBN 9780762482221 (hardcover) | ISBN 9780762482238 (ebook)
Subjects: LCSH: Asian Americans in motion pictures. | Motion pictures—United States—Encyclopedias.
Classification: LCC PN1995.9.A77 Y36 2023 (print) | LCC PN1995.9.A77 (ebook) | DDC 791.43/6520395073—dc23/eng/20230110
LC record available at https://lccn.loc.gov/2022048925
LC ebook record available at https://lccn.loc.gov/202204892

ISBN: 978-0-7624-8222-1 (hardcover), 978-0-7624-8223-8 (ebook)

Printed in Malaysia

PCF

10 9 8 7 6 5 4 3 2 1

Contents

Foreword

In *Everything Everywhere All At Once,* the weird, wonderful movie I made with the Daniels [Daniel Kwan and Daniel Scheinert], I played Evelyn Wang, a woman who journeys through a myriad of different universes to ultimately learn more about herself. Looking at the many movies in this book—works of creative minds that span eras and span across the world—it is humbling to realize how many diverse voices there are out there in the world of filmmaking.

When I started acting in Hong Kong, filmmaking was new to me. Ballet had been my life up to that point and action films felt like a good fit for my physicality and love of choreography. I didn't know what to expect, and the industry was booming so fast no one stopped to think about what we couldn't do. Fall off an overpass into a flatbed truck? I did that for *The Stunt Woman*. Ride a motorcycle at high speed onto a moving train? Just another day at work on *Supercop*.

It was when I first went to Hollywood that I realized how special the things we were doing in Hong Kong were. People in Hollywood would ask me: "How did you guys do the visual effects for that motorcycle jumping on the train?" I said, "What visual effects? We did that for real!"

And yet, even though we had much smaller budgets and less technical know-how, we found our own way to tell our stories. As far as representation is concerned: Telling authentic Asian stories was never something we had to *think* about. These stories were our world! We just shrugged and jumped our motorcycles onto the train it took Hollywood decades to eventually board.

After the Broadway-to-big-screen adaptation of *Flower Drum Song* in 1961, three decades passed before *The Joy Luck Club* was produced as the first major studio drama to feature an all-Asian cast. It took another three decades for the next one to be made with *Crazy Rich Asians*. But *Shang-Chi and the Legend of the Ten Rings* quickly followed—and then *Everything Everywhere All At Once*.

I was fortunate to have been a part of these last three breakthroughs, something that was made possible by the emergence of a global community of wonderfully talented filmmakers, writers, and producers, who are finally getting the chance to create content in our own authentic voices and who needed actors like me to bring stories to life. Making films is never easy—it's still not easy today.

But hopefully, the 136 films featured in this book, films that span history, circle the world, and reflect all of the many varied facets of our diaspora, will give the next generation of new filmmakers the inspiration and courage to tell their own diverse and moving stories—expanding our Asian multiverse.

And for those of you reading this because you simply love movies—watching them, sharing them, and talking about them—sit back and enjoy, because the train is leaving the station, the motorcycle is in midair, and you're in for an amazing ride . . . .

—MICHELLE YEOH

Introduction

I always remember the quote that my longtime friend and sometimes collaborator Parry Shen—star of *Better Luck Tomorrow*—frequently shares when asked about why representation on the silver screen matters: "If you see a three-dimensional person, 40 feet tall on-screen, you can't help but fall in love with him or her—and when that figure is accompanied with an Asian face, that begins to change perceptions." He's always attributed it to Maxine Hong Kingston, though I've never been able to hunt down the exact source. (His wife of twenty years, Kim, maintains that Parry made it up to get her to fall in love with him. Hey, it worked!)

Apocryphal or not, it sums up the power of cinema to change hearts and minds, a power that is unique to the medium. Movies are simultaneously intimate and larger than life, a shared yet private experience. In the darkness of the theater, we're enveloped and immersed, yet we retain the agency to bring something of ourselves to what we see on-screen. The truth of a movie emerges at the experiential interface between our memories—our identities—and those flickering, mesmerizing forty-foot-tall images.

For most of Hollywood's existence, Asian Americans have been ghosts at the cinematic feast: invisible in the magic mirror of the silver screen, or reflected only in twisted, toxic, or tasteless fashion. Our stories were so rarely represented with any kind of truthfulness—or even empathy—on the biggest screens that we sought out the smallest crumbs of affirmation that we did exist, as lovers, fighters, heroes, explorers. Most of all, as *humans*.

The importance of seeing ourselves rendered with depth and color and truth wasn't just about yearning for validation. Whether we like it or not,

a big part of who we become is shaped by what we watch. Psychologist Albert Bandura's groundbreaking experiments in the '70s demonstrated the power of "social modeling" via media, in which watching filmed or televised footage encouraged people, especially children, to mimic the behaviors or attitudes they saw. His work also underscored that the more closely a viewer identifies with the "protagonist" of these works, the greater the impact of this social modeling. When you watch media with characters you believe to be like yourself, you're significantly more likely to embrace their beliefs and follow their lead.

So, what did this mean for those growing up in the 1930s, '40s, and '50s—decades in which Asians were depicted in movies almost exclusively as demented buffoons, vicious thugs, alien outsiders, and servile sidekicks to heroic, charismatic non-Asian protagonists?

These representations normalized the treatment of Asians with casual mockery, unwarranted suspicion, social exclusion, and subordination. Among Asians, they contributed to the inclination to passively accept these kinds of abuse, to avoid taking up space, to defer to louder voices, and to discount one's achievements, needs, and value. After all, the larger-than-life pictures on that big screen told them they should. As a result, generations of Asian Americans grew up to be real-life Junes from *The Joy Luck Club*, constantly taking the bad crab instead of the "best quality"—because that's what the media's social modeling made them feel they deserved.

With the arrival of the '60s and '70s, however, glimmers of change appeared on the cinematic horizon. Stars like James Shigeta, Nancy Kwan, George Takei, Miyoshi Umeki, and the one and only Bruce

Lee crashed the gates of Hollywood. A swelling tide of immigrants from Asia—following the end of racist restrictions that put America largely off-limits to those from the so-called Asiatic Barred Zone—brought along with them the burgeoning cinemas of Japan, Hong Kong, and India. These movies featured entire casts full of Asians, albeit ones speaking languages and representing cultures that were often equally foreign to Asians in the US as to their white neighbors.

By the '80s, Asian American independent cinema was in full swing, offering an authentic if low-rent alternative to big-budget studio works. By the '90s, diversity had become an aspirational buzzword, and most multiracial ensemble casts featured an Asian (if rarely more than one), while studios began to tentatively develop stories set in Asia's past, present, and future, and in ethnic immigrant enclaves.

The marking of the millennium saw the first flush of high-profile movies featuring Asian Americans who spoke English, lived acculturated urban or suburban lives, and modeled the social experiences that the majority of US-born-and-raised Asians might find familiar, leading up to the release of a blockbuster that proved to be transformative for the cinematic representation of Asian Americans: 2018's *Crazy Rich Asians*.

After its $240 million global box office take proved there was a large and hungry audience for Asian stories starring English-speaking Asian actors, Hollywood's cynical resistance to such projects seemed to dissipate. Dozens of Asian-forward projects were suddenly greenlit; dozens of other such projects, already in development prior to *Crazy Rich Asians*, were suddenly front-burnered, with an extra zero or two added to their marketing budgets.

Now, half a decade later, a new generation has arrived at prime moviegoing age—though they've grown up watching films on streaming platforms, not in theaters. They have a lifetime's library of Asian and Asian American cinematic works available at the touch of a remote, with more constantly being created and added to the canon, from animated classics to rom-coms, science fiction to spy thrillers, historical fiction, heart-stopping horror, intimate character studies, and dimension-spanning epics.

This book, *The Golden Screen*, is about those movies: the ones that shaped us and shaped how the world saw us. Not all of these works are good—indeed, some of them are barely watchable: Asian stories told by white actors in comically monstrous makeup; propaganda films designed to stimulate rage toward the Asian-faced enemy (both those afar and right next door); tales that showcase unrecognizably grotesque Asian caricatures. The good ones, however, have shown us how our pioneers endured the challenges of the migration across oceans, and how our communities have found common ground with those around us; they've brought to life warriors to cheer for and lovers to ship; they've helped us explore the disturbing shadows of our subconscious and the depths of the gender and generational divides; and they've lifted up the untold stories of our past and present, inserting us into conversations that all too often treat us as silent bystanders. Above all, they've given us hope, inspiration, and of course, endless hours of entertainment.

And this is just the beginning: The narrative plenitude of our communities has still barely been tapped, and the march of our forty-foot-tall figures has only just begun.

Across the Diaspora

FLOWER DRUM SONG · A GREAT WALL · EAT A BOWL OF TEA · FORBIDDEN CITY, USA · HEAVEN AND EARTH · PICTURE BRIDE · THREE SEASONS · LOST IN TRANSLATION · THE GRACE LEE PROJECT · THE NAMESAKE · JOURNEY FROM THE FALL · SEOUL SEARCHING · GHOST IN THE SHELL · THE PROBLEM WITH APU · GO BACK TO CHINA · LUCKY GRANDMA · TIGERTAIL · BLUE BAYOU

"I'm 100 percent Asian and 100 percent American. Or maybe just 200 percent bad at math."
A Talk with **Janet Yang** and **Bao Nguyen**

ILLUSTRATION (OPPOSITE) BY TOMA NGUYEN

One of the most powerful aspects of cinema is how it enables us to reveal the hidden and bring the distant close. Where Asian Americans are concerned, this has sometimes been used to paint our customs, languages, and traditions as exotica, as we've seen in films like *Lost in Translation* and *Ghost in the Shell*, where Asian people and cultures are used in ways that highlight differences and make them weird, alien, and forbidding. But movies also allow people, places, and communities that have been sealed away by closed doors, closed borders—or closed minds—to be brought forward, centered, and seen, in all their myriad complexities.

The vibrantly joyous Chinatown of *Flower Drum Song*, the insular and gossipy one in *Eat a Bowl of Tea*, and the gray and grumpy one in *Lucky Grandma* are each in their own way real and revelatory views of an immigrant-enclave experience that's rarely observed by those who don't reside within these communities.

Movies like *A Great Wall, Seoul Searching, The Namesake, Go Back to China*, and *Tigertail* highlight the cultural disconnect between those on opposite sides of global migration and generational divide.

The many ways in which we arrive across oceans— by boat and by plane, seeking prosperity or fleeing adversity—can be seen in the rich narrative tapestry of films like *Heaven and Earth, Picture Bride*, and *Journey from the Fall*, while the unique and diverse challenges that Asian immigrants (and their off-spring) negotiate in integrating with the new world unfold in films like *The Grace Lee Project, The Problem with Apu*, and *Blue Bayou*.

Together, these movies deepen and enrich our understanding of not just the Asian American experience but also the mixing and migration of peoples across national borders and physical boundaries, and the ways that the foreign slowly evolves toward the familiar.

Flower Drum Song

1961, NOT RATED, 133 MINUTES, UNIVERSAL PICTURES, USA

DIRECTOR: Henry Koster

STARRING: Nancy Kwan, James Shigeta, Miyoshi Umeki, Jack Soo, Benson Fong, Kam Tong, Juanita Hall

WRITER: Joseph Fields

BASED ON THE NOVEL BY CHIN YANG LEE

This adaptation of the hit 1958 Rodgers and Hammerstein Broadway musical was notable for having a virtually all-Asian cast and, if you over-looked its liberal sprinkling of fanciful stereotypes, its familiar and contemporary San Francisco setting. For many viewers, it represented the first time they'd seen *so many Asians* being *so American* on-screen at once—singing, dancing, romancing, and wisecracking in all the sassy, swoonworthy, and slapstick ways that Hollywood made famous. For Asian audiences, it was a transformative experience: proof that we could own the stage, command the spotlight, and be the stars of our own stories, if only given the chance.

In the film, Chinese immigrant Mei Li (Umeki) and her father, the eminent Dr. Han Li (Tong), make their way to America via the cargo hold of a trans-pacific freighter, seeking to marry her off to Wang Ta (Shigeta), the dreamy eldest son of his old friend Master Wang (Fong). Unfortunately, Wang Ta has a dazzling distraction in the form of Linda Low (Kwan), a showgirl at Celestial Gardens nightclub (and the sometime significant other of its owner, Sammy Fong, played with hangdog brilliance by comedian Jack Soo). The multiway love knot untangles itself over the course of a few hours, made brisk by the earworm tunes and bang-up choreography of numbers like Kwan's eye-popping "I Enjoy Being a Girl" and show-stopping "Grant Avenue"; odes to generational and cultural gaps like "The Other Generation" and "Chop Suey"; and hilarious set pieces like "Sunday" and "Don't Marry Me." Over the decades, *Flower Drum Song* has gone from guilty favorite to must-watch classic—though one whose problematic elements continue to be acknowledged.

The songs are dollar-store chinoiserie (save for the camp affectations of "I Enjoy Being a Girl"), and I absolutely loathe how orange is the dominant color scheme. But stumbling across *Flower Drum Song* one night on cable when I was a kid, I was spellbound by the spectacle of Asian Americans singing and dancing, and I still carry a flame for it now. James Shigeta should be in the ranks of the heartthrob canon. Nancy Kwan, in love with her own reflection while clad in a white towel and heels in front of a tripartite mirror, gives us a master class in charisma. Jack Soo's the dude I'd want to get drunk with on tiger bone wine at the Li Po Lounge on Grant Avenue. And I'm forever struck by the perversity of the "Sunday" dream sequence when an Asian American child in cowboy getup mimics a TV screen Western, only for the image to go full-out *Ringu* and break the Fourth Wall in miniature to wreak terror on the nuclear family. The horror of assimilation, indeed!

—ANTHONY KIM ON *FLOWER DRUM SONG*

Reiko Sato and James Shigeta (right)

My immigrant parents adored musicals and played Rodgers and Hammerstein soundtracks continuously, searing the lyrics into my young brain. When *Flower Drum Song* finally appeared on TV, my parents gathered us around the small screen—me in middle school and my three brothers, all around my age. My excitement quickly turned to pubescent embarrassment as sexy Nancy Kwan kicked and strutted with other scantily clad Asian showgirls to such ridiculous lyrics as "Moo goo gai pan." In her next number, wearing only lingerie, she extols being an ultra-femme sex object—something every girl should enjoy—yuck! Counterpoint to her Asian-Americanized hypersexuality was the soft-spoken, compliant, pushover foreigner played by Miyoshi Umeki. With its majority Asian American cast (a feat that would not recur for another thirty years), the film could have opened new narratives but instead reified old ones.

—HELEN ZIA ON *FLOWER DRUM SONG*

Peter Wang, Qinqin Li, Kelvin Han Yee (right)

A Great Wall

1986, PG, 97 MINUTES, ORION CLASSICS, USA

DIRECTOR: Peter Wang

STARRING: Peter Wang, Kelvin Han Yee, Sharon Iwai

WRITERS: Shirley Sun, Peter Wang

Billed as the first American movie to be shot (with permission!) in mainland China, *A Great Wall* is a modest comedy of cultural contrasts, featuring its director Peter Wang as Leo Fang, a Chinese American tech exec who, after smashing his head against Silicon Valley's glass ceiling, decides to take his first trip to his nation of birth since childhood, bringing his very Asian American family—wife, Grace (Iwai), and son, Paul (Yee)—on an extended visit to his sister's family in Beijing. Though its modern-West-meets-traditional-East narrative may come off as quaint today given China's decades of economic transformation, the groundbreaking nature of this film remains evident: It is the rare film to explore differences and disconnects among Asians and Asian Americans with humor and humanity, and without dwelling on displacement and loss.

Eat a Bowl of Tea

1989, PG-13, 102 MINUTES, COLUMBIA PICTURES, USA

DIRECTOR: Wayne Wang

STARRING: Cora Miao, Russell Wong, Victor Wong, Siu-Ming Lau, Eric Tsang

WRITER: Judith Rascoe

BASED ON THE NOVEL BY LOUIS CHU

Set in the years immediately after the end of World War II, this resplendent period film adapts Louis Chu's pioneering novel of the same name, which explores the nearly all-male immigrant "bachelor society" of New York Chinatown—the result of the Chinese Exclusion Act's restrictions against Chinese American men bringing wives or families to join them in the US.

Ben Loy (Russell Wong) is the US-born son of BMIC (Big Man in Chinatown) Wah Gay (Victor Wong, no relation). An army veteran with the legal right via the War Brides Act to bring a wife home from overseas, Ben is pushed by his father to accept an arranged marriage with Mei Oi (Miao), the daughter of Wah Gay's oldest friend, and brings her back with him to New York. Fortunately, Mei Oi is beautiful and willing, and their contractual union seems destined to become a love match, until overbearing pressure from Wah Gay and his Chinatown buddies for the couple to produce an immediate heir causes Ben to become impotent. A confused Mei Oi accuses Ben of not loving her, and the couple drifts apart, paving the way for sleazy gambler Ah Song (Hong Kong funnyman Tsang) to sweep Mei Oi into an illicit liaison. When the affair is discovered and Mei Oi is found to be pregnant—and not sure whether Ben or Ah Song is the father—the teapot of Chinatown society boils over, which only settles when Mei Oi and Ben decide they need to build a life together beyond the prying eyes and wagging tongues of their fathers' generation.

Eat a Bowl of Tea aptly illuminates a unique slice of Chinese immigrant history, without flinching from its harsher aspects, yet it ultimately flies on the wings of its performers: Russell Wong's rakish, goofy charm; Victor Wong's pop-eyed bluster; and Miao's sweet-and-sour innocence.

Russell Wong and Cora Miao

ased on Louis Chu's 1961 novel, *Eat a Bowl of Tea* shows how sex and racist immigration laws make for hostile bedfellows in the postwar Chinese American boudoir. In this comedy of marriage, the third party is the Chinese Exclusion Act. Unable to consummate with all of Chinatown's hopes riding hard on his loins, the community's golden boy Ben Loy (played by an impossibly beautiful Russell Wong with a perfect coif) confesses to his new bride (Cora Miao), "I just feel like everybody's watching us." One thing's for sure: No matter the budget or the gloss of the cinematic joints he found himself in, Victor Wong—here as the cantankerous and screwy patriarch Wah Gay and director Wayne Wang's self-proclaimed on-screen "alter ego"—guaranteed that the rough-hewn, boisterous cacophony of the world beyond the frame was never too far away. Watch for the sequence scored to Japanese American chanteuse Pat Suzuki's slowed and stripped-down cover of "How High the Moon," during which Wang expertly moves us through pathos, suspense, slapstick comedy, and back to pathos all over the course of a song.

—ANTHONY KIM ON *EAT A BOWL OF TEA*

Forbidden City, USA

1989, 56 MINUTES, DEEPFOCUS PRODUCTIONS, USA

DIRECTOR: Arthur Dong

STARRING: Larry Ching, Frances Chun, Charlie Low, Mary Mammon, Toy Yat Mar, Jackie Mei Ling, Dottie Sun, Dorothy Fong Toy, Noel Toy, Tony Wing, Jadin Wong, Paul Wing

WRITERS: Arthur Dong, Lorraine Dong

This documentary by Arthur Dong pulls the curtain back on a fascinating fragment of history that postwar generations have largely forgotten or never encountered: the world of Asian American variety and cabaret performers of the swinging thirties and forties. Centered largely in San Francisco Chinatown, which boasted a half dozen nightclubs featuring live, all-Asian entertainers, none were bigger, brighter, or brassier than Charlie Low's Forbidden City, which packed in crowds by the hundreds nightly. It boasted charismatic players and star attractions aplenty, such as Larry Ching, the "Chinese Frank Sinatra"; Dorothy (Takahashi) Toy and Paul Wing, a married couple billed as the "Chinese Ginger Rogers and Fred Astaire"; singer and dancer Jadin Wong; and burlesque performer Noel Toy, the "Chinese Sally Rand." Forbidden City gave these Asian American performers and many dozens more their first opportunity to perform before enthusiastic crowds—and to get paid for it.

The crowds were mostly non-Asian, drawn in by a combination of curiosity, the lure of the exotic, and naturally, the sex appeal of the City's scantily clad showgirls. But in addition to novelty seekers and mobs of sailors on shore leave, the club boasted celebrity patrons, including Hollywood luminaries Humphrey Bogart, Lauren Bacall, and Bing Crosby; Black icons like Duke Ellington and Lena Horne; and the future governor of California and president of the United States Ronald Reagan. Forbidden City's entertainers got their share of attention in newsreels and magazines and even launched a national tour, bringing their coastal Chinatown glamour to military bases, the small-town Midwest, and the segregated Deep South (the segment when the performers recall whether they ended up choosing "white" or "colored" bathroom options while on the tour is a gut punch). But the prevailing racism of the times prevented most of them from joining the handful of Asians who'd managed to break into Hollywood. For the former performers Dong interviewed for the documentary, Forbidden City was a career highlight, a brief flash of glamour in lives that quickly returned to the

As a young girl, I devoured musicals like *Singin' in the Rain* and *The Music Man*. To me, Gene Kelly, Fred Astaire, and Ginger Rogers were the most glamorous stars to ever grace the silver screen. It wasn't until I saw *Forbidden City, USA*, a documentary directed by Arthur Dong on Forbidden City, an all-Chinese nightclub in 1930s and 1940s San Francisco, that I saw Asian American entertainers from this era, and it blew my mind. Up until this point, I never imagined anyone who looked like me could dance like Fred Astaire and Ginger Rogers.

—NANCY WANG YUEN ON *FORBIDDEN CITY, USA*

ordinary once they became too old for the grueling six-shows-a-week lifestyle. They became supermarket clerks, truck drivers, homemakers, and real estate brokers, whose grandkids might never have learned about the secret histories of their yeyes and nai nais until this documentary came along.

One major Asian American Hollywood star did get his start at Forbidden City: Goro Suzuki, who worked as the revue's emcee under the Chinese-ified name of "Jack Soo." When Rodgers and Hammerstein wrote the musical *Flower Drum Song*, whose antics were largely set at the Celestial Gardens, a fictional Chinatown nightclub inspired by Forbidden City, Soo found himself cast as the Gardens' owner, both in the Broadway run and the subsequent movie. His standout performance in the film set him on a path to becoming one of Hollywood's enduring comic staples, most memorably in the long-running sitcom *Barney Miller*, until he passed away of cancer during the show's fifth season.

A Forbidden City flyer

Heaven and Earth

**1993, R, 140 MINUTES,
WARNER BROS., USA**

DIRECTOR/WRITER: Oliver Stone

STARRING: Tommy Lee Jones, Joan Chen,
Haing S. Ngor, Hiep Thi Le

BASED ON THE MEMOIRS *WHEN HEAVEN AND EARTH CHANGED PLACES* BY LE LY HAYSLIP WITH JAY WURTS AND *CHILD OF WAR, WOMAN OF PEACE* BY LE LY HAYSLIP WITH JAMES HAYSLIP

This biopic inspired by the life story of author and humanitarian Le Ly Hayslip, *Heaven and Earth* stands nearly alone as a Hollywood Vietnam film told from the first-person perspective of a Vietnamese woman. Billed as the third installment in Oliver Stone's "Vietnam War Trilogy," which includes *Platoon* and *Born on the Fourth of July*, it's admittedly the weakest of the three narratively, due in no small part to the contortionist stretch required for a director whose canon is defined by male psychodrama to channel the voice of an Asian female protagonist. (Stone's real self-insert is Steve Butler, the character he created for the movie as Hayslip's white-savior GI husband, played with tragic gravitas by frequent Stone collaborator Jones.) That's too bad, as Hayslip's life story is remarkable and compellingly embodied by first-time actor Hiep Thi Le. Over the course of the film, Hayslip faces repeated brutality at the hands of men, loses her home and loved ones multiple times, yet manages to survive, bring up three sons, and reconnect with the family she left behind in Da Nang. In real life, Hayslip also bridged the gap between two nations with charitable work, establishing foundations that have built school and library networks, extended healthcare to rural Vietnamese villages, and provided hundreds of thousands with emergency relief in times of crisis—though the movie gives short shrift to that aspect of the real-life Hayslip.

Hiep Thi Le

One of my first experiences in a cinema was watching this film with my entire family. Since my parents worked late, there weren't many opportunities for our family to spend time together, so watching a film in a theater was a massive luxury. Barely past the age of ten, the brutal scene of Le Ly Hayslip's character being raped by a Vietnamese soldier shook me to my bones. But I'm fortunate that this scene was not the one that made the most lasting memory on me, as visceral as it was. It was the scene of Hayslip's blue áo dài floating through the endless maze of an American supermarket that dazzled my eyes. For the first time in my life, I saw my mom, who was sitting right next to me, and her story unfolding before my eyes. When I turned to my mom after the credits started rolling, I saw tears streaming down her face. For many reasons, I think she finally realized her story as a Vietnamese refugee now had value.

—BAO NGUYEN ON *HEAVEN AND EARTH*

Picture Bride

1994, PG-13, 94 MINUTES, MIRAMAX, USA

DIRECTOR: Kayo Hatta

STARRING: Youki Kudoh, Akira Takayama, Tamlyn Tomita, Cary-Hiroyuki Tagawa, Kati Kuroda, Toshiro Mifune

WRITERS: Kayo Hatta, Mari Hatta

Youki Kudoh

Set in the early years of Japanese immigration to Hawaii, *Picture Bride* tells the story of Riyo (Kudoh), a sixteen-year-old sent to the territory to meet and marry Matsuji (Takayama), a man whom she'd only seen in a decades-old photograph. Now wed to a man her father's age, Riyo finds herself thrust into the hard life of a plantation worker, cutting sugarcane by day and secretly doing laundry at night hoping to earn enough money to return to Japan. But mentored by an older "picture bride" named Kana (Tomita), Riyo gradually finds her place in the tight-knit society of the cane workers, embracing both her new life and, ultimately, the affections of her husband.

Kudoh is as stunning as the movie's lush Hawaiian backdrop; she and Tomita display lovely sister-worker chemistry in a film that won the Audience Award at Sundance and, for director Hatta, the Independent Spirit Awards' Best First Feature honors. (Sadly, it would also be her last feature: She passed away in 2005, only forty-seven years old, without making another film.) Given that Asian American history is frequently seen through the eyes of men, when seen at all, *Picture Bride* is a remarkable achievement, and deserving of far more attention than it has received.

***P**icture Bride* was one of the few 1990s films that I identified with because the characters looked like me and acted like my family. As it turned out, my connection was deeper than I expected. While I knew Japanese picture brides sought their "matched" husbands only to find much older men than those in the photos, it never occurred to me that my maternal obachan might herself be a picture bride until I saw the film. It made sense. She was eighteen years younger than my ojichan. I left the theater anxious to talk to my mother. She confessed that just like in the movie, her mother was tricked into marrying her father because she saw a much younger photo of him. I was shocked because I was unaware of this, saddened for the life that my obachan had to live, but proud of what she endured. I am grateful that *Picture Bride* helped divulge my own family history!

—RICK NOGUCHI ON *PICTURE BRIDE*

Zoe Bui, as Lan from *Three Seasons*

Three Seasons

1999, PG-13, 104 MINUTES, OCTOBER FILMS, USA/VIETNAM

DIRECTOR: Tony Bui

STARRING: Don Duong, Nguyen Ngoc Hiep, Tran Manh Cuong, Zoe Bui, Nguyen Huu Duoc, Harvey Keitel

WRITERS: Timothy Linh Bui and Tony Bui

Tony Bui's gorgeously shot and lyrically told first feature imbues three interwoven tales of contemporary Vietnam with all the magical realism that cinema has to offer. In one story, a group of girls sells lotus flowers to help support a revered poet who has gone into seclusion after becoming disfigured by leprosy; in another, a cyclo driver named Hai (Duong) seeks to win the heart of a prostitute named Lan (Zoe Bui) by bringing to life her most cherished dream: a full night in an air-conditioned hotel; in the last, a soldier named Hager (Keitel) seeks out the half-Vietnamese daughter he left behind, hoping to apologize and, perhaps, reconnect. The characters meet and interact at the margins of their stories, in both trivial and meaningful ways; taken together, the movie ultimately serves as the director's love letter to the imagined home he left at the age of two and didn't return to until he was an adult. *Three Seasons* won a host of awards, including Sundance's Cinematography Award, Audience Award, and the coveted Grand Jury Prize. It's still quite shocking that this honors haul didn't end up launching Bui's big-screen directorial career; since then, he's made just one more feature film, a 2015 spy thriller called *The Throwaways*.

I was born in Vietnam but left in 1975 as an infant with my parents when Saigon fell. Growing up in America, everything I'd seen on the screen about Vietnam was bathed in bloodshed, combat, and conflict and made by non-Vietnamese filmmakers' "Vietnamese" characters running around in the background spewing incoherent gibberish waiting to be shot. When I watched *Three Seasons*, I saw Vietnamese people as main characters speaking actual Vietnamese and being filmed in Vietnam, not in Asian countries masked to look like Vietnam. It transported me in a way that no prior film had done before. It took us away from the battlefield and into the common yet complex lives of everyday people—graceful scenes of women working on a lotus pond; a seemingly mundane conversation between two cyclo drivers drinking sugarcane juice out of a plastic bag in front of a bright red Coca-Cola ad. Don't get me wrong: The film features tired tropes like poverty, prostitution, and a GI returning to look for his child, but the mastery of storytelling in *Three Seasons* is how it portrays hardships with nuance. This film illustrated the complexity of the human condition with a meditative mood that made me pause, think, and feel, changing how I, as Vietnamese American, felt about my birthplace.

—THAO HA ON *THREE SEASONS*

Lost in Translation

**2003, R, 102 MINUTES,
FOCUS FEATURES, USA**

DIRECTOR/WRITER: Sofia Coppola

STARRING: Bill Murray, Scarlett Johansson,
Giovanni Ribisi, Anna Faris, Fumihiro Hayashi

For white critics and audiences, *Lost in Translation* is a gentle, moving exploration of disconnection and loneliness, of psychological miasma created by the passage of time, the shock of the unfamiliar, and the sense of being an outsider even in one's own life. But for many Asians, Sofia Coppola's critically beloved sophomore feature hits differently. Set in a cartoonishly exaggerated Tokyo, the film turns Japan and Japanese people into a luridly exotic backdrop and comic foil for its white main cast, headlined by Johansson as Charlotte, a young wife pulled along in the wake of her busy and distracted husband, and Murray as Bob Harris, a past-his-prime movie star trying to milk his fading fame for overseas dollars.

While undoubtedly funny, visual gags about how 6'2" Bob towers above the Japanese fellow occupants of an elevator and is unable to use a hotel showerhead because for him it's set at chest level play off the notion that Murray is a human giant among alien Lilliputians. So do constant dialogue jokes about Japanese English speakers unintelligibly switching *L*s and *R*s. Meanwhile, Japanese men are depicted as tech-obsessed, porn-consuming empty suits; Japanese women, as over-the-top fetish queens or voiceless service workers.

ABOVE: Scarlett Johansson and Bill Murray

OPPOSITE: If *Lost in Translation* hadn't leaned into racialized tropes, perhaps it could have accommodated a wider perspective on being an outsider in an unfamiliar world. Here **Jun Cen** imagines a remake of the film featuring a diverse cast and a more humane way of engaging with foreignness.

I struggled while watching *Lost in Translation*. The film is beautifully shot; the scenes of being a stranger in a strange land resonated with me and my 2003 self. A young, talented female director, making a thoughtful film—hooray! Bill Murray and Scarlett Johansson play not-very-likeable characters, but their chemistry and acting drew me into the film. And yet, the film bothered me. The exoticism and otherness of how Tokyo and Japanese people were depicted bothered me. I felt embarrassed at being Asian, of hearing conversation about accents and had flashbacks to now-vague memories of taking offense. It felt sloppy, like Sofia Coppola could have taken more time and care to bring a portrayal of a complicated, beautiful city during a fictional complicated time in the main characters' lives. I haven't watched the film since. I might watch it again.

—THERESA LOONG ON *LOST IN TRANSLATION*

A deeply flawed but beautiful work, *Lost in Translation* plays out as a diary entry for a sensitive young woman venturing out of her comfortable spaces for the first time in her life to find the world is impossibly larger, and emptier, than she could have imagined. I did connect hard with Bill Murray's character, who sees in Scarlett Johansson's Charlotte a reflection of himself at a crossroads, facing the choice to start living again or to continue dying. But the only way to forgive the portrayal of the Japanese in this paean to alienation and loneliness is to consider it all as part of the ingrained bias of its protagonist.

—WALTER CHAW ON *LOST IN TRANSLATION*

Coppola's wandering, Oscar-winning reverie of a screenplay certainly could have depicted a pair of people out of joint with the world around them without leaning so hard on stereotypical tropes and easy humor at foreign expense. But as it is, her portrait of disorientation has a heavy accent on the "Orient."

The Grace Lee Project

2005, 68 MINUTES, WOMEN MAKE MOVIES, USA

DIRECTOR: Grace Lee

What's in a name? Does a common moniker make the people who wear it more homogenous or less unique? This is what one filmmaker, Grace Lee, sets out to discover in this clever documentary, rooted in an Asian in-joke: Most of us know at least one Grace Lee, and maybe more than one. Lee takes it upon herself to hunt down as many other Grace Lees as she can to deconstruct their stereotypically common name and the cliché nice-girl attributes it always seems to invoke. It evolves into something much bigger and more consequential—an examination of immigrant roots, the pressures of assimilation, and the corrosive stereotype of the model minority. After hundreds of interviews, Lee constructs a composite portrait of the "average Grace Lee": Korean American, born in the US and living in California, twenty-five years old, 5'3", with three and a half years of piano lessons and at least one master's degree. But she also highlights the ways that the dozens of Grace Lees she speaks with diverge from the norm and, in some cases, break the mold: They're artists, rebels, iconoclasts, and, as in the case of the doc's most famous Grace Lee, organizers and activists. Lee's interview of pioneering social justice advocate and public intellectual Grace Lee Boggs is a highlight of the film.

The Namesake

2006, PG-13, 122 MINUTES, SEARCHLIGHT PICTURES, USA/INDIA

DIRECTOR: Mira Nair

STARRING: Tabu, Irrfan Khan, Kal Penn, Zuleikha Robinson, Jacinda Barrett, Sebastian Roché, Sahira Nair, Ruma Guha Thakurta, Sabyasachi Chakrabarty, Supriya Devi

WRITER: Sooni Taraporevala

BASED ON THE NOVEL BY JHUMPA LAHIRI

The Namesake is a story about how names define and divide us—shaping the way we're seen and the way we see ourselves. An intimate portrait of the diaspora, vividly told by Mira Nair, it perfectly adapts the bestselling book of the same name by Jhumpa Lahiri. The film follows Ashoke (Khan) and Ashima (Tabu), two Bengali Indians who immigrate to America after their marriage. Though they were paired by arrangement, the match between them works, and they grow to love one another and raise two children, Gogol (Penn) and Sonia (Sahira Nair, the director's niece). As he grows older, Gogol becomes the film's protagonist, struggling under the unusual name that he's been burdened with by his parents—given in honor of the great Russian author Nikolai Gogol because, as we learn later, Ashoke was reading Gogol's short story "The Overcoat" when a train he was riding overturned; the page of the story that a buried and broken Ashoke was clutching is what allowed rescuers to find and save him.

Ashoke's story doesn't comfort Gogol, who pushes himself away from his family and his Indian heritage out of resentment at the choices his parents have made for him without his assent (a feeling that his parents can't understand, given that they weren't even able to choose who to marry). He confronts his culture in his romantic relationships—first with a white woman named Maxine (Barrett), who comes from an archetypal WASP background, and later with an old childhood friend, Moushumi (Robinson), who happens to also be Bengali. But ultimately, neither Maxine nor Moushumi can help Gogol find his complete self; that journey is one he must take on his own, within himself, which he begins when he reads the book of stories written by his namesake, the graduation gift his father had given him that he never opened.

Made for under $10 million and earning over twice that amount, *The Namesake* was both a commercial and a critical success—and a major turning point in the career of its star, Kal Penn, who had, prior to this film, been seen as a purely comic actor. Ironically, it was Penn's perfor-mance in the raucous *Harold and Kumar* buddy comedies that led to his taking the role: His co-star in those films, John Cho, had pushed Penn to read the book, which he fell in love with, and Nair's

Tabu, Kal Penn, and Jacinda Barrett

then-fifteen-year-old son Zohran, a big fan of the *Harold and Kumar* franchise, pushed his mother to cast him in the adaptation.

*T*he Namesake is one of the only films I've ever walked out of the theater while watching—not because it was bad but because it made me weep uncontrollably, and I didn't want to disturb others. In *The Namesake*, when his father Ashoke dies, we see his son Gogol put on his father's wing tips. That detail eviscerated me. I had done that too. A deluge of grief engulfed me, and I was grateful the theater lobby in Georgetown was deserted. I washed my face and anxiously tiptoed back in for the ending, feeling both broken and seen.

—ANNA JOHN ON *THE NAMESAKE*

*W*hen I first read *The Namesake*, it was a life-changing experience because South Asian American novels just didn't exist (much less South Asian American movies). As soon as I was done reading it, I gave it to my mom. It changed our relationship: She saw herself in the story line, and in my reading of the book, she saw herself being seen. I watched the movie adaptation in a special screening at UCLA full of South Asians. I could hear the collective gasps and tears at Brown moments I thought I alone could relate to, making it a truly communal empathy experience. My mother watched the movie on her own and loved it—but not as much as the book, of course.

—TAZ AHMED ON *THE NAMESAKE*

Jayvee Mai The Hiep and Long Nguyen (right)

Journey from the Fall

2006, R, 135 MINUTES,
IMAGINASIAN ENTERTAINMENT, USA

DIRECTOR: Ham Tran

STARRING: Kieu Chinh, Long Nguyen,
Diem Lien, Cat Ly, Nguyen Thai Nguyen

WRITERS: Ham Tran, Lam Nguyen

Tran's startlingly accomplished first feature begins
with the Fall of Saigon in 1975 and, as the title
suggests, follows the journey of a family from the
brutal oppression of the new North Vietnamese com-
munist regime to a new life in America, setting sail in
one of the makeshift refugee boats that took many to
safety and many others to their deaths.

Among the survivors is the Nguyen family: Mai
(Lien), her son Lai (Nguyen Thai Nguyen), and her
mother-in-law Ba Noi (Chinh). They are delivered
from the threat of imprisonment and torture, into a
set of new-world pressures: poverty, cultural alienation, and harsh discrimination. Mai's husband, Long
(Long Nguyen), remains behind even as he sends his
family off on their terrifying trip, held back by his
loyalty to ideals and homeland; imprisoned before he
can set off to rejoin them, he nearly succumbs to his
hellish captivity, until he gets word that they made it
to the US and are alive. He then decides he must risk
escaping—a flight that requires running across an
active minefield. Tran's fictional story shook refugees
who first saw it so deeply that some tried to stop him
from distributing it, to avoid transmitting the trauma

of this history to innocent younger generations. It is fortunate he did distribute it: While any number of films tell the story of US soldiers during the war, few other movies document the Vietnamese experience of the conflict and its aftermath with such power and authenticity.

Seoul Searching

2015, NOT RATED, 105 MINUTES, WONDER VISION, USA/SOUTH KOREA/CHINA

DIRECTOR/WRITER: Benson Lee

STARRING: Justin Chon, Jessika Van, Teo Yoo, Esteban Ahn, Rosalina Lee, Kang Byul, Albert Kong, Cha In-pyo, Nekhebet Juch

Hollywood coming-of-age movies tend to converge on well-worn and universal ground, given how much young adulthood is shaped by surging hormones and halting steps toward independence. But the most interesting expressions of the genre focus on unique situations, locations, and cultural circumstances; *Seoul Searching*, a passion project for director Lee, is a prime example.

For post-immigrant generations of Asians, the "summer culture camp" is a staple means to reconnect with the "motherland." Inspired by Lee's youthful mid-eighties experiences at one such study program, the period comedy follows a group of high schoolers from all over the world—the US, Germany, Mexico, the UK—as they converge in the nation of their shared roots, South Korea, for a program that will immerse them in their ancestral language and enrich their knowledge of Korean culture and heritage. Just kidding! It's an opportunity to make friends, meet cute, and if they're lucky, to get lucky, in the tried-and-true teen-com tradition.

Punky Sid (Chon) and his roommates, buckled-down Korean German Klaus (Yoo) and Korean Mexican lothario Sergio (Ahn), are the trio at the narrative's core. All three match up by movie's end, as Sid connects with rebellious pastor's daughter Grace (Van); Klaus bonds with Kris (Lee), an adoptee searching for her birth parents; and Sergio gets a lesson in respecting women from taekwondo expert Judy (Juch). Lee made it as an homage to John Hughes, maestro of the American coming-of-age movie. But for Asian viewers who blanched at the casual racism of Hughes's movies, *Seoul Searching* was less of an homage than a welcome antidote.

Crystal Kay and Esteban Ahn

Growing up, I never thought of myself as a Korean American. If anything, I purposefully distanced myself from any kind of cultural understanding, so my parents sent me to a summer program in Korea after graduating high school. Until then, it didn't even occur to me that Koreans would live anywhere but Los Angeles. It was amazing to meet Koreans from all over the world speaking with unfamiliar accents. And as different as we all were, it was obvious we all shared a common glitch—that we were all searching for something. My parents hoped the experience would distill in me an appreciation for the motherland they had failed to foster. And it worked. I learned to drink and party harder than any of my friends back home and I even taught myself to read Korean phonetically by going to noraebangs. So to see *Seoul Searching* by director Benson Lee nearly twenty-five years later was a refreshing reminder of my wayward youth. The film articulates the feelings of alienation one suppresses when visiting a foreign motherland, the conflict we feel against parental expectations, the need for acceptance from our peers, the lust for the popular girls, and the envy for the cooler kids—all wrapped in a language I'm acutely fluent in: eighties John Hughes movies and New Wave music. And just like my experience of visiting Korea back then, the film itself is a rite of passage for Asian American stories to be shared in the cinema.

—NICK CHA KIM ON *SEOUL SEARCHING*

Ghost in the Shell

2017, PG-13, 107 MINUTES, PARAMOUNT PICTURES, USA

DIRECTOR: Rupert Sanders

STARRING: Scarlett Johansson, Takeshi Kitano, Michael Pitt, Pilou Asbæk, Chin Han, Juliette Binoche

WRITERS: Jamie Moss, William Wheeler, Ehren Kruger

BASED ON THE MANGA BY MASAMUNE SHIROW

Aloha (2015), *The Great Wall* (2016), and *Doctor Strange* (2016) all represented notorious examples of "whitewashing"—the revisionist casting of white performers in Hollywood movies with clearly delineated Asian settings. *Aloha* cast Emma Stone as a character named Allison Ng; *Doctor Strange* gave the canonically Tibetan (and male) role of the Ancient One to British actress Tilda Swinton. *The Great Wall* inexplicably managed to make Matt Damon the hero of a movie about Chinese people fighting an invading army of dragons. All these choices were called out by advocates and castigated on social media, and they triggered apologies from their creators and performers. But for Asian Americans, this movie was, if you will, the ghost that broke the camel's shell.

Based on a hugely popular anime franchise by visionary director Mamoru Oshii, *Ghost in the Shell* tells the story of a cybernetically enhanced operative, the Major, who leads a counterterrorism unit known as Section 9. In the anime, the Major is Japanese and named Motoko Kusanagi. In the live-action adaptation, the Major is Scarlett Johansson and named Mira Killian. The name change was clearly chosen to make Johansson's casting more plausible, despite the movie's setting in a futuristic Tokyo, replete with moody neon, Japanese gangsters, and murderous robo-geisha. But a bizarre twist in the plot gives away the game: Late in the movie, Killian discovers that her memories have been falsified and that her true identity is . . . Motoko Kusanagi, a murdered Japanese activist whose soul has been digitally pirated and uploaded into a mechanical shell that somehow happens to look exactly like Scarlett Johansson. Intended as an Easter egg for fans of the original, this "race transplant" plot device underscored the ludicrousness of the entire enterprise, while further enraging Asian Americans. The movie ended up an expensive flop and a persistent shadow over Johansson's otherwise brilliant career.

I did not read manga as a kid, but whoa, when I saw the original *Ghost in the Shell* anime in 1995, it blew my mind. *Ghost* was a meditation on existence, technology, terrorism, surveillance capitalism, and what it means to be human—a serious animated film that made me think. The visuals of a futuristic Japan! The haunting music by Yoko Kanno! The cybernetic prosthetics and technology! I loved all the animated iterations of *Ghost*, including its numerous animated series and subsequent films. As a disabled person who considers herself a cyborg, I felt a tenuous kinship with the Major. Which is why seeing her embodied as Scarlett Johansson in the live-action version felt like such a betrayal, multiple times over.

—ALICE WONG ON *GHOST IN THE SHELL*

Rila Fukushima

Hari Kondabolu

The Problem with Apu

2017, NOT RATED, 49 MINUTES, TRUTV, USA

DIRECTOR: Michael Melamedoff

STARRING: Hari Kondabolu, Utkarsh Ambudkar, Aziz Ansari, W. Kamau Bell, Samrat Chakrabarti, Shilpa Dave, Noureen DeWulf, Whoopi Goldberg, Dana Gould, Sakina Jeffrey, Aasif Mandvi, Hasan Minhaj, Vivek Murthy, Ajay Naidu, Aparna Nancherla, John Ortved, Maulik Pancholy, Kal Penn, Russell Peters, John Powers, Mallika Rao, Rohitash Rao, Sheetal Sheth

For fans of the long-running animated hit *The Simpsons*, Apu Nahasapeemapetilon is readily remembered as the Indian owner of the Kwik-E-Mart convenience store. He's a cheery, heavily accented immigrant whose business success is the result of both hard work and absolutely disgusting safety and hygiene practices. But as comedian Hari Kondabolu and a legion of other Desi celebrities highlight in this sharply pointed documentary, Apu represents a confluence of offensive stereotypes that have long been used to mock, diminish, and exclude people of South Asian descent—and the popularity of *The Simpsons* means that it's virtually impossible to escape his shadow. Worse yet? Apu wasn't even being voiced by an Indian American voice actor, having been played by Hank Azaria since the character's 1990 introduction. The controversy over the performance as "animated brownface," spotlighted by this documentary, eventually led Azaria to announce he would no longer voice Apu, prompting a wave of decisions across the animation industry to recast nonwhite characters being played by white actors.

Go Back to China

2019, TV-14, 95 MINUTES, GRAVITAS VENTURES, USA/CHINA

DIRECTOR/WRITER: Emily Ting

STARRING: Anna Akana, Richard Ng, Lynn Chen, Kelly Hu

YouTube creator Anna Akana, in her first movie lead, plays Sasha Li, a recent fashion school grad whose glam LA lifestyle is fueled by remote infusions of cash from her estranged father Teddy (Hong Kong cinema superstar Ng), the Chinese owner of a successful stuffed toy factory. When Sasha finds her credit cards suddenly cut off, Teddy explains to her that the free ride is over: If she wants her trust fund back, she'll need to join him in China and spend a year earning her keep with the family business.

In Shenzhen, Sasha is reconnected with her older half-sister from Teddy's prior marriage, Carol (Chen), and introduced to her younger siblings, who are Teddy's children with his much younger mistress. Despite her awkward relationship with her newfound family, Sasha's bold ideas invigorate his

Lynn Chen (standing left), Anna Akana (center), and Richard Ng

business—before a mistake by Sasha nearly leads the business into economic disaster. Sasha's party-girl friends end up making a suggestion that saves the day, but the experience makes it clear to both Sasha and Carol that if they want to preserve any kind of relationship with their father, they can't be dependent on him for survival.

Ting's sophomore feature is assured and authentic, offering up a gently comic warts-and-all glimpse at the dynamics of modern Asian families divided by diaspora. And there's a real joy in seeing the intergenerational, transpacific chemistry between Akana, a sparkling product of America's digital landscape, and vintage Cantonese movie star Ng, with his trademark hangdog look and grumpy bark recalling the heyday of Hong Kong comedy.

Lucky Grandma

2019, NOT RATED, 87 MINUTES, GOOD DEED ENTERTAINMENT, USA

DIRECTOR: Sasie Sealy

STARRING: Tsai Chin, Hsiao-Yuan Ha, Michael Tow, Woody Fu, Eddie Yu, Mason Yam

WRITERS: Banban Cheng, Sasie Sealy

Powered by the force of nature that is Tsai Chin, *Lucky Grandma* brings to life a particular tribe of Chinatown residents, those leather-tough elders of uncertain age who plow through crowds shoulder first, gleefully engage in vices from gambling to chain-smoking with seemingly zero repercussions, and command respect from everyone around them

Tsai Chin

because they've been around forever and probably will be decades into the future. Chin's character, known only as Grandma, sees auspicious signs all around her and decides to head to Atlantic City to test her fortune, as one does; while the casino doesn't pay off, the sudden death of her seatmate on the bus ride back and the briefcase full of cash that ends up in her arms as a result certainly seems like a lucky windfall—until she discovers that the money is the stolen property of a Chinatown gang. Naturally,

Grandma's choice isn't to return it but to hire a "security guard" from a rival gang to keep her safe. While she finds herself unexpectedly bonding with the oversized lug they assigned as her detail, Big Pong (Ha), Grandma's luck can't last forever. Or can it? Shot on a million-dollar budget—won via the annual minority filmmaker pitch competition run by the Tribeca Festival—*Lucky Grandma* feels much bigger, in no small part because of Chin's outsized and indelible performance.

*L*ucky Grandma is the kind of movie I never knew I needed until I saw it. A one-of-a-kind crime comedy with a cranky Chinese nai nai as its antihero. Its next-generation representation of AAPI culture goes well beyond the well-trodden immigrant story or kung fu flick. And can we talk about the sly, irascible slow-cigarette-burn performance of octogenarian star Tsai Chin? The sixty-year veteran of stage and screen must've had so much fun playing the world-weary, "I'm too old for this sh*t" elder. Can we have more movies like this please?!

—DAN WU ON *LUCKY GRANDMA*

Tigertail

2020, PG, 91 MINUTES, NETFLIX, USA

DIRECTOR/WRITER: Alan Yang

STARRING: Tzi Ma, Christine Ko, Hayden Szeto, Hong-Chi Lee, Kunjue Li, Fiona Fu, Kuei-Mei Yang, James Saito, Joan Chen, Zhi-Hao Yang, Yo-Hsing Fang

In his directorial debut, producer and television writer Alan Yang tells a story loosely based on his father's life, which began in a small town in Taiwan called Huwei (literally "tiger tail"). Yang notes that obtaining his tiger dad's tale proved to be a challenge: Like many immigrants, Yang's father was resistant to sharing his past, and it was only over time and late in life that his full history came out. As a result, the fictionalized *Tigertail* ends up being not just a biopic but a musing on the psychic walls that prevent generations from communicating, and on the slow path to coming to terms with and sharing the secrets of the past.

Born into a poor family, after the death of his father, a boy named Pin-jui (Zhi-Hao Yang) is sent to live with his grandparents in the rice-farming rural outskirts of his province. It's in the idyllic countryside that Pin-jui meets a girl named Yuan, with whom he forms an instant bond. After being called back to Huwei, however, they lose touch, until they reunite as young adults, beginning a hot-blooded romance. But the adult Pin-jui (Lee) is a blue-collar factory worker, and grown-up Yuan (Fang) is the privileged daughter of a wealthy family, a class divide that Pin-jui believes dooms their relationship. After his mother suffers an accident, the only possible path forward for Pin-jui seems to be the deal proposed by the factory boss: Marry his quiet daughter, Zhenzhen (Li), in exchange for the boss helping the newlywed couple immigrate to America. Pin-jui accepts the offer and leaves Huwei with Zhenzhen, too heartbroken to even say goodbye to Yuan. The couple have a daughter, Angela (Ko), but Pin-jui is as unable to communicate with her as he is with Zhenzhen. It takes a brief reunion with Yuan, his long-lost love, to finally convince Pin-jui to open up to his child and tell her about his past. The question that lingers behind *Tigertail*'s unfolding tapestry: How many other such stories have gone untold among our elders, and how many have been lost forever as a result?

Blue Bayou

2021, R, 117 MINUTES, UNIVERSAL PICTURES HOME ENTERTAINMENT, USA

DIRECTOR/WRITER: Justin Chon

STARRING: Justin Chon, Alicia Vikander, Mark O'Brien, Linh Dan Pham, Sydney Kowalske, Vondie Curtis-Hall, Emory Cohen

This film was one of the first to bring the Korean adoptee story to the big screen in narrative fashion, and it created a whiplash eruption of acclaim and backlash—the latter rooted in concerns that the fictionalized narrative failed to properly acknowledge the real-life adoptees whose stories inspired it. The movie itself is a gripping, emotional work, in part due to incredible performances by Chon, Vikander, and the movie's entire supporting cast.

Antonio LeBlanc (Chon) is a fitfully employed ex-con, barely making ends meet for his family as a tattoo artist; we learn that his criminal record, his functional illiteracy, and the systemic racism of his surroundings have conspired to plant him

Sydney Kowalske (top), Justin Chon, and Alicia Vikander

permanently in Louisiana's underclass. After being taunted into a fight and brutally arrested by New Orleans cops Denny (Cohen) and Ace (O'Brien)—the latter being the jealous biological father of Antonio's young stepdaughter—Antonio is told that his adoptive parents never had him naturalized as a US citizen, and his criminal recidivism has led his case to be transferred to ICE. Horrified at the thought of leaving his family behind, he seeks out high-powered legal help but is quoted a price that's well beyond his meager income. A desperate Antonio participates in another crime to make the money for his defense, but in the process triggers a chain of events that puts him at risk of losing everything. The movie's climax is a gut punch, but not one without real-life precedent: After the final fade to black, Chon unveils a scrolling montage of actual transnational adoptees who were never naturalized and were deported as a result, along with shocking statistics about the phenomenon from the Adoptee Rights Campaign.

> **P**eople who make films about being Asian American tend to be upper middle class and college educated, and the stories that they tell tend to come from their experiences. So I appreciate that Justin Chon tells stories about messed-up people with messed-up lives, and that he digs into issues that often go unexplored. I love that he used his platform to tell an overlooked and untold story of undocumented adoptees. This is not *Crazy Rich Asians*. This is the opposite of the model minority. And to me, that made this movie very refreshing.
>
> —JENNIFER 8. LEE ON *BLUE BAYOU*

"I'm 100 percent Asian and 100 percent American. Or maybe just 200 percent bad at math."

A Talk with **Janet Yang** and **Bao Nguyen**

Asian ethnic enclaves are thriving sites of cultural fusion and laboratories for social change, providing a first home for new immigrants and serving as the staging ground through which fads, food, and entertainment from Asia—including cinema—have arrived in the US and eventually get discovered by wider audiences. In this Q&A, filmmaker Bao Nguyen (*Be Water*) and producer and Motion Picture Academy president Janet Yang (*The Joy Luck Club*) discuss the inherently transnational nature of Asian American identity, the ways that their storytelling journeys have stretched across oceans, and the global future of Asian American cinema.

How did you end up making movies that focused on the connections between Asian communities across oceans?

JANET YANG: My parents had come to the US from China in the mid-1940s to study as grad students, but right in the middle of their education, the revolution happened, and they had no real choice but to stay. I was the youngest of their three kids, so I had a little less pressure from my parents to pursue a respectable profession, like doctor or lawyer. And I was always a bit of a seeker—someone looking for hidden truths, whether in religion, or romance, or storytelling. Then in 1972, after Nixon opened up relations, China put out the message that Chinese Americans should visit their relatives "back home."

My mother worked at the United Nations at the time, and the ambassador from China gathered up all UN employees of Chinese descent and said, "Seriously, guys, you can come. Please. We're not these scary monsters." So, we took this trip, and that was my introduction to China. I became obsessed with finding out more about my heritage, ended up majoring in China studies in college, and a professor got me a job that brought me back to Beijing. I arrived during a real period of transition—I literally watched as giant portraits of Marx and Lenin and Stalin were being taken down from walls. And while this was happening, I was meeting all these now-famous movie directors. I realized growing up I hadn't known the name of a single Chinese filmmaker; these artists just didn't exist in our American world. When I got back to the US, I started organizing Chinese film festivals. That led to me running a company in San Francisco that was trying to become the first distributor of mainland Chinese films in North America. From there, I went to work for Universal, and worked with Spielberg, and then ran Oliver Stone's production company—I'd met him while organizing film festivals. The rest is history.

BAO NGUYEN: For me, I had a head start on a lot of my peers, as far as developing a kind of borderless sensibility. My parents had come to the US from Vietnam as part of the second wave of boat people in the late 1970s, but I began visiting Vietnam regularly when I was only nine years old. I feel like a lot of my Vietnamese American peers only went back for the first time in their twenties, so they had sort of a fully formed version of who they were as artists by the time they first "went back." Transpacific movement has deeply informed my identity as a filmmaker—I moved to Vietnam after school and worked on my first film productions out there. I ended up staying there for seven years. And I hate to always bring Bruce Lee into the conversation, but that's one of the things that attracted me to his story and prompted me to make *Be Water*—because I felt like we had a similarity as two people who "went back" to the ancestral homeland to establish our careers.

What convinced you that there was an opportunity to make global stories?

JANET: Yeah, well, I certainly wasn't motivated by money! When I first got to China, I saw how films were shown out in the countryside: People would be sitting in fields, watching movies projected on sheets that were hung up on poles. It was really funny to watch everyone rush into China in the decades that followed, having been there from the very beginning. But the truth is, long before the "China market" became something that filmmakers wanted to go after, and long before most people in the US even realized that mainland China made movies, I knew there was an opportunity. Because I saw how Chinese audiences were stirred—how they laughed and cried and shouted the same way American audiences did. And when I first watched Chinese movies, I was moved by the stories they were telling too. It underscored for me how movies create a connection that supersedes culture. We get distracted these days by the politics and economics that surround the industry, but to me, it's just that simple: Movies show us what it means to be human.

BAO: When you're in America, America feels like the center of the universe. But when you get what James Baldwin called "critical distance" from America, it helps you realize there are other markets and other creative industries, and they are equally vital and essential. I went to Vietnam to work on my first narrative feature—*Saigon Electric*— as cinematographer for Stephane Gauger, a fellow Vietnamese American director. Before that, I'd only done shorts and documentaries. My entry point into fiction filmmaking was on a transnational production, with a crew made up of both Vietnamese and Vietnamese Americans. Anderson Le, who runs the Hawaii International Film Festival, was one of the executive producers. Ham Tran, who made *Journey from the Fall*, helped edit the movie. After that, we all just kept working on each other's films. And then when Stephane passed away in 2018, we

founded a production company in his memory, East Films, that's focused on making transpacific movies bridging Southeast Asia and the US. *Be Water* was one of the first films that East coproduced, followed by Ham Tran's *Maika*.

But the truth is, it's still hard to convince people that stories can cross boundaries of language and culture, isn't it?

JANET: Absolutely. Take *The Joy Luck Club*—it was based on this huge bestseller, a beloved book, but if it wasn't for Jeffrey Katzenberg at Disney, who had the vision to accept that it could be a movie, it might never have been made. Everyone else had passed on it. And even then, no one knew how to market it. There was no attempt to outreach to Asian Americans—they didn't even think we were a targetable demographic. They just put the movie out and aimed all their marketing at the so-called mainstream. So no ads in Chinese media. No attempt to rally community organizations. Social media didn't exist. It was just: Do your ads, do your trailer, cross your fingers, hope for the best.

BAO: It's hard whichever side of the ocean you're on. When I was living in Vietnam, I realized that no matter how long I stayed there I was never going to be fully accepted as Vietnamese, because being Vietnamese American, being Asian American, is a distinct identity. The diaspora has a different viewpoint from the mother country. I want to say that as an Asian American I'm 100 percent Asian and I'm 100 percent American. Or maybe just 200 percent bad at math.

Do you think that it's harder for stories set in diasporic communities to get "mainstream" respect?

JANET: Well, let's put it this way—we got great reviews, we had people watching it multiple times, walking in with tissues because they knew they were going to cry. We made a critically acclaimed, commercially successful movie without having to put a bunch of white people in it. We had an acclaimed director, an Oscar-winning screenwriter, all our wonderful actresses—Tsai Chin, who delivered a performance for the ages!—and still the film didn't get nominated for anything. But my observation is that social change occurs very slowly, and then all at once. You have to build up a wave of pressure behind the dam before the floodgates open. Back then, having an all-Asian cast and bilingual dialogue was seen as a handicap. Today, all the kids want to watch Asian movies, and they want to watch them with subtitles.

BAO: That's because there's a certain authenticity to watching films in their original language. I can't stand watching dubbed films—I have to watch subtitled movies, even when I can't understand the language in which the film is made. And I think it's because diaspora communities have seen people appropriate our culture in so many ways, so all we can hear when those dubbed English voices hit our ears is the sound of our culture becoming commoditized. I go back to Bong Joon-ho talking about how "Once you overcome the one-inch-tall barrier of subtitles, you will be introduced to so many more amazing films" as he accepted the best foreign film Oscar for *Parasite*. That, to me, is the basic entry point for respect: being willing to watch a movie in its original language, even if that means reading it. Like, *Parasite* is basically a perfect movie. I can't imagine watching it in any other way.

What do you think the future holds for transnational filmmaking? At one point, it felt like making movies across borders was the inevitable future—particularly for Asian Americans. That seems much farther off now.

JANET: Where China is concerned, it's an understatement to say that relations are currently "challenged." But this isn't the first time this has happened. In the 1980s, I spent all my time going back and forth between the US and China, building bridges between the movie industry here and there. And then at the end of that decade, everything froze. So, I focused on learning how to make global movies in Hollywood and trying to get Asian American movies made, and then a decade later, everyone was talking about China again . . . until they weren't. I've had my heart broken multiple times already. Right now, the anti-Chinese propaganda is so strong here and anti-American propaganda is so strong over there; who wants to swim in those waters? And yet we can only hope for the best, or at least for better.

BAO: I grew up watching cinema from all over the world. I even lived in Italy for a brief period and studied Italian neorealist cinema. They weren't making those films thinking of global audiences, yet those movies are classics of global cinema. What makes them universal is their honesty and authenticity, their sense of intimacy through specificity. The future of transnational filmmaking won't be about pandering to American tastes or to the demands of other big regional markets. It's going to be about incubating unconventional voices and unique stories, and then bringing those to the world. You can't create great films with focus groups; there's no passion in art that's made like that, and if there's one thing that translates across borders, it's passion.

As far as Asian Americans are concerned, there's a generation coming up that's looking to create new worlds without being beholden to history. Ocean Vuong often talks about how we're often expected to be tour guides of our own trauma. Well, I'm tired of how every time you see "Vietnam" in a headline, people assume it's referring to the war, something that's not true for Germany or Korea. In 2014 I shot and produced *Nuoc 2030*, a dystopian SF feature about a near future when most of the southern part of Vietnam is underwater. After one screening, an older white gentleman stood up and asked, "Why isn't there any mention of Agent Orange in your film?" It just boggles the mind how much Americans always want to recenter things around their experiences. That's why in Vietnam we call it the American War.

2

Crossed Cultures

THE CRIMSON KIMONO · STAR TREK VI: THE
UNDISCOVERED COUNTRY · THE GOONIES · MISSISSIPPI
MASALA · TOMORROW NEVER DIES · RUSH HOUR ·
BEND IT LIKE BECKHAM · ROBOT STORIES · HAROLD AND
KUMAR GO TO WHITE CASTLE · UP · THE BIG SICK ·
BE WATER · THE ETERNALS · AFTER YANG

"When we bond, we flow together."
A Talk with **Daniel Kwan** and **Diane Paragas**

ILLUSTRATION (OPPOSITE) BY TOMA NGUYEN

For much of Hollywood's history, Asian American cinematic representation was either all, none, or one. There are indie films and occasional studio movies set in Asian countries or ethnic neighborhoods that offer the opportunity for a cast consisting of all or nearly all Asian performers. There are the vast bulk of motion pictures that simply pretended Asians didn't exist as a demographic, even in dense urban areas. And then there are those movies in which a single token Asian appears, inserted for diversity or comic relief. What has largely been missing are films in which Asians are showcased as full peers with people of other circumstances, in ways that allow the exploration of cultural contrasts and human commonalities.

When these rare pairings do occur, they're sometimes romantic, as in *The Crimson Kimono*, *Mississippi Masala*, and *The Big Sick*; they're sometimes professional, like in *Rush Hour* and *Tomorrow Never Dies*; they sometimes showcase bonds of unlikely friendship, as in *The Goonies, Bend It Like Beckham*, and—in one of the rare team-ups featuring Asian protagonists of different ethnicities—*Harold and Kumar Go to White Castle*; and sometimes they focus on the deep bonds of the family we choose, as in *Up* and *After Yang*.

Together, they demonstrate a reality that the great Bruce Lee may have spoken to best: "You know what I want to think of myself? As a human being. Because . . . under the sky, under the heavens, there is but one family. It just so happens that people are different."

The Crimson Kimono

1959, NOT RATED, 82 MINUTES, COLUMBIA PICTURES, USA

DIRECTOR/WRITER: Samuel Fuller

STARRING: Victoria Shaw, Glenn Corbett, James Shigeta

A groundbreaking movie that takes a remarkably complex approach to exploring race in America, this frequently overlooked noir from auteur Sam Fuller stars James Shigeta in his cinematic debut—prior to this film, the Hawaiian-born, third-generation Japanese American, unable to break into Hollywood, moved to Tokyo and had become a popular singer and musical theater performer whom the media dubbed the "Frank Sinatra of Japan."

The Crimson Kimono proved Shigeta was more than capable of commanding the big screen, starring as Detective Joe Kojaku, an LA cop tasked with investigating the murder of a showgirl performing at a Little Tokyo burlesque theater. He and his white partner, Detective Sergeant Charlie Bancroft (Corbett), uncover a key witness, student artist Christine Downs (Shaw); as the two protect her from the murderer's attempts on her life, they both are increasingly attracted to her. With Downs clearly preferring Kojaku, tension grows between the friends, finally exploding when the two find themselves competing against one another in a kendo tournament. Kojaku attacks Bancroft aggressively; in a heated conversation afterward, Bancroft flashes Kojaku a look that the latter interprets as disgust at the idea of a white woman being attracted to an Asian man.

The revelation that his longtime friend harbors secret racist feelings disillusions Kojaku, who resolves to quit the force, despite Bancroft's protests that his look was driven by envy, not bigotry. Later, Kojaku discovers that a similar misinterpretation was the trigger for the murder the pair had been investigating, and attempts to reconcile with Bancroft, but the latter admits that his jealousy over Downs will always stand between them. The film ends with an interracial kiss between Kojaku and Downs, which back then was lurid enough that it became the focus of the movie's sensational (and wildly misleading) marketing campaign: The film's poster tagline was "Yes, this is a beautiful American girl in the arms of a Japanese boy!"

When I saw *The Crimson Kimono* during my years living on the East Coast, the footage of Nisei Week and East First Street storefronts made me homesick, because much of the action is set in LA's Little Tokyo, a place that's been central to my family's life for a century—the scene at the Nisei soldier memorial in Evergreen Cemetery still chokes me up. Meanwhile, Shigeta is a heartthrob who doesn't merely challenge the stereotype of the unappealing Asian male, he demolishes it. American screen culture that demonizes and emasculates Asians has always been at odds with the real world. Here, the Nisei detective thrashes his white partner at kendo, he's the one who solves the case—and he gets the girl in the end! It's an upside-down world, and I'm so here for it.

—RENEE TAJIMA-PEÑA ON *THE CRIMSON KIMONO*

Victoria Shaw and James Shigeta

Leonard Nimoy and William Shatner

Star Trek VI: The Undiscovered Country

1991, PG, 110 MINUTES, PARAMOUNT PICTURES, USA

DIRECTOR: Nicholas Meyer

STARRING: William Shatner, Leonard Nimoy, DeForest Kelley, James Doohan, Walter Koenig, Nichelle Nichols, George Takei, Kim Cattrall, David Warner, Christopher Plummer

WRITERS: Nicholas Meyer, Denny Martin Flinn

Space: the final frontier. To boldly go where no man has gone before. The cultural influence of *Star Trek* is so broad today it's hard to imagine that the original series lasted just seventy-nine episodes across three seasons—two years shorter than the USS *Enterprise*'s stated "five-year mission." A decade after it aired its last episode, the franchise was revived through *Star Trek: The Motion Picture*, fulfilling the dreams of a legion of *Trek* fans who'd kept the Federation torch burning for a generation. Five direct sequels would follow, of which this was the final one to feature the original crew and cast. For Asian American fans of the franchise, however, *Star Trek VI* represented a transformative moment.

When the series was first introduced in 1966, with its defiantly utopian representation of a racially integrated future focused on peaceful scientific discovery (and the occasional phaser battle), Sulu (the iconic George Takei) was one of the few non-stereotypical Asian representations on network TV. But Sulu was the ship's helmsman, navigating but never commanding. From its earliest moments, *The*

Undiscovered Country showcased Hikaru Sulu for the first time as the captain of his *own* starship, the USS *Excelsior*. Sulu's vessel happens to be the first to discover that the longtime nemesis of the Federation, the Klingon Empire, has been put at existential risk by an interplanetary catastrophe, forcing it to petition for peace. Not everyone agrees with the decision to bring the half-century-long war to an end; a secret attempt to sabotage negotiations and assassinate the Federation President is revealed and ultimately thwarted by the joint efforts of Captains Kirk (Shatner) and Sulu. The final moments of the movie truly go where no prior installment has gone before, as Kirk, a famously bombastic presence both on and off camera, salutes his fellow captain as a peer.

The Goonies

**1985, PG, 114 MINUTES,
WARNER BROS., USA**

DIRECTOR: Richard Donner

STARRING: Sean Astin, Josh Brolin, Jeff Cohen, Corey Feldman, Kerri Green, Martha Plimpton, Ke Huy Quan

WRITER: Chris Columbus

Goofy, raucous, blissfully innocent, and barely coherent, *The Goonies* could easily have been scripted by a backyard full of eight-year-olds. Instead, it was the brainchild of Steven Spielberg, which naturally meant that it was (a) greenlit immediately and (b) a giant hit, making $125 million, over six times its $19 million budget. The eponymous Goonies are five kids—Mikey (Astin), his big brother Brandon (Brolin), loquacious Mouth (Feldman), awkward Chunk (Cohen), and, in his second big-screen performance, Ke Huy Quan as Richard "Data" Wang, an aspiring inventor whose home-brewed gadgets work slightly better in his mind than in reality. Together with Brandon's crush Andy (Green), the crew goes on a gleeful adventure through the underground wilds of Astoria, Oregon, seeking the lost treasure of One-Eyed Willy, evading both the pirate's deadly traps and the Fratellis, a family of local thugs hunting for the same hoard. After a roller-coaster ride of thrills, surprises, and disappointments, the kids return home in one piece, with just enough of Willy's wealth to save their neighborhood, the Goon Docks, from foreclosure.

While each member of the gang has a starring moment, there's no question that Data and his gizmos—the Suction Belt! The Pinchers of Power! The Bully Blinders! The Slick Shoes! The Pop-Out Boxing

The whole *Goonies* gang is great fun, but for Asian Americans, the real star of the show was Ke Huy Kwan as Data—the guy with the gear and the plan, even if neither worked quite the way he intended. Here (opposite) **Yu-Ming Huang** imagines what the movie might have looked like with our hero front and center.

Ke Huy Quan (left), Sean Astin, Josh Brolin, Corey Feldman, Jeff Cohen

I spent so much of my childhood reenacting scenes from *The Goonies*. I truffle-shuffled in front of the mirror, walked the plank off the diving board, "swam" in the bathtub searching for pennies. I channeled Mikey when I used my inhaler, and Brandon when I got rid of my training wheels. Andy taught me how to kiss with my eyes closed. I still hear Mama's voice in my head every time I "hit puree!" on my blender. But of course it was Data and his family I related to the most. I couldn't believe he was so respected for his inventions and adventurous spirit. That he had a little sister who looked like me and a father he spoke Cantonese with—as a child of the eighties, that gave me hope that I, too, could feel accepted in my mostly white American town.

—LYNN CHEN ON *THE GOONIES*

Glove!—play an outsized role in both the success of the quest and the movie's fun. Sadly, despite its huge success, this essentially marked the end of Quan's career as a child star; the lack of available roles led him to retire as an actor—only returning to the big screen nearly four decades later, in 2022's *Everything Everywhere All at Once.*

Mississippi Masala

1991, R, 118 MINUTES, JANUS FILMS, USA

DIRECTOR: Mira Nair

STARRING: Denzel Washington, Roshan Seth, Sarita Choudhury, Charles S. Dutton, Joe Seneca, Sharmila Tagore

WRITER: Sooni Taraporevala

Rarely have the fault lines of race, nationality, and culture been explored with as much subtlety, grace, and heat as in Mira Nair's sophomore feature, a

Sarita Choudhury and Denzel Washington

It was our third date—I, a Bangladeshi Angeleno obsessed with rom-coms, and he, a Black Muslim convert obsessed with kung fu. We had met organizing a Muslim poetry night and we were tentatively feeling each other out in an awkward cultural exchange. Would I enjoy the bean pie he made for me? Would he enjoy this Muslim punk band I was into? For this date, we decided *Mississippi Masala* was the perfect movie-watching compromise—romance, politics, economic struggles, coming-of-age trope. I was the Sarita to his Denzel. At the time, movies would always have the Desi girls fall for the white boy as a rebellion to parents, or Desi girls would fall for the Desi boy version of Holden Caulfield. It's silly to say that watching *Mississippi Masala* like that together on that date night helped us imagine a possibility where we could exist, but it kind of did.

—TAZ AHMED ON *MISSISSIPPI MASALA*

charming and brainy romantic drama enlivened by fantastic performances by Denzel Washington, newcomer Sarita Choudhury, and a supporting cast of veterans of Hollywood, Bollywood, and the British film industry.

Set in the seventies, after Ugandan dictator Idi Amin declared that he was "returning Uganda to the ethnic Ugandans" and forcibly expelled eighty thousand Asian Indians from the country, *Mississippi Masala* focuses on Jay (Seth), his wife Kinnu (Tagore), and their daughter Mina (Choudhury), who end up settling in Greenwood, Mississippi, helping their relatives operate a chain of motels along the Delta. After Mina literally bumps into carpet-cleaning entrepreneur Demetrius (Washington)—a fender bender serves as their meet-cute—the pair slowly begin to fall for one another, sending rumbles through both communities and triggering rage in Mina's father, whose memories of the family's treatment under Amin has fostered in him a buried antipathy toward Black people. The couple decide to flee the state to be together and seem to find both freedom to love and freedom from hate—albeit in a form that feels elliptical and symbolic, dancing together alone in a Mississippi cotton field. That the lovers' fate remains open seems intentional; as Washington's Demetrius says to Mina, "Racism gets passed down like recipes. The trick is, you gotta know what to eat and what to leave on your plate. Otherwise, you'll be mad forever," to which Mina has the very Asian response, "And you'll never eat." In *Mississippi Masala*, director Nair serves up a banquet.

Tomorrow Never Dies

1997, PG-13, 119 MINUTES, UNITED ARTISTS, USA

DIRECTOR: Roger Spottiswoode

STARRING: Pierce Brosnan, Jonathan Pryce, Michelle Yeoh, Teri Hatcher, Joe Don Baker, Judi Dench

WRITER: Bruce Feirstein

There are Bond girls who are mostly eye candy, there are Bond girls designed primarily as plot devices to spur Bond into action, and rarely, there are Bond girls who are neither Bond's nor "girls"—they're agents with full agency, incredible competency, and the effortless capability of taking on the bad guys or Bond himself as needed. The top of *that* list? Michelle Yeoh's Wai Lin.

Yeoh plays a Chinese operative sent to help 007 prevent World War III after media baron Elliot Carver (Pryce) triggers a superpower nuclear

When Pierce Brosnan took over as Bond in 1995, he seemed like he could handle warfare, weapons, women, and words—e.g., the bare minimum to be 007. But he couldn't handle Wai Lin: Michelle Yeoh, playing Bond's Chinese counterpart, was more than his equal. In both hand-to-hand combat and strategic thinking, she flat-out kicked his ass. Yeoh was in control, physically tough, and super sexy all at once. And she looked like me! Well, only in the being-a-Chinese-woman department—I'm not like her character in most of the other ways. But neither are the guys who are obsessed with Bond. In the twenty-five years since *Tomorrow Never Dies*, Yeoh continues to be the best Bond co-star that ever was.

—CYNTHIA WANG ON *TOMORROW NEVER DIES*

Pierce Brosnan and Michelle Yeoh

showdown to boost his cable news ratings. There isn't a scene in which Yeoh appears where she doesn't make you wonder why she's not the top-billed name in the film, most notably her solo bike-shop fight against a gang of thugs and the motorcycle chase scene in which she copilots the cycle while handcuffed to Bond and facing backward. Just turn off the film before the final mandatory "Oh, James" scene, where Wai Lin implausibly falls for Bond's charms, despite outwitting, outfighting, and outdoing him at every turn. At one point MGM floated a spin-off franchise focused on Wai Lin, but scheduling and budget-balking ended those plans before they began. Action fans are the poorer for it.

Chris Tucker and Jackie Chan

Rush Hour

**1998, PG-13, 98 MINUTES,
NEW LINE CINEMA, USA**

DIRECTOR: Brett Ratner

STARRING: Jackie Chan, Chris Tucker, Tzi Ma,
Tom Wilkinson, Ken Leung, Elizabeth Peña,
Mark Rolston, Rex Linn, Julia Hsu

WRITER: Jim Kouf

Rush Hour wasn't the first time that Hong Kong superstar Jackie Chan attempted to break into the US market—a feat the king of comedy kung fu always saw as his ultimate challenge. He'd made a handful of middling stabs at crossing over in the eighties, in the form of *The Big Brawl* (1980), Burt Reynolds's

wacky racer comedy *The Cannonball Run* (1981), and *The Protector* (1985); none of them delivered him the respect or financial reward Chan felt he deserved.

For the next decade, Chan rejected other Hollywood entreaties, instead building his own unique library of films that includes some of the greatest action classics in history, while establishing himself as an action hero who'd risk every bone in his body if it meant he'd surprise and delight his fans. By the time director Brett Ratner called him with the pitch for *Rush Hour*, Chan was well into his forties and largely resigned to only being one of the most visible and popular stars in the entire rest of the world beyond America. But Ratner was persistent and assured Chan that pairing him up with a Black comic actor—martial arts plus motormouth—was the formula that would finally win over US audiences. Ratner was right: Though far from Chan's best, his team-up with Chris Tucker grossed over $140 million in the US, setting the scene for two hit sequels (and counting).

Chan plays Detective Inspector Lee of the Royal Hong Kong Police, sent to investigate cultural treasures that have been stolen during the former colony's reunification with China. The trail leads him to Los Angeles and a plot to kidnap Soo Yung (Hsu), daughter of the head of LA's Chinese consulate (Ma). Lee and his LAPD "partner," Detective James Carter (Tucker), must overcome their cultural divide, their mutual antipathy, and a secret conspiracy within the consulate itself to save Soo Yung and US-China relations. In the process, they affirmed how martial arts cinema in the US represents a shared pop culture obsession for both Black and Asian audiences.

Bend It Like Beckham

2002, PG-13, 112 MINUTES, SEARCHLIGHT PICTURES, UK

DIRECTOR: Gurinder Chadha

STARRING: Parminder Nagra, Keira Knightley, Jonathan Rhys Meyers, Anupam Kher, Juliet Stevenson, Shaznay Lewis, Archie Panjabi

WRITERS: Gurinder Chadha, Guljit Bindra, Paul Mayeda Berges

Parminder Nagra and Keira Knightley

There's a committed fandom around *Bend It Like Beckham* that stretches well beyond the love that people have for those cast members who've gone on to major stardom, like Keira Knightley and Jonathan Rhys Meyers. That's because Gurinder Chadha's delightful follow-up to *Bhaji on the Beach* (1993) and *What's Cooking?* (2000) scores a hat trick on issues of race, gender, and sexual orientation, while treating the subject of its premise—women's football—with respect and enthusiasm.

As football-loving Jess, who hides her passion and talent for the sport from her traditional parents, Parminder Nagra shines. But it's her chemistry with fellow femme footballer Jules (Knightley) that makes the film sing, to the point where it's not exactly surprising that Jess and Jules mistakenly suspect the two are lesbians—Jess and Jules are a much more convincing couple than Jess and actual love interest Joe (Meyers), coach of the women's amateur football team to which both belong, the Hounslow Harriers. But then again, after plenty of family interference, fibs, false assumptions, and football, football, football, it's Jess and Jules who fly off together at the movie's end (having both earned scholarships to play football, er, soccer at the University of Southern California). Knightley has gone on record saying that there should have been a sequel where Jess and Jules end up together, so who knows where the story truly ends?

We do—in our imaginations.

Tamlyn Tomita

Robot Stories

2003, NOT RATED, 85 MINUTES, PAK FILM, USA

DIRECTOR/WRITER: Greg Pak

STARRING: Tamlyn Tomita, James Saito, Wai Ching Ho, Greg Pak, Sab Shimono

This debut feature from director Greg Pak—a quartet of thematically aligned short films—has proven to be well ahead of its time, both in its ideas and the angle it takes in exploring them. The stories here are about robots, yes, but it's more delicately about the thin line between intelligent machines and humanity, tracing out territory that later works—from TV series like *Black Mirror*, *Humans*, and *Love, Death, and Robots* to films like *Her*, *Ex Machina*, and *After Yang*—would mine in depth. In "My Robot Baby," Marcia (Tomita) is challenged with taking care of a robot baby to "qualify" for adopting a human one. In "The Robot Fixer," Bernice (Ho) finds a path to accepting her son's imminent death by completing his broken collection of toy robots. In "Machine Love," a robot office worker named Archie (Pak), shunned by his human coworkers, finds connection (and maybe more) in the form of a female office robot he sees through a window in the building facing his. And in "Clay," an old and dying sculptor (Shimono) is asked to consider eternal life as a virtual being but resists the temptation, recognizing that the very limitations of human senses and mortality are in some ways a gift. A subtle facet of each of the stories is metaphorically emphasizing the alienating experience of being a visibly different outsider in a world that ignores or erases your priorities and agendas—making the *Robot Stories* a quintessentially Asian American film, and perhaps underappreciated as much as its director and cast.

Harold and Kumar Go to White Castle

**2004, R, 88 MINUTES,
NEW LINE CINEMA, USA**

DIRECTOR: Danny Leiner

STARRING: John Cho, Kal Penn,
Neil Patrick Harris

WRITERS: Jon Hurwitz, Hayden Schlossberg

Fans of *Harold and Kumar* inevitably wonder how the film's white creators, Jon Hurwitz and Hayden Schlossberg, created a pair of characters who feel so true to the Asian American experience: Harold and Kumar spar over the lameness of Asian college organization parties! Harold worries about being called out as a Twinkie—"yellow on the outside, white on the inside"! There are references to *The Joy Luck Club* and—Easter egg!—*Better Luck Tomorrow*! The answer, of course, is that relentlessly buckled-down investment banker Harold Lee (Cho) and pre-med rebel Kumar Patel (Penn) are based on actual high school buddies of Hurwitz and Schlossberg. True story: Over time, the real-life Harold Lee met and became fast friends with his doppelgänger Cho. But it's not just its surprising cultural authenticity that makes *Harold and Kumar* special; it's the combination of that realness with the absolute surrealness of the setting and story in which they're planted.

After Patel convinces his roommate Lee to indulge in their favorite hobby, getting extremely stoned, the duo decides to seek out the ultimate panacea for the munchies—a rack of White Castle sliders. The ensuing on-the-road movie forces the pair to overcome enraged raccoons, even more enraged immigrant parents, weird mutants, annoying friends, police brutality, an escaped cheetah, and Neil Patrick Harris. Along the way to its destination, the movie manages to both normalize diversity and disrupt every expectation of it, blending the genuinely progressive and wildly offensive into a slurry that is as shockingly affecting as it is frequently hilarious. In the process, it gave a boost to the rising careers of John Cho and Kal Penn, who'd go on to be two of the highest profile and most reliably interesting Asian American performers of their generation.

John Cho and Kal Penn

What second-gen East Asian among us hasn't gotten super-baked with their Desi roommate to watch *Harold and Kumar*, resulting in a moment of weed epiphany where you realize that the movie mirrors the Asian diaspora and its endless absurd quest to access the Castle of White Privilege? Forget *Crazy Rich Asians*—this movie was the diaspora's first truly satisfying, self-aware Asian-led mainstream comedy that showed us that if you let go of your need for a movie to be as smart as your parents think you should be and embrace for just one night the experience of being Asian burnouts taking a break from overachieving for capitalism, you could laugh your ass off with your best homie.

—TZE MING MOK ON *HAROLD AND KUMAR GO TO WHITE CASTLE*

When *Harold and Kumar* came out, I was there opening night. Kal Penn was already a household name for us, thanks to his work in the pass-the-videotape-around-to-my-high-school-Indian-friends cult classic *American Desi*, and so I celebrated seeing one of the first times I'd ever seen an Indian American in a Hollywood leading role. As one of those Desi kids who was actively in the process of trying to figure out how to tell her parents she didn't want to be a doctor, this stoner comedy was deeply validating. We got to see Indian kids like us being f*ck-ups and rebelling. We got to see them make the jokes, instead of being the butt of them. It was nothing short of cathartic.

—PREETI CHHIBBER ON *HAROLD AND KUMAR GO TO WHITE CASTLE*

Up

**2009, PG, 96 MINUTES,
WALT DISNEY STUDIOS, USA**

DIRECTOR: Pete Docter

STARRING: Ed Asner, Jordan Nagai,
Christopher Plummer, Bob Peterson

WRITERS: Pete Docter, Bob Peterson

There's something beautiful about how deeply weird and firmly grounded this Pixar film is—perhaps because its premise is loosely inspired by a pair of real-life stories: The first is that of "Lawnchair Larry" Walters, the truck driver who attached dozens of weather balloons to a folding patio chair and flew a forty-minute flight, sixteen thousand feet into the sky, until he was able to safely land by shooting balloons one by one with a pellet gun. The second is the story of eighty-four-year-old Seattle resident Edith Macefield, who refused to sell her tiny one-story home to developers, forcing them to build over and around it instead. Docter and the rest of the Pixar brain trust saw something brilliant in the pairing of Walters's absurd aspiration of escapist flight and Macefield's steadfast refusal to move, and created *Up*, the story of an old man named Carl Fredricksen (Asner), who uses balloons to float his entire home into the sky in the hopes of flying it to South America.

The trip is a posthumous homage to his wife, Ellie, who passed away before ever getting to see the continent both had always dreamed of visiting. But Carl finds an unexpected stowaway: an Asian American Wilderness Explorer named Russell (Nagai), who's persistently been seeking a way to help Carl so he can earn his "Assisting the Elderly" merit badge. Russell's eight-year-old innocence and excitement play brilliantly off Carl's dour and cranky bitterness, which comes in part from the recognition that Russell represents another wish Carl was never able to fulfill for Ellie: having a child of their own.

It's a Pixar movie, so as you might expect, by the end of their journey—which requires them to first defeat a murderously obsessed explorer and then save an endangered species of giant bird—Carl has embraced Russell as a proxy son, Russell has gotten his merit badge and a brand-new grandpa figure, and Asian Americans kids have received the gift of a character who reflects their identity in moving, but unassuming, fashion. Russell is Asian, but that fact is never really mentioned or addressed; he's just . . . a kid. Which, for kids who've grown up rarely seeing themselves on-screen, is sometimes enough. (Why did Docter make Russell Asian American? Because in personality and appearance, he's based on Russell Jang, Docter's real next-door neighbor and his son's best friend.)

The Big Sick

2017, R, 120 MINUTES, AMAZON STUDIOS, USA

DIRECTOR: Michael Showalter

STARRING: Kumail Nanjiani, Zoe Kazan, Holly Hunter, Ray Romano

WRITERS: Emily V. Gordon, Kumail Nanjiani

Cowritten by Nanjiani and his wife, Emily V. Gordon, and based on the actual story of how they met and matched, *The Big Sick* was nominated for an Oscar for Best Original Screenplay, while wowing critics and becoming one of the most successful independent films of 2017. It's at its core both a love story and a tale of how deeply relationships are shaped by family memories, expectations, and aspirations.

Kumail Nanjiani plays his younger self, a child of successful Pakistani immigrants who's dodging the LSATs and driving for Uber while trying to break through as a stand-up comedian. His parents

Zoe Kazan and Kumail Nanjiani

are okay with his weird show business dreams but want him to settle down with a nice young Pakistani woman and are constantly trying to set him up for dates with perfectly nice options. But fate has different plans: After a show, Kumail talks to a lovely young lady heckler, and the two end up having a one-night stand, which stumbles toward becoming something more. But Kumail's anxieties about whether his parents will accept his having a relationship with a white woman (spoiler: they won't) end up torpedoing their budding romance. What rekindles it is the darkest of circumstances—a friend of Emily's calls out of the blue to let him know that she's been hospitalized with a disease severe enough to require she be put into a medically induced coma. With no easy choices, Kumail signs off on the permission form allowing Emily to be put under, then contacts her parents (Romano and Hunter), whom he's never met before and who know the two have already broken up. Nevertheless, the shared experience of

> This movie is about something that could have been a tragedy, and pulling it off with humor and nuance while deftly handling interracial and interfaith differences is why Kumail Nanjiani and Emily Gordon were nominated for an Academy Award. On a side note, I also love how the movie shows what it's like to be a struggling stand-up. *The Big Sick* really shows the truth of what it was like for Kumail to be a South Asian Muslim man trying to make it as a comedian without having to lean into ethnic material.
>
> —JENNIFER 8. LEE ON *THE BIG SICK*

Bao Nguyen

caring for and worrying about Emily brings the three of them together. Secrets are revealed, parental confrontations occur, and Kumail comes to the realization that Emily is the one for whom he's destined.

He also remembers something important that proves to be the key to unlocking Emily's sickness and triggering her recovery, but just because she's well doesn't mean she wants Kumail back. Yet the ending ends up a happy one: Emily sees a video of Kumail's train wreck of a stand-up audition, in which he explains his feelings for her, and is moved enough to hunt him down in New York—reconnecting with him as they'd first met, by heckling him during one of his shows. The story itself is extraordinary; the acting, including by Nanjiani, who demonstrates an easy charm worthy of a romantic comedy lead, takes it to another level and makes you wonder if Nanjiani and Gordon's life together has paved the way for any sequels to this satisfying tale.

Be Water

2020, NOT RATED, 105 MINUTES, ESPN, USA

DIRECTOR: Bao Nguyen

There have been numerous attempts, both narrative and nonfiction, at Bruceography—that is to say, telling the story of Lee Jun-Fan, known to most as Bruce Lee (or "the Dragon" if you're nasty). Bao Nguyen's *Be Water* is an exceptional entry in the genre, telling the story of Lee's birth, struggles, triumphs, and untimely demise with a particular focus on issues of race, representation, and identity.

Born in San Francisco but relocating to Hong Kong just a few months later, Lee was a child actor, a juvenile delinquent, and a self-trained ballroom dancer who won the Cha-Cha Championship of Hong Kong as a teen, months before heading to America for college. But he was also the son of a famed Cantonese opera performer, which provided him with his entrée both into show business and the world of martial arts. His father introduced him to Wing Chun grandmaster Ip Man, who would become Lee's teacher and lifelong mentor; Lee's exceptional passion and aptitude for kung fu provided him with a means of sustaining himself in the US, teaching fighting skills first in Seattle while attending the University of Washington and then in San Francisco, where he began to gain fame for his free-flowing, open-minded approach to both the practice of martial arts—which would shape the development of his own proprietary technique, Jeet Kune Do—and racial inclusion, based on his willingness to accept all comers as students. The latter raised the ire of other kung fu teachers, but Lee scoffed at their assertions that only Chinese should be allowed to learn these skills.

As Nguyen's documentary points out, Lee saw martial arts as a natural point of solidarity between the Black and Asian communities, since they were initially developed as a tool of resistance and self-protection against oppression. One of Lee's first students and most trusted friends, Jesse Glover, had shared with him his own experiences with police brutality, shaping Lee's desire to reach out and teach other African Americans, including Hall of Fame NBA star Kareem Abdul-Jabbar, whom Lee would cast in his unfinished final work, *Game of Death* (completed posthumously and released in 1978). But as the documentary notes, Lee had firsthand brushes with racism as well, both on the streets of Hong Kong, where he was frequently bullied and pulled into brawls as a child of quarter-European

I love how *Be Water* explores Bruce Lee's impact across race and time. I've watched the film multiple times with different people, and I always enjoy seeing the range of their reactions. I will never forget that because of him, when we first immigrated to the US in the eighties, a little boy in South Carolina innocently asked my mom, "Are you Bruce Lee's sister?" Sure, it's a question that leans into stereotype, but for those of us who grew up in small towns in the places like the American South, it shows how Bruce gave us some kind of anchor for cultural recognition. Because of him, even in places where we were all alone, we weren't.

—MOMO CHANG ON *BE WATER*

(From left) Kumail Nanjiani, Lauren Ridloff, Ma Dong-seok, Angelina Jolie, Richard Madden, Salma Hayek, Gemma Chan, Lia McHugh, Brian Tyree Henry, Barry Keoghan

The Eternals

ancestry, and among the gatekeepers of Hollywood, who diminished him, denied him opportunity, and dismissed his vision—when they weren't stealing it for projects showcasing white actors, most notably the 1970s TV series *Kung Fu*, which cast David Carradine, who was neither Asian nor a martial artist, as its Asian lead over Lee. Drawing from a rich trove of archival material, interviews with contemporaries and family, and considerable footage of the man himself, some of which has only recently been uncovered, the documentary is a complex portrait of a man whose depths continue to be plumbed, and a sweeping record of his legacy, showing how his influence stretches beyond pop culture and into the worlds of social justice and global activism.

2021, PG-13, 156 MINUTES, WALT DISNEY STUDIOS, USA

DIRECTOR: Chloé Zhao

STARRING: Gemma Chan, Richard Madden, Kumail Nanjiani, Lia McHugh, Brian Tyree Henry, Lauren Ridloff, Barry Keoghan, Don Lee, Harish Patel, Kit Harington, Salma Hayek, Angelina Jolie

WRITERS: Chloé Zhao, Patrick Burleigh, Ryan Firpo

> I usually get bored pretty quickly when I watch Marvel movies, but *The Eternals* is a refreshing change from the standard bombastic Spandex-hero product, no doubt because of director Chloé Zhao's ethereal cinematic vision. Although the film underperformed at the box office, I really like its New Agey faux-Greek mythology aesthetic, subdued color palette, and stately pace, as well as its angsty emo characters. Not unlike *Rogue One: A Star Wars Story*, which also featured the most culturally and ethnically diverse cast of its franchises, *The Eternals* has a completely different vibe from its sibling films in the Marvel universe. But I thought Don Lee and Angelina Jolie's relationship was oddly muted, in comparison to Gemma Chan and Richard Madden, who were all about the skinship. And I was very let down when—spoiler!—they killed off Gilgamesh, because Don Lee deserves better. It just goes to show that even in the twenty-first century, Hollywood is still a bit frightened of Asian men as lovers or as heroes.
>
> **—VALERIE SOE ON *THE ETERNALS***

Greater in scope, cast, and running length than all but the two halves of the Avengers "Infinity Gauntlet" arc, *The Eternals* is wildly ambitious—a story of gods, not heroes, beginning in 5000 BC and ending in the present day. Its premise is complicated and, for anyone who'd been following Marvel's Spandex-clad superhero adventures until that point, somewhat problematic: It establishes that even as Earth's Mightiest Heroes have spent twenty-five or so movies saving the planet, and sometimes the universe, from existential threats, there were actually even mightier heroes lurking *right beneath their eyes*, refusing to participate in the relatively trivial conflicts of mortals and demigods in favor of working day jobs, raising families, baking bread, or sulking in various wilderness compounds. But the emergence of an even more existential threat, a group of interstellar predators known only as the Deviants, rouses the Eternals—Ajak (Hayek), Sersi (Chan), Ikaris (Madden), Kingo (Nanjiani), Sprite (McHugh), Phastos (Henry), Makkari (Ridloff), Druig (Keoghan), Gilgamesh (Lee), and Thena (Jolie)—from hiding. We learn that the Eternals are emissaries of the Celestials, sent to exterminate the Deviants, a corrupted wave of earlier Celestial creations who seek to ravage planets that support sapient life.

But the shocking murder of the Eternals' original leader Ajak soon reveals a new set of truths:

> I'm a fan of basically every movie and TV show from the Marvel Cinematic Universe, so I was thrilled to learn that there was going to be a big new story that featured a diverse cast, including Gemma Chan as the lead Sersi, and Kumail Nanjiani and Don Lee as Kingo and Gilgamesh, with Chloé Zhao as the director. *The Eternals* did not disappoint; I thrilled to see how each of the roles allowed the actors to do what they do best: Sersi showing empathy and heart, Gilgamesh demonstrating strength and loyalty, Kingo offering infectious, fun-loving bravado. When the sequels emerge as inevitably as Celestials being born from the depths of a planet, I'll be first in line to cheer for all my favorite Asian American superheroes, hoping that one day they'll join up with Shang-Chi, Katy, and Wong for an epic night of karaoke.
>
> **—LORI LOPEZ ON *THE ETERNALS***

The Eternals weren't sent to protect humans but to cultivate them for their psychic energies, feeding the embryonic Celestial seeded at the Earth's core until it is ready to hatch and shatter the planet. Having fallen in love with Earth and its inhabitants, all but one of the Eternals choose to rebel against the cosmic cycle, leading to an epic final intrafamily battle.

The Eternals is aesthetically and tonally as different as one can imagine from the rest of Marvel's canon, thanks to director Chloé Zhao's unique eye and storytelling ethos. The film's visual grandeur is undeniable, and the inclusive casting is inspiring. It features several firsts for Marvel: its first openly LGBTQ character (Henry), one of its small handful of characters played by Latin actors (Hayek), its first disabled superhero to be played by a disabled actor (Ridloff, who is deaf and communicates via ASL), and, of course, three Asian ensemble leads in Gemma Chan, Don Lee, and Kumail Nanjiani. Chan, who assumes leadership of the Eternals upon Ajak's death, is the movie's heart, but Lee and Nanjiani are delightful in their smaller turns as Thena's bearlike protector Gilgamesh and the gleefully narcissistic Kingo, respectively. Those asking why the first twenty or so Marvel movies were so overwhelmingly white now have their answer: An immortal set of mostly nonwhite heroes were there all along—they were just waiting for their turn in the spotlight.

After Yang

2022, PG, 96 MINUTES, A24, USA

DIRECTOR: Kogonada

STARRING: Colin Farrell, Jodie Turner-Smith, Justin H. Min, Malea Emma Tjandrawidjaja, Haley Lu Richardson

WRITER: Kogonada

BASED ON THE SHORT STORY "SAYING GOODBYE TO YANG" BY ALEXANDER WEINSTEIN

At first glance, it's hard to know what to make of mononymic director Kogonada's sophomore feature; it opens with a giggle-inducing montage featuring the main cast and, apparently, other families around the movie's world doing a synchronized dance routine in a kind of global interactive competition, which ends when Yang (Min), the elder son of the family, seems to lose control of himself. We later learn that Yang is a robot, and a secondhand one at that, purchased to serve as an "elder brother" for Jake (Farrell) and Kyra (Turner-Smith)'s adoptive daughter, Mika (Tjandrawidjaja). Something has

> **T**his movie debuted right after I'd lost my aunt Lorna to cancer. She helped raise me in the formative years of my life, and her death, along with my grandmother's passing two years prior, was a huge blow to our family. These losses, the COVID pandemic, and a globe plagued with social and political volatility fed a grief in me that at the time I did not know how to navigate or comprehend. This poetic reflection on loss and mourning didn't exactly show me how to navigate grief, but it helped me realize that it's okay to feel it.
>
> **—DINO-RAY RAMOS ON *AFTER YANG***

gone wrong in his operating system, and if he can't be repaired, he'll rapidly decompose. Jake, a tea leaf vendor by trade, sets off to get Yang fixed, leading him to discover things about his recycled "son" that he couldn't possibly have imagined.

As he unlocks Yang's memory bank and reviews archival footage of both the family and the world beyond the family, Jake learns that Yang spent his free hours with a young woman named Ada (Richardson). After speaking to Ada, Jake tracks down Yang's prior owner, who points Jake to an even deeper level in Yang's archives—unlocking memories of Yang's life with another woman named Ada, who turns out to be the younger Ada's great-aunt. All these revelations force Jake and Kyra to reconsider how human their

robot son was, and whether they'd treated him as truly "one of them."

Min's affectless yet somehow deeply expressive performance as Yang is a standout, bringing sharper lines to the film's hazy philosophical drift. Yang and his human sister Mika both being Asian makes the question of who gets to be perceived as human that much more charged. Is Yang's humanity more in question because of his Asian appearance? What of Mika, a war orphan who's been transracially and transnationally adopted? Was she, too, seen by their parents as a commodity, secured like Yang to play the role of Jake and Kyra's child? It's proof of the film's power that these questions keep rippling long after its final credits.

"When we bond, we flow together."

A Talk with **Daniel Kwan** and **Diane Paragas**

For decades, nearly every studio movie featuring an Asian main character featured a cross-cultural couple or transnational team-up, in part because this was Hollywood's go-to way of minimizing risk by maximizing potential audiences. But in the process, these films have created indelible pairings and exposed unexpected truths about how people of different backgrounds can find unlikely common ground. In this Q&A, filmmakers Daniel Kwan (with Daniel Scheinert, codirector of *Everything Everywhere All at Once*) and Diane Paragas (*Yellow Rose*) share their thoughts on what it's like to tell stories that cut across racial and ethnic boundaries.

It feels like the game has changed for Asian Americans, in terms of the kinds of stories we're "allowed" to tell on-screen.

DANIEL KWAN: We are obviously standing on the shoulders of giants who blew open doors—the most recent one being *Crazy Rich Asians*, which not only inspired Ke Huy Quan to come back to acting, but which also made our film viable in the marketplace. *Crazy Rich Asians* blew open the door for us. Our movie, *Everything Everywhere All at Once*, just kind of snuck in afterward to represent the Weird Asians. It was suddenly possible for us to put stranger, alternative layers of what an Asian can be on-screen.

DIANE PARAGAS: I started pitching the story for *Yellow Rose* a decade and a half ago, telling people I wanted to create this story about an undocumented Asian woman immigrant who dreams of singing country-western music. And people just looked at me blankly and said, "What are you talking about?" Everyone tells you to "write what you know," and I did, and then everyone said no. So, I put it aside for a long time and focused on directing more commercial projects. But then I saw Mira Nair talking at the Toronto International Film Festival, and she was saying how when she stopped making films about South Asians, those movies just stopped getting made. That made me feel an obligation to go back and do this film. This time I went to the Filipino community and ended up financing the entire film 100 percent through Filipino money. It was such a different experience.

Feeling free to be yourself—even the weirdest version of yourself—is such a liberating thing.

DANIEL: Filmmaking saved my life. For the longest time, I felt like Evelyn—that this is the worst version of me. I was the worst Boy Scout. I was the worst soccer player on my team, which was the worst soccer team in town. It was my mom who told me I should go into filmmaking. She saw I was a really good storyteller and eventually she told me, "Maybe you should make movies." Later I found out a friend of a friend of hers, who was a Christian soothsayer, had come up to her and was like, "Your son is going to become a very famous filmmaker one day, and he's going to spread the word of God." [Laughs.] Hey, it's not too late! My career is just beginning!

DIANE: Well, for me, it took going out and being unafraid to be "weird" to get Hollywood to pay attention! Sony Pictures stepped in to release what we'd made. That felt symbolic of a tide that was changing. I started meeting people, and getting attached to different projects, some of which had all-white casts. But I often still feel like I'm the sore thumb, you know? I'll still be in boardrooms where it's just me and eighteen powerful white people in this room, and I'm explaining to them things that are like "So here's what it feels like to be a multiracial Asian woman."

Being Asian American has historically been an obstacle for creatives—in the sense that it's put us in a box, or forced us to choose between our identity or our art.

DANIEL: Well, I didn't have the intention when I was starting out of "representing my people." I had such trouble even thinking of myself as a director that I kind of let that part of me fall to the wayside, you know? But when I met my directing partner Daniel Scheinert, he'd been good at everything he'd ever done. And he's good at recognizing what's interesting about a person and trying to cultivate and protect it. He was the one who pushed me to star in the music video we made for "Turn Down for What." He said, "No one else dances like you! It needs to be you!" And he was so adamant that he overcame my resistance. I was concerned that people just did not want to see an Asian guy in a Lil Jon hip-hop video. Having that nice straight white male ego wrapped around me was the perfect way for me to gain the confidence to understand that I actually belong.

DIANE: I've seen so many people who are very talented face that *Sophie's Choice* moment in their careers where they had to decide *Am I going to stick to my guns and tell this very personal and intimate story for me, or am I going to pay my rent?* It's a hard choice to make financially and professionally. And I was lucky, because I was making a decent living as a commercial director—I had the privilege to be able to wait to tell the story I wanted. But my career would have been very different if somebody had said yes earlier. What has made the difference has been seeing Asian executives on the studio and production side. It feels a lot less like you're on your own, trying to convince a jury that's not your peers, you know?

It shows how people from different cultural contexts bring different things to the table.

DANIEL: Absolutely. In some ways Scheinert and I are like water, which—science!—is made up of hydrogen and oxygen. On our own, we're totally different and potentially explosive, but when we bond, we flow together. The stuff we create together is way more interesting and maybe more resilient than the things we'd create ourselves.

DIANE: *Yellow Rose* is focused on a story that's about an older white man mentoring a younger Asian female in a musical genre that has by and large been only safe and open for people like him. That was a tricky story line to navigate, because in many ways it was an aspirational fable. But aspirational fables are common in country music. I think the key to us was emphasizing empathy, and showing white characters that are allies, not saviors. A critical step in our evolution is when someone sees us as more than just our race or our gender, but as a talent, and reaches out with an open hand.

A lot of what you've done in your work has been to break down walls between worlds.

DIANE: I grew up in Lubbock, Texas, and I was that girl trying to make my eyes big and wanting to be blond. That was me looking in the mirror and feeling like I didn't want to be in this body or have this face—that's how I grew up. I just wanted to escape everything. I wanted to escape myself. And music was what got me through it. But when I wrote *Yellow Rose*, I realized it was about a character who *didn't* want to escape—who wanted to stay in the world where she already was. Like, sometimes walls give us comfort, you know? They keep the roof up over our head. So what I ended up doing was showing all these shots of her shoes by the door. To me, that was a shorthand for constantly having to move. I love how much of an Asian American shorthand it is for us, to see an image of shoes by a door.

DANIEL: For me, breaking down barriers is what making change is about. I hope we get to keep doing it, and I hope we've inspired other people to do it. It reminds me of something my mom used to say to me all the time: "The way things are isn't how they have to be." That was a very terrifying thing to hear as a kid, but now as an adult, it's very freeing.

3

Fists of Fury

SEVEN SAMURAI · COME DRINK WITH ME · ENTER THE DRAGON · THEY CALL ME BRUCE? · THE KARATE KID · A BETTER TOMORROW · DRAGON: THE BRUCE LEE STORY · THE MATRIX · CROUCHING TIGER, HIDDEN DRAGON · ONG BAK: THE THAI WARRIOR · KUNG FU HUSTLE · IP MAN · THE RAID: REDEMPTION · ROGUE ONE: A STAR WARS STORY · THE PAPER TIGERS · MORTAL KOMBAT · SNAKE EYES · SHANG-CHI AND THE LEGEND OF THE TEN RINGS · RRR

"Anything worth doing is kung fu."
A Talk with **Ronny Chieng** and **Daniel Wu**

ILLUSTRATION (OPPOSITE) BY TOMA NGUYEN

Poison fists and silent blades in the night, bone-shattering kicks, and impossible acrobatic feats. Many Asian Americans grew up immersed in the world of martial arts cinema, absorbing the classics in the laps of immigrant parents, and then hungrily seeking out badly reproduced and poorly subtitled examples of the canon wherever we could find them.

There are stories of the sword like *Seven Samurai, Come Drink with Me, Crouching Tiger, Hidden Dragon*; tales of closed fist and open hand, from kung fu classics like *Enter the Dragon* and *Ip Man*; works featuring a kaleidoscope of other combat styles like *Ong Bak: The Thai Warrior*'s Muay Thai and *The Raid: Redemption*'s Pencak Silat. The elasticity of martial arts as a genre allows it to extend into comedy, in works like *Kung Fu Hustle* and *The Paper Tigers*; superhero fantasy, as in *Mortal Kombat, Shang-Chi and the Legend of the Ten Rings, Snake Eyes*, and the epic Indian historical fiction film *RRR*; and even science fiction, through the *Matrix* franchise and *Rogue One: A Star Wars Story*.

But as much as we love martial arts films, we can't help but occasionally cringe at the microaggressions others direct at us because of them—the chop-socky gestures and wild screeches we experience as schoolyard taunts—and the more macro aggressions that follow when taunts escalate into bullying demands to demonstrate our (presumably inborn) fighting skills. Yet the films remain an indelible part of our heritage, and a persistently beloved element in our popular culture. If martial arts can continue to exist in movies alongside starships and laser blasters, we can assume they'll be with us forever.

Seven Samurai

1954, NOT RATED, 207 MINUTES, TOHO COMPANY, JAPAN

DIRECTOR: Akira Kurosawa

STARRING: Toshiro Mifune, Takashi Shimura, Keiko Tsushima, Isao Kimura, Daisuke Kato, Seiji Miyaguchi, Yoshio Inaba, Minoru Chiaki, Kamatari Fujiwara, Kokuten Kodo, Yoshio Tsuchiya, Eijiro Tono, Jun Tatara, Atsushi Watanabe, Yoshio Kosugi, Bokuzen Hidari, Yukiko Shimazaki

WRITERS: Akira Kurosawa, Shinobu Hashimoto, Hideo Oguni

Frequently in conversation as one of the greatest movies of all time, Akira Kurosawa's *Seven Samurai* is certainly one of the most influential, having brought ideas, imagery, and tropes to the screen that have been duplicated, quoted, and repurposed time and again across cinema and pop culture at large. (Its most famous direct remake: John Sturges's Wild West take on the film, 1960's *The Magnificent Seven*, itself an influential film, though far less than its source.) For Kurosawa, *Seven Samurai* represented a career pivot and a tremendous bet on his own ability to tell a story in a new genre for him—the chanbara film, named after the onomatopoeia for the clashing of swords ("chan chan bara bara"). Depicting martial exploits, heated rivalries, self-sacrificing loyalty, and the traditional bushido code of the samurai, chanbara were period epics focused on delivering action and entertainment.

In the years after the end of World War II, chanbara production largely shut down due to concern from US occupation censors over their deeply nationalistic underpinnings. But by the early fifties, the studios slowly began to return to the milieu, and Kurosawa, coming off the back-to-back successes of *Rashomon* (1950) and *Ikiru* (1952), felt compelled to help lead the charge. Secluding with his favorite screenwriters for a month-and-a-half-long writing retreat, he emerged with the script for *Seven Samurai*—the tale of a village beset by bandits, whose people pool their meager resources to hire a group of warriors to defend their home. (An elder, noting that they can only pay with

I grew up as a half-Asian kid in the suburbs of Dallas in the 1970s and 1980s, camping with the Boy Scouts, playing D&D with my friends, and absorbing every kind of outdoor adventure storytelling, from fantasy to Westerns. So when I discovered Akira Kurosawa, Toshiro Mifune, and *Seven Samurai*, my head pretty much exploded. I was thrilled by the action, dazzled by the companionship and humanity, harrowed by the raw vulnerability of Mifune's performance, and deeply impressed by the monumental decency of Takashi Shimura's character. I was also hit hard in the best of ways by the sheer confidence of every other actor in the movie. I was used to seething over stereotypical depictions of Asian people in American media. But here was an epic movie filled with Asian actors who commanded the screen, full of charisma, dazzling us with every virtue and flaw of their characters, never apologizing, never fading back, never questioning their right to command their moment in the spotlight, no matter how big or small. Kids today might call it main character energy. All I know is that back then, they opened a door in my brain that will never, ever close.

—GREG PAK ON *SEVEN SAMURAI*

food, advises the villagers to "find hungry samurai.")

The story is simple, but there was room in it for Kurosawa to bring together an ensemble of veterans from his prior films, most notably the great Toshiro Mifune, and to stage incredibly intricate battle sequences that together bring the film's running time to a gargantuan three and a half hours. The production took almost a year to complete and ran three times over budget, making it the most expensive Japanese film in history—but the costs were worth it, as it earned over $100 million at the Japanese box office and millions more abroad, while reaping universal critical acclaim.

While *Seven Samurai* is undoubtedly a work of visionary genius and technical mastery, it is at its core an action film, and one that truly transformed a hidebound genre. Chanbara fight sequences were conventionally shot with single cameras at static distances using repeated takes, a filming style that was adequate given their Kabuki-inspired, stylized combat. Kurosawa wanted his battles to look raw, vicious, and chaotic, and to thrust viewers into their center. He pioneered the use of multiple cameras set to simultaneously capture different framings and angles of each scene, and telephoto lenses to provide an immersive POV on the fight. The final siege sequence, an alternatingly sweeping and

Seven Samurai movie poster

claustrophobic brawl set against rainy darkness and across gore-drenched mud, is a brutal masterpiece, highlighting the individual costs of war and the psychic burden of taking a life. No other film has ever put the "art" into martial arts cinema to this degree since. The resulting victory, as the leader of the seven Kambei (Shimura) says, does not belong to the handful of surviving samurai but "to the peasants."

Come Drink with Me

1966, NOT RATED, 95 MINUTES, FRANK LEE INTERNATIONAL, HONG KONG/CHINA

DIRECTOR: King Hu

STARRING: Pei-Pei Cheng, Hua Yueh, Chih-Ching Yang, Hung-Lieh Chant

WRITERS: King Hu, Shan-Hsi Ting

It's not a coincidence that martial arts films have been a staple of Greater Chinese film since its earliest days. The first movies made in Shanghai, Taiwan, and Hong Kong—the region's original cinematic trinity—were filmed adaptations of Chinese opera, capturing not just the music and dance of the medium but also its staged combat, which, in the Cantonese version of the form, was particularly replete with acrobatic tricks and fanciful weapon-work. As a result, many early Hong Kong actors were well trained in the fundamentals of martial arts performance from childhoods spent with opera companies, and audiences were primed to embrace the more realistic depictions of combat in opera-inspired movies.

But it was this film, King Hu's second directorial effort, that revolutionized cinematic martial arts in Hong Kong and, subsequently, for the world. Starring ballet-trained dancer Pei-Pei Cheng as its heroic protagonist Golden Swallow, the film features combat sequences that are at once more stylized—the film's fights have a symmetry and precision that betray their opera origins—and grittier and more substantial: There are no coy cutaways when blades meet flesh, blood spurts, limbs tumble, and death in all its horror is shown.

The story was also revolutionary for centering on a female warrior, as Swallow is tasked by her father with rescuing her kidnapped brother, and aptly demonstrates fighting skills worthy of that task in her first interaction with the bandits behind the crime. Swallow isn't operating alone—a beggar named Drunken Cat (Yueh) is seen secretly protecting her from ambush and shares with her key clues as to the location of her brother and the leader of the gang through his intoxicated singing. Later, we discover that Drunken Cat is actually a martial arts master named Fan Da-Pei, who was trained in the temple that has become the villains' headquarters. Fan's former martial arts brother, Liao Kung (Yang), has thrown in with the villains; out of residual loyalty and fear of Liao's skill, Fan is unable to move against Liao himself. As a result, he is guiding Swallow toward the monastery as his proxy.

> Seeing virtually no leading Asian American faces on-screen growing up, I hardly knew what I was missing until I caught Chinese star Pei-Pei Cheng tearing through an inn filled with armed thugs in *Come Drink with Me*. Lithe and lethal with a steely grace, she was effortless cool personified—blades in hand, eyes on her enemies, a thinking warrior woman in a man's world. In her iconic role as Golden Swallow, Cheng paved the way for the many badass female Hong Kong stars who followed and reached across borders and generations to give me the kind of heroine I still haven't stopped looking for at the movies.
>
> —JEN YAMATO ON *COME DRINK WITH ME*

In the film's climax, as Swallow leads her squad of female fighters against the bandits, Fan finds himself thrust into a showdown with Liao, and—inspired by Swallow's heroism—he summons the strength to defeat him. Hu's style and themes became the foundation for the cinematic wuxia genre, and inspired directors from Ang Lee, whose *Crouching Tiger, Hidden Dragon* (2000) has Hu's fingerprints all over it, to Quentin Tarantino, who at one point was threatening to helm a Hollywood remake of *Come Drink with Me*. (It never happened—thank God.)

Enter the Dragon

1973, R, 102 MINUTES, WARNER BROS., USA

DIRECTOR: Robert Clouse

STARRING: Bruce Lee, John Saxon, Jim Kelly, Ahna Capri, Bob Wall, Shih Kien, Bolo Yeung

WRITER: Michael Allin

Every scene of this movie begs one to consider what the world missed due to Bruce Lee's untimely demise. A foundational masterpiece by the most influential action star of all time, *Enter the Dragon* established many of the core conceits we associate with the modern martial arts genre, from the underground fighting tournament to the multicultural backgrounds of its protagonists. Video games like *Street Fighter* and *Mortal Kombat* wouldn't exist without it; neither, one could argue, would professional MMA. The film was also a blockbuster hit on a scale rarely seen before or since: With a budget of just $850,000, it earned over $350 million in worldwide box office sales—the equivalent of over a billion in present-day dollars. In the process, it turned Bruce Lee into a global superstar, though he never reaped the benefits of his newfound fame, nor did he even see the finished cut of his breakthrough film: Lee died July 20, 1973, over a week before *Enter the Dragon*'s Hong Kong premiere.

In the movie, Lee plays a character very much like himself, a martial artist and martial arts teacher from Hong Kong, who's asked by British intelligence to enter a global combat competition sponsored by drug lord and supervillain Han (Shih). (We know he's a supervillain because he has a deadly metal fist that he can exchange for an even deadlier metal claw.) Lee has personal incentive to participate: The man who murdered his sister (played by legendary martial arts star Angela Mao Ying) is Han's bodyguard and a sure

Decades before any marvelous Asians suited up for cinematic universes, we actually had our very own superhero: Bruce Lee, a one-man revolution who single-handedly and shirtlessly changed the game for martial arts, Asian masculinity, and international underdogs on the silver screen. The first time I saw Bruce Lee—as a kid—I felt an aggressive collision of emotions: absolute awe that such a person could exist; annoyance that no one had yet bothered to tell me about him; and disappointment to learn that he was, in fact, no longer alive. Released just weeks after his sudden death in 1973, *Enter the Dragon* inadvertently became both Bruce's magnum opus and swan song. The plot? Who cares. Okay, the plot: There's an island. Bruce kicks everyone's ass. And looks unbelievably cool while doing it. The end. In the history of action flicks, there are only two eras: Before and After Bruce.

—PHIL YU ON *ENTER THE DRAGON*

bet to also fight in the contest. Lee accepts the mission and finds a pair of compatriots in Roper (Saxon) and Williams (Kelly), two war buddies each hoping to win the tournament's prize. Lee's snooping during the tournament triggers Han to order the execution of the guards who were supposed to ensure that contestants stayed in their rooms. After the guards are brutally killed by Bolo (Yeung), Han's giant enforcer, on the tournament's first day, Lee is paired to fight O'Hara (Wall) and kills him after the latter attempts a cowardly ambush. That night, Williams and Lee both sneak out; the former is murdered by Han, and the latter is once again discovered by guards. He delivers a thorough beating to dozens of Han's island security staff before being trapped in a tiger pit sealed with metal doors. The next day, Han demands that Roper fight Lee; when Roper refuses, he's assigned to fight Bolo instead. Roper barely wins using somewhat dirty tactics, and an enraged Han orders his men to kill them both. A general melee begins between the tournament contestants and Han's guards. In the chaos, Han tries to escape but is hunted down by Lee and killed in an epic final duel in the island's "mirror room." The end of the movie holds open the possibility of following Lee and Roper's continued adventures in future sequels, but of course, real-life tragedy would intervene.

They Call Me Bruce?

1982, PG, 97 MINUTES, FILM VENTURES INTERNATIONAL, USA

DIRECTOR: Elliott Hong

STARRING: Johnny Yune, Margaux Hemingway, Raf Mauro, Pam Huntington

WRITERS: Elliott Hong, David Randolph, Johnny Yune

For Asians, there were two immediate consequences of Bruce Lee's death at the height of his fame. The first was that everyone around him—and a lot who weren't around him—tried to cash in on his iconic name, face, and identity, with a slew of Z-grade martial arts movies starring Wanna-Lees with knockoff

Johnny Yune

stage names like Bruce Li, Bruce Lai, Bruce Le, Bruce Ly, and Dragon Lee. The second consequence was that Asian guys found themselves being perceived as kung fu experts by random white strangers, as if Lee's halo was so large that it encircled anyone who even vaguely shared his features. This could be a good thing (striking a pose and making a high-pitched keening noise has made more than a few bullies back

off) or a bad one ("You think you're tough, chop-socky guy? Why don't you *show* me how tough you are?"). This low-budget action comedy, starring Korean American comic Johnny Yune and directed by Elliott Hong, was the first movie to satirize both halves of the "We Are All Bruce Lee" phenomenon.

The plot is skeletal: Yune is an immigrant cook for an Italian mafia clan whose members call him

As much as having a role model like Bruce Lee kicking ass on-screen was empowering and important, it wasn't until I saw Johnny Yune that I felt I actually saw myself. Johnny Yune proved that you could be Asian *and* funny. I was never going to get a black belt in kung fu, but I definitely knew how to tell a good fart joke. Johnny Yune showed me that there were other ways to be powerful—even if his comedy is dated and often inappropriate now.

—MICHAEL KANG ON *THEY CALL ME BRUCE?*

Ralph Macchio and Pat Morita

Bruce (after Lee) because they can't pronounce his real name. Seeking a way to get a huge shipment of cocaine to their distributors without risking a bust, the don hits upon the solution of having Bruce unwittingly drive it cross-country, telling him that it's just special "Chinese flour." But no one really cares, because the movie is just a vehicle for Yune to deliver as many cringe-inducing jokes as possible, like "I am a sex object. I always ask women for sex, and they object." Or a scene in which a geisha girl offers to join Bruce in a hot tub, leading him to say, "You are a ten!"—until she removes her kimono, at which point he corrects himself: "You are a ten where you should be a thirty-six!" Nevertheless, Yune was a true pioneer and often-overlooked superstar of comedy, appearing a staggering thirty-four times on *The Tonight Show Starring Johnny Carson*, and while the movie isn't great, it had the last laugh—it earned a stunning $17 million at the box office, enough to spawn a sequel: 1987's *They Still Call Me Bruce*.

The Karate Kid

1984, PG, 126 MINUTES, COLUMBIA PICTURES, USA

DIRECTOR: John G. Avildsen

STARRING: Ralph Macchio, Noriyuki "Pat" Morita, Elisabeth Shue, William Zabka, Martin Kove, Randee Heller

WRITER: Robert Mark Kamen

By the seventies, martial arts had become a staple of America's urban environment, driven predominantly

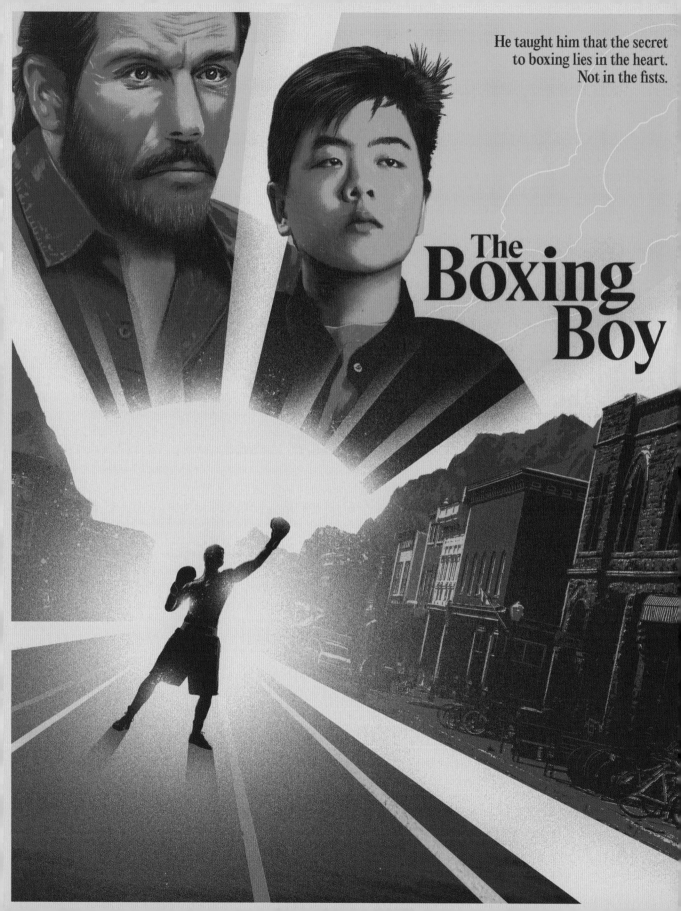

He taught him that the secret
to boxing lies in the heart.
Not in the fists.

The Boxing Boy

by Black fans of Bruce Lee and subsequent kung fu icons. A decade later, *The Karate Kid* brought martial arts into the suburbs, inducing a vast wave of white minivan drivers to enroll their kids in strip-mall kwoons and dojos across the country. But John G. Avildsen's celebration of white-on-white violence was nearly perfect multiplex fare, with a brilliant performance by Pat Morita as Mr. Miyagi, the wise and whimsical World War II vet who teaches karate to troubled youth Daniel LaRusso (Macchio). The sweetly goofy fantasy world the film concocts—where high schoolers put more stock in martial arts than football and the All-Valley Karate Championships are a big enough event to grind business to a halt and fill a fifty-thousand-person arena—still holds up today, as can be seen from the amazing success of the franchise's TV continuation, *Cobra Kai*.

For Asian Americans in particular, *The Karate Kid* is a mixed bag. On the one hand, it stings that the movie's youthful ensemble contains not a single Asian face, despite being a martial arts movie set in California. On the other, the movie is thoughtful enough to depict Miyagi as a Medal of Honor–winning veteran of the all-Japanese 442nd Infantry Regiment, which earned more battlefield decorations

Few who grew up in the eighties have anything but nostalgic feelings for *The Karate Kid*, but there's no question that the movie is an enormous act of cultural appropriation. So why not a remake that appropriates right back? **Ashraf Omar** shows us (opposite) what that might look like.

and suffered more casualties than any other fighting unit in the war; it also explains that as he was bravely serving his country, his wife died in childbirth—while incarcerated in the Manzanar internment camp. This character note represents the first time most viewers of the film were likely exposed to that part of our American history—a small victory that offsets any number of ridiculous "Daniel-san" crane kicks.

A Better Tomorrow

1986, NOT RATED, 95 MINUTES, RIM, HONG KONG/CHINA

DIRECTOR: John Woo

STARRING: Ti Lung, Leslie Cheung, Chow Yun-Fat, Emily Chu, Waise Lee, Kenneth Tsang, Shi Yanzi, Tien Feng, John Woo, Kam Hing-Yin, Leung Ming, Shing Fui-On, Wang Hsieh

WRITERS: Hing-Ka Chan, Suk-Wah Leung, John Woo

Chow Yun-Fat

A Better Tomorrow reinvented the action game in Hong Kong and, eventually, Hollywood. It brought the inventive staging and acrobatic choreography of the martial arts genre to gunfighting, while updating the timeworn tropes of wuxia for a high-caliber contemporary landscape: honor lost and regained, loyalties broken and remade, manhood demonstrated through bloody sacrifice.

Prior to *Tomorrow*, John Woo had made some forgettable kung fu films, finally earning success with a pair of slapstick comedies, *Money Crazy* (1977) and *From Riches to Rags* (1980). Both took a comic approach to demonstrating the lengths to which poor people might go for money. But having grown up poverty-stricken himself in the slums of Hong Kong, Woo felt the urge to show the grittier reality of the class divide, and how even those with nobility in their hearts could be driven to crime in the absence of opportunity. *A Better Tomorrow* was his ode to modern chivalry and brotherly bonds that exist even without blood ties.

Ti Lung plays Ho, a counterfeiter for the Hong Kong Triad; pop idol Leslie Cheung plays his younger brother Kit, a police academy cadet who doesn't know about his elder sibling's gang affiliations. But it's Chow Yun-Fat, playing Ho's best friend and bodyguard Mark, whose star went supernova in this film.

I saw my first John Woo film, *The Killer*, at a student screening of a dubbed and vinegared print my freshman year of college. The elation of that crowd—packed with young people of every race and creed, yelling and laughing—made me proud, truly proud, to be an Asian American for the first time in my life. When I caught up with *A Better Tomorrow* on VHS later that year, I tracked down Mark's sunglasses and made living life in the imitation of Brother Chow my brand. I wasn't alone. Woo's film about the heroic bloodshed genre's key themes of brotherhood, shadows, and fusillades of bullets changed the direction of not just the Hong Kong film industry but Hollywood too. There would be no John Wick without John Woo.

—WALTER CHAW ON *A BETTER TOMORROW*

A Taiwanese banknote deal goes sour, leading to Ho's arrest and imprisonment, as well as the murder of Ho and Kit's father to keep the former silent. An angry Mark retraces Ho's steps to Taiwan, killing the Taiwanese gang members responsible for Ho's betrayal in a scene that, to this day, remains iconic: Wearing his signature black duster, Mark enters the restaurant where the gangsters are celebrating, while secretly hiding loaded pistols in potted plants along the hallway, knowing he'll need extra firepower if he plans on taking out the whole crew. He bursts into the room and launches a savage gunfight that sprawls back out into the hall, where Mark eliminates the Taiwanese Triad boss and a dozen thugs. The aftermath of this blaze of violence leaves Mark unable to walk without a leg brace.

Three years later, Ho is released from prison and fulfills his promise to Kit to abandon crime. Taking a job as a cab driver, he sees Mark, broken and disabled, having been ejected from the Triads by Shing (Lee), Ho's junior partner in the Taiwan deal and now the boss of bosses. Mark and Ho uncover evidence that Shing was the turncoat who sabotaged Ho's Taiwan mission and murdered their gang's former chief. Everything ends in a disastrous shootout on the Hong Kong waterfront, with the cavalry arriving in the form of Mark, still in his black trench coat, guns blazing, saving the brothers at the expense of his own life. In the film's wake, black trench coats and pilot sunglasses became the preferred uniform of Hong Kong adolescent boys seeking to look cool (and, it must be admitted, more than a few Asian American teens as well).

Dragon: The Bruce Lee Story

1993, PG-13, 120 MINUTES, UNIVERSAL PICTURES, USA

DIRECTOR: Rob Cohen

STARRING: Jason Scott Lee, Lauren Holly, Nancy Kwan, Robert Wagner, Michael Learned, Lim Kay Tong, Ric Young, Luoyong Wang, Sterling Macer, Sven-Ole Thorsen, John Cheung, Ong Soo Han, Eric Bruskotter, Van Williams, Shannon Lee, Rob Cohen

WRITERS: Rob Cohen, Edward Khmara, John Raffo

This loose biopic in 1993 was the first attempt by Hollywood to tell the story of Bruce Lee's brightly blazing and all-too-short life, and for many it remains their first introduction to the man behind the myth. But the myth is all too present in *Dragon* as well, as director Cohen couldn't resist incorporating fictional characters and situations into the story to amplify the drama—for example, creating a nonexistent rival for Lee named Johnny Sun (Cheung)

I vividly remember going to the theater to watch *Dragon: The Bruce Lee Story* as a junior in high school. I'd grown up admiring Bruce Lee and his ephemeral but legendary film career, so I was skeptical going in, since Jason Scott Lee looked nothing like him. But the film exceeded my expectations; the acting, the art direction, the writing, all of it was on point. I still get chills whenever I hear the epic score. And when Bruce walks out of the infamous Mickey Rooney yellowface scene while watching *Breakfast at Tiffany's*, he was all of us.

—DAVE LU ON *DRAGON: THE BRUCE LEE STORY*

Jason Scott Lee

and his revenge-seeking brother (Han); suggesting that Lee suffered a broken back in a secret trial by combat staged by disapproving kung fu masters; and inventing a "demon," supernatural or metaphorical, whose curse led to Lee's death. The last addition is the most problematic of all the choices made in the movie, turning a tragic-heroic tale into a fantastical one and adding exotic orientalist filigrees to Lee's very human, very imperfect demise. Some of *Dragon*'s fictional choices are brilliant, however—notably the inclusion of a scene in which Lee, played by Jason Scott Lee, takes his future wife, Linda (Holly), out for a movie date and is forced to watch Mickey Rooney's ghastly yellowface performance as Mr. Yunioshi in *Breakfast at Tiffany's*, which remains one of the deftest and most memorable examples of Hollywood calling out its own racism in US motion picture history.

The Matrix

1999, R, 136 MINUTES, WARNER BROS., USA

DIRECTORS/WRITERS: The Wachowskis (Lana and Lilly)

STARRING: Keanu Reeves, Laurence Fishburne, Carrie-Anne Moss, Hugo Weaving, Joe Pantoliano

It's important to remember that when he was cast in *The Matrix*, Keanu Reeves was already a star, having

Keanu Reeves

established his box office creds in *Point Break* (1991), *Speed* (1994), and *The Devil's Advocate* (1997). *The Matrix*, however, turned him into a superstar.

The Wachowskis' anime-inspired, Hong-Kong-action-infused cyberpunk opus looked like nothing audiences had ever seen, spawning three sequels, an animated series, and a plethora of new cinematic technologies, including "bullet time," a temporal freeze effect the Wachowskis invented to highlight the surreal nature of combat in their imaginary computer-generated reality. But none of it would have stuck without Reeves, whose transcendently flat performance and raw physicality brought the movie's impossible hero, Neo—a drifting, empty office drone turned cyber-messiah—to life in a way that couldn't have been imagined with the other leading candidates for the part, which was first offered to Will Smith, then in turn Nicolas Cage, Brad Pitt, Val Kilmer, and Leonardo DiCaprio, before landing on two final options: Reeves, whom the studio wanted, and Johnny Depp, who was the Wachowskis' choice—a shining example of what it looks like when the studio's instincts are far sharper than those of the auteur-creators.

The film imagines a future dystopia where most of humanity exists as living batteries, plugged into pods that harvest their electrical energies as a power source for a race of sentient machines. To tamp down rebellion, the machines have created a simulation of reality, the Matrix, that pod-humans experience as real life. A small but growing number of humans have managed to escape from this consensual illusion, "taking the red pill" and joining a ragged resistance that continues to fight the machines' AI agents in the Matrix, recruiting new rebels and searching for a prophesized savior called the One. By this point in the story, it's obvious that Neo is the One (reflected even in his name), and resistance leader Morpheus (Fishburne), his trusted deputy Trinity (Moss), and other members of their crew succeed in releasing Neo from machine captivity. But the path to Neo becoming the One is long and uncertain, and a rogue AI known as Agent Smith (Weaving) is determined to cut it off before he arrives at his goal.

Though it isn't referenced in the film, Reeves's multiracial Asian Pacific heritage is a critical aspect of making the film work, selling *The Matrix*'s jumbled Asian references in a way that, say, Will Smith or Nic

Cage could not. The non-Asian rest of the ensemble do their best to hold it down while operating in environments inspired by anime classics like *Neon Genesis Evangelion* (1995) and *Ghost in the Shell* (1995), demonstrating Yuen Woo-Ping kung fu choreography in bullet-ballet battles that include direct quotes of John Woo. Without Reeves, the "Asian aesthetics without Asian people" flavor of the film and its subsequent franchise would be overpowering.

Crouching Tiger, Hidden Dragon

2000, PG-13, 120 MINUTES, SONY PICTURES, USA

DIRECTOR: Ang Lee

STARRING: Chow Yun-Fat, Michelle Yeoh, Zhang Ziyi, Chang Chen, Sihung Lung, Cheng Pei-Pei

WRITERS: Hui-Ling Wang, James Schamus, Kuo Jung Tsai

BASED ON THE BOOK BY WANG DU LU

By anyone in Hollywood's predictions, Ang Lee's wildly ambitious and lyrically epic wuxia movie—with an entirely ethnic Chinese cast, speaking dialogue exclusively in Mandarin—should have been a disaster. Instead, it was a unicorn whose horn pointed the way to the boundless opportunity at hand if Hollywood would only embrace inclusive casting and tell global stories, earning an unbelievable $213 million against its $18 million budget. Naturally, the studios drop-kicked the unicorn into the sun, calling *Crouching Tiger* a fluke and continuing to make America-focused, English-language films with mostly white casts until burgeoning demographic diversity and the surging Chinese market forced their hand.

Meanwhile, there was *Crouching Tiger*, a swordsman drama in the grand Chinese tradition, set in the Qing dynasty of the nineteenth century, a time in which mystical sects proliferated and wandering heroes and rogues populated the murky shadow society known as the jianghu, or martial world. Chow Yun-Fat stars as Li Mu Bai, a renowned Wu Tang warrior on the verge of retirement; Michelle Yeoh plays Yu Shu Lien, his longtime friend and equal as a fighter. The two hide deep-rooted feelings for one another, never explored because of Shu Lien's status as the fiancée of Mu Bai's long-dead friend. As the film begins, they're on the road to Beijing to deliver Mu Bai's fabled sword, the Green Destiny, to his patron, Sir Te (Lung); while they're en route to doing so, the sword is stolen by a masked thief, who turns out to be Jen (Zhang), the young and defiant daughter of the provincial governor. Jen has been learning

Zhang Ziyi

sword skills from Jade Fox (Cheng), a rogue warrior who was the former mistress—and murderer—of Mu Bai's teacher. With the Green Destiny in hand, Jen has the ability to supersede her instructor. The conflict over the sword ends in tragedy: Mu Bai and Jade Fox die at each other's hands, but not before Mu Bai finally admits his feelings to Shu Lien; Jen, who instigated everything, takes her own life in regret.

The ending isn't neat, nor is it happy, which is one more reason why the film stands out from most Hollywood fare. But the acting and action are both superb, the latter choreographed by the great Hong Kong action director Yuen Woo-Ping and exquisitely delivered by its cast, who did their own stunts using suspension harnesses, hard work, and practical effects. The scene in which a pouty Jen defeats

Bruce Lee's *Enter the Dragon* was my introduction to martial arts movies, but my main education came through "Kung Fu Theater," the weekend series that aired on KTLA in Los Angeles. It broadcast original Hong Kong movies from the seventies, overly dramatic sound effects and unintentionally comedic dubs included. Back then, it was the only consistent way I ever saw faces like mine on a screen. So watching *Crouching Tiger, Hidden Dragon* in 2000, I flashed back to those days in front of the family TV, enraptured with "Kung Fu Theater." Ang Lee's film was superior to its predecessors in practically every way: the acting, the cinematography, the interweaving of complex emotional stakes with thrilling, balletic action choreography. But at its core, I'd like to think Lee also understood and shared the same delight I first experienced as a kid, watching Asian bodies doing amazing things.

—OLIVER WANG ON *CROUCHING TIGER, HIDDEN DRAGON*

an entire two-story inn full of dozens of heroes and rogues while boasting about her (invented) past adventures in the martial world would be an unparalleled spectacle—if it weren't for her bamboo treetop battle with Mu Bai, and her training hall fight with Shu Lien using every weapon in the hall's arsenal.

Ong Bak: The Thai Warrior

2003, R, 105 MINUTES, MAGNOLIA PICTURES, THAILAND

DIRECTOR: Prachya Pinkaew

STARRING: Tony Jaa, Petchtai Wongkamlao, Pumwaree Yodkamol, Chattapong Pantana-Angkul, Suchao Pongwilai, Wannakit Sirioput, Chumphorn Thepphithak, Rungrawee Barijindakul, Cheathavuth Watcharakhun

WRITER: Suphachai Sittiaumponpan

Tony Jaa training for his role in *Ong Bak*

The evolution of martial arts cinema has been driven by new forms and new performers—fresh combat disciplines and previously undiscovered talent bringing their novel takes and techniques to the table. *Ong Bak* offers both, highlighting the bone-crunching art of Thai kickboxing (strictly speaking, Muay Boran, the more ancient root discipline of Muay Thai) and a sensational new screen practitioner of that art in Tony Jaa. The movie's premise is thin: Thieves steal the head of a rural village's sacred Buddha statue, bringing the artifact to the big city as a gift for an aging crime lord. (Why the decapitated head of a statue? The crime lord in question asks the same thing when he receives it.) Ting (Jaa), a young man

with extraordinary boxing skills, sets off to Bangkok to retrieve it, meeting up with his cousin Humlae (Wongkamlao) and Humlae's female pal Muay Lek (Yodkamol). Gambling addict Humlae steals Ting's money to bet on an underground fighting tournament, forcing Ting to participate and win with ease. That doesn't prevent thrill-seeker Humlae from getting into further scrapes, all of which end up with him, Muay Lek, and Ting engaged in wild chase scenes culminating in a new display of the latter's martial prowess.

Because this is a movie, Humlae redeems himself, making the ultimate sacrifice to save Ting's life, and charging him with taking care of his best girl. But the film is first and foremost a showcase for Jaa and his skills, something underscored by the sassy fourth-wall-breaking graffiti its creators added to background walls ("Hi, Spielberg, let's do it together!"; "Luc Besson, we are waiting for you!"). To that end, it's one of the most impressive debuts of any martial artist in history, turning Jaa's bone-crushing strikes and Jackie Chan-worthy stunts and acrobatics into the gold standard for a new generation of action performers, while signaling to the world that Southeast Asia was entering the fight.

Kung Fu Hustle

2004, R, 99 MINUTES, SONY PICTURES CLASSICS, HONG KONG/CHINA

DIRECTOR: Stephen Chow

STARRING: Stephen Chow, Danny Chan, Yuen Wah, Yuen Qiu, Eva Huang, Leung Siu-Lung

WRITERS: Man-Keung Chan, Stephen Chow, Xin Huo, Kan-Cheung Tsang

It took far too long for the West to discover Stephen Chow, the Hong Kong comedic genius who virtually created an entire new genre of cinematic humor in the region, dubbed "mo lei tau" (or "total nonsense"). The style is marked by fast-paced verbal pyrotechnics, sudden absurdist shifts in tone, visual and linguistic puns, and a slapstick physical humor that brings cartoon physics into live-action settings. Chow's early works of this type tended to be wild farces and pop culture parodies (such as his 1994 James Bond satire *From Beijing with Love*). But it wasn't until the early 2000s that Chow would perfect the form, moving away from chaos for chaos's sake

(the finale of his 1999 *King of Comedy* randomly turns into a blatant ad for Pringles potato chips, with the dialogue suddenly shifting to marketing slogans and every character shoving chips into their mouths) and imbuing his unpredictable hilarity with new sophistication and emotional depth. *Shaolin Soccer* (2001), a sports comedy featuring a group of motley monks playing football to generate attention for shaolin kung fu arts, paved the way.

In *Kung Fu Hustle*, Chow's evolved style reaches its acme, with the star playing a con man named Sing who seeks to join the Axe Gang, a brutal hatchet-wielding, line-dancing criminal outfit that has established total control over the town. He's told that he can join the gang only if he kills someone first, so he heads to Pigsty Alley, a boardinghouse packed with penniless oddballs, seeking to kill the building's chain-smoking, curler-wearing Landlady (Yuen Qiu). It's just his luck that the Landlady—and her husband (Yuen Wah) and most of her tenants—are incredible martial artists who've chosen to retreat and hide away from the world, a discovery that enrages Sing, who tried to learn martial arts from a street vendor's pamphlet as a young child in order to defend a pretty, mute girl from bullies (and is totally humiliated as a result).

The Landlady and Landlord defend Pigsty Alley from a pair of deadly assassins sent by Brother Sum (Chan), leader of the Axe Gang; Brother Sum then commissions Sing to retrieve an unspeakably powerful and insane martial artist known only as the

Stephen Chow

My first exposure to Stephen Chow was in high school when *King of Comedy* played on a Bay Area Chinese channel. Though it was one of his smaller films, it hit me so hard that I went out to Chinatown and looked for a VCD of it (definitely bootlegged). His balance of slapstick humor with raw emotions was something I'd never seen in any Western media, and it deeply resonated with me. A couple years later, *Shaolin Soccer* came out and became an instant classic with its mix of traditional cultural references and modern commentary. That in turn set the stage for *Kung Fu Hustle*, a massive hit that perfectly blended classical Chinese imagery with Stephen's unique style of humor. Though Stephen had been a superstar for decades in Hong Kong, *Kung Fu Hustle* was the West's first time seeing his work, and it cemented his place not just in Asian cinema but also around the world. It shaped my own storytelling—you bet I made some parody clips in my dorm room—and it's still a dream of mine to work with Mr. Chow someday.

—PHILIP WANG ON *KUNG FU HUSTLE*

Mike Tyson and Donnie Yen at the premiere of *Ip Man 3*

Beast (Leung) from the asylum in which he's being held as an ultimate weapon against the Landlady and Landlord. The rescue is successful, but Sing, who has slowly been experiencing an evolution of both his heart and his hidden martial arts, changes his allegiance and joins the Landlady and Landlord in fighting back against the Beast.

By movie's end, Sing has come to terms both with his kung fu and with Fong, the mute girl he'd tried to defend as a child. There isn't a wasted beat in this film, even when it's at its most preposterous, such as a sequence in which Sing tries to escape his nemesis, the Landlady, using Looney Tunes–style CGI, and the result has influenced filmmakers from Spike Lee to *Shang-Chi*'s Destin Daniel Cretton.

Ip Man

2008, R, 106 MINUTES, WELL GO USA ENTERTAINMENT, HONG KONG/CHINA

DIRECTOR: Wilson Yip

STARRING: Donnie Yen, Simon Yam, Lynn Hung, Gordon Lam, Fan Siu-wong, Xing Yu, Chen Zhihui, Hiroyuki Ikeuchi, Tenma Shibuya

WRITERS: Tai-Lee Chan, Edmond Wong

Ip Man, starring veteran Donnie Yen in a career-defining role, tells the Wing Chun prodigy's story beginning in 1935, in the middle of his career, already renowned among kung fu insiders but uninterested in fame or public attention. Ip's true mastery is exposed after a local layabout observes him defeating Liu (Chen), one of the town's most revered masters, in a private fight. Shortly afterward, the Second Sino-Japanese War breaks out, and General Miura (Ikeuchi) and his Imperial Japanese Army troops invade and subjugate the town of Foshan, contemptuously offering a bag of rice to any Chinese master who can defeat the army's karate-trained soldiers. Liu is shot to death after beating one karateka but refusing a subsequent challenge of defeating three at once. Hearing the news, Ip avenges Liu by offering to challenge ten karate experts at once—handily winning with the most ruthless Wing Chun demonstration in martial arts movie history, shattering bones, dislocating joints, and pummeling already-downed fighters until they're bloody and unconscious. Ip refuses his prize of rice, satisfied with having humiliated the invaders. But Miura is not yet satisfied. He demands that Ip train his soldiers how to use his art; Ip responds by challenging Miura himself to a public duel. Miura, his honor at stake, accepts the challenge, and the two fight an extended bout on a high platform, ending with Ip proving Wing Chun's superiority, and by extension, that of China over Japan. A crowd suffused with fervor attacks the Japanese Army, and in the chaos that ensues afterward, Ip escapes to Hong Kong with his wife and son, a faceless war refugee like hundreds of thousands of others. Yen plays Ip Man with the solemn grace of a family man, set in his ways and sure of his abilities. If Bruce Lee was a warrior of blood and fury, Jackie Chan a pure entertainer, and Jet Li a sparkling diamond polished by endless practice, Yen is a methodical craftsman, a scholar of martial arts seeking to demonstrate them in thorough and authentic fashion. His Wing Chun is exemplary here, and *Ip Man* a master class in how to showcase it.

The Raid: Redemption

2011, R, 101 MINUTES, SONY PICTURES CLASSICS, INDONESIA

DIRECTOR/WRITER: Gareth Evans

STARRING: Iko Uwais, Joe Taslim, Donny Alamsyah, Yayan Ruhian, Pierre Gruno, Ray Sahetapy, Tegar Satrya, Eka "Piranha" Rahmadia

Watching *The Raid*, in which rookie cop Rama (Uwais) and his fellow members of Jakarta's organized crime unit run hell's own gauntlet through a building teeming with monstrous gang members, is very nearly a traumatic experience—there isn't a minute that passes once Rama and company enter the ambush-filled upper floors of the apartment tower that isn't filled with hyperkinetic violence or heart-stopping dread over imminent violence.

Throughout the journey, the block's mob boss, Tama (Sahetapy), watches the unfolding torture on a bank of security monitors, savoring the action along with the audience, at least until the surviving cops get too close. It turns out that Rama joined the mission to search for his estranged brother, revealed to be Tama's right-hand man, Andi (Alamsyah). Meanwhile, Wahyu (Gruno), the lieutenant who ordered the raid, and Dagu (Rahmadia), one of the unit's other skilled fighters, manage to reach the fifteenth floor, Tama's personal abode. It's revealed that Wahyu is a corrupt cop who staged the mission as a cover for assassinating the crime lord and eliminating the last witness to Wahyu's criminal activities. Wahyu executes Tama and Dagu before attempting to take his own life and failing, discovering he's out of ammo. Rama, having fought through endless waves of savage killers to do so, arrives just in time to arrest Wahyu and confront his brother, asking him to come home. But Andi responds that he is in a better position to protect Rama where he is—now the head of the biggest gang in Jakarta. Rama is unable to rebut Andi's argument, and leaves with the two survivors as Andi's face lights up in a grin of triumph. The fighting-style deployed by Rama throughout the movie is Pencak Silat, a largely unregulated Indonesian martial art that emphasizes incapacitating the enemy through kicks, punches, throws, and joint locks. Uwais smashes through the residents of the building like a wrecking ball, relentless, merciless, unstoppable. Both critics and audiences rightly hailed this film as not just the arrival of a fresh international face in the action genre but a transformative pivot for the genre itself.

Rogue One: A Star Wars Story

2016, PG-13, 133 MINUTES, WALT DISNEY STUDIOS, USA

DIRECTOR: Gareth Edwards

STARRING: Felicity Jones, Diego Luna, Ben Mendelsohn, Donnie Yen, Mads Mikkelsen, Alan Tudyk, Riz Ahmed, Jiang Wen, Forest Whitaker

WRITERS: Chris Weitz, Tony Gilroy

The most interesting of the Disney-era *Star Wars* movies, *Rogue One* fills in the story of how the Rebel Alliance identified the "vulnerability" that allowed Luke Skywalker's well-placed proton

torpedoes to destroy the monstrous Imperial planet-killer. Cassian Andor (Luna), a Rebel spy, and Jyn Erso (Jones), the daughter of the research scientist who'd been forced against his will to help design the super-weapon, disobey Alliance Council orders and assemble a ragtag group of volunteers to steal the Death Star's schematics from a heavily guarded Imperial base. Dubbing their suicide mission "Rogue One," the team infiltrates the base, obtains the schematics, and transmits them to the Rebel fleet, dying one by one as they sacrifice themselves for various parts of the plan. The final survivors, Cassian and Jyn, die when the surface of the planet is destroyed by an enraged Grand Moff Tarkin, while Darth Vader, at the peak of his power, slaughters the officers and troops on the orbiting Rebel command ship. Nevertheless, the uploaded schematics escape, via a tiny spaceship piloted by Princess Leia Organa—harbinger of the galaxy's "new hope."

The plot, deeply influenced by the classic *Seven Samurai*, is one of the Star Wars franchise's strongest, and the casting of the film is exemplary. Perhaps the most indelible characters are Chirrut Îmwe (Yen), a blind martial artist with a sensitivity to the Force and a playful sense of humor, and Baze Malbus (Jiang), his wry and taciturn mercenary companion—the first two major roles played by Asian actors in any of the Star Wars films to date. Their combat scenes in *Rogue One* stand out as highlights, beginning with their very first fight, where Chirrut takes out over a dozen stormtroopers with nothing more than a staff and his preternatural sense of perception—before Baze saves him from another half dozen with a barrage of precision blaster bolts. But it's the bantering chemistry between the pair that made them fan favorites. On the heels of that brawl, Chirrut snaps to Baze, "You almost shot me!" To which Baze laconically replies, "You're welcome," before ambling off. If only they'd had a bit more screen time.

The Paper Tigers

**2020, PG-13, 108 MINUTES,
WELL GO USA ENTERTAIMENT, USA**

DIRECTOR/WRITER: Bao Tran

STARRING: Alain Uy, Ron Yuan, Mykel Shannon Jenkins, Jae Suh Park, Joziah Lagonoy, Roger Yuan, Matthew Page, Yuji Okumoto

A labor of love that took writer-director Bao Tran a decade to make, *The Paper Tigers* is first and foremost an ode to classic martial arts cinema. It takes some of the genre's familiar themes—harsh training, brotherly loyalty, vengeance for a slain mentor, and implausible victory over a stronger and more skilled foe—and brings them into our modern world of single-parent childcare and dead-end jobs, minivans and midlife crises.

Three decades after training under the same kung fu master, Sifu Cheung (Roger Yuan), a trio of friends, Danny (Uy), Hing (Ron Yuan), and Jim (Jenkins), finally reunite when they hear their sifu has died—now on the wrong side of forty, with their youthful kung fu dreams having long since faded. But after discovering that their sifu was murdered, the Three Tigers, as they were known as cubs, take it upon themselves to hunt down his killer and bring him to justice. Unfortunately, the world has moved on and grown only more complicated. Divorced Danny is trying his best to not disappoint his young son Ed

Alain Uy and Mykel Shannon Jenkins

(Lagonoy) or his ex-wife Caryn even more than he already has. Hing is overweight, injured, and, we find out after a wig slip, bald. Jim works as a coach and personal trainer, but he's replaced his traditional kung fu skills with trendy jujitsu moves aimed at MMA-loving Gen Z clients. All of which means they're totally unprepared to take on their master's mysterious motorcycle-riding murderer, or the trio of obnoxious kids who've claimed their childhood title as the new Three Tigers, or even Carter (Page), their Caucasian childhood rival who, unlike the Tigers, went on to make kung fu his life. (Page steals every scene he's in with his snotty passive-aggression and penchant for delivering fortune-cookie wisdom prefixed with the phrase "We Chinese have a saying . . .")

Still, because this is that kind of kung fu movie, everything works out in the end. Danny goes into turbo mode with the killer, defeats him, and resists the urge to take a life for a life. Kung fu brings the three friends back together again, revives their joy in life—and even repairs Danny's relationship with his son, who becomes the first student at the revived Cheung school of martial arts. *The Paper Tigers* is a loving exercise in nostalgia that surely spurred many audience members to revisit their favorite old-school classics—which, ten

years after Tran embarked on the journey to make this film, was surely his goal in the first place.

Mortal Kombat

2021, R, 110 MINUTES, WARNER BROS., USA

DIRECTOR: Simon McQuoid

STARRING: Lewis Tan, Jessica McNamee, Josh Lawson, Tadanobu Asano, Mehcad Brooks, Ludi Lin, Chin Han, Joe Taslim, Hiroyuki Sanada

WRITERS: Greg Russo, Dave Callaham

The buzz behind this reboot of the *Mortal Kombat* movie franchise, inspired by the gore-drenched fighting game of the same name, began long before it was even fully cast. After all, the original *Mortal Kombat*

Lewis Tan (right)

had been a surprise box office hit, earning over $120 million on a $20 million budget back in 1995, spawning a sequel and two TV series adaptations. The gaming franchise has stood the test of time, having produced twenty-four different games available on virtually every platform on the planet (at least the ones that allowed graphic depictions of severed heads and spines being ripped out of bodies).

Nearly twenty-five years after its big screen debut, a fresh installment seemed almost overdue. But Warner Bros., whose New Line Cinema division had made the original, decided to shake up the reboot's development and marketing—trickling out cast announcements one by one while zealously guarding what seemed to be the movie's biggest secret. Actor and martial artist Lewis Tan had leaked that he would be playing a major role in the movie—but which character would he play? Fans were stumped. It was a shock when the answer was revealed: Tan would be the movie's main protagonist, but a totally new and original character, a down-on-his-luck MMA fighter named Cole Young.

As it turns out, Young is the descendant of a seventeenth-century ninja named Hanzo Hasashi (Sanada), which explains why he's included on a list of warriors who've been invited via the appearance of a mystical dragon mark to compete in an interdimensional martial arts tournament called, natch, Mortal Kombat. On one side, the contest features villainous warriors representing the evil realm of Outworld, the domain of the sorcerer Shang Tsung (Han); on the other, a selection of Earth's most powerful human and superhuman fighters, led by the thunder god Raiden (Asano). Much of the movie is spent introducing and assembling the familiar characters of the game franchise, followed by a training arc where each fighter seeks to unleash his or her "arcana," a special power-up move that's critical to victory in the Kombat. And then the fighting begins, very much shaped by the over-the-top violence and absurdist gore of its video game source: Hearts are ripped out of chests, torsos are sliced in half, heads are imploded, bodies are immolated with hellfire. It's all in good fun, if not exactly appropriate for kids. (Then again, the kids have probably been playing the game since they were toddlers.) The film earned $85 million in theaters despite the impact of the Covid-19 pandemic and proved to be a huge success on streaming as well—all despite a hard-R rating and a predominantly Asian main cast.

Snake Eyes

2021, PG-13, 121 MINUTES, PARAMOUNT PICTURES, USA

DIRECTOR: Robert Schwentke

STARRING: Henry Golding, Andrew Koji, Úrsula Corberó, Samara Weaving, Iko Uwais, Takehiro Hira

WRITERS: Evan Spiliotopoulous, Joe Shrapnel, Anna Waterhouse

The announcement of *Snake Eyes*—a movie that would simultaneously provide a reset for the G.I. Joe live-action movies (2009's *G.I. Joe: The Rise of Cobra* and 2013's *G.I. Joe: Retaliation*) and a fresh origin story for its most popular character, silent ninja Snake Eyes—generated both anticipation and concern among the franchise's stalwart fans. Could it be a worthy new beginning for a beloved world whose legend has sprawled across almost six decades of toy figurines and comic books, only to stumble at the cinematic box office? Would the new film do justice to the fan-favorite hero's established canon? The answer, it turned out, is: Sort of!

While visually impressive and more narratively ambitious than its predecessors—both of which were anchored in the continued conflict between the Joes and the global terrorism operation known as Cobra—the movie was generally received negatively by critics and die-hard fans, and made $40 million at the box office, though this total reflects the complete shutdown of movie theaters in the US market.

It was the casting news for the movie that made waves, however. While Snake Eyes has traditionally been depicted as white, the movie cast British Malaysian dreamboat Henry Golding as its lead, and Andrew Koji, best known for his role as hero in Cinemax's period kung fu series *Warrior*, playing Tommy Arashikage, Snake Eyes's friend, rival, and eventual nemesis. The film establishes Snake Eyes as an underground pit fighter recruited by a Yakuza boss, Kenta (Hira), to infiltrate and eventually steal a powerful mystic artifact. Snake Eyes accepts, knowing that the mission will end with Kenta giving him the information he seeks—the name of his long-dead father's killer. But the artifact's owners, the Arashikage, are an incredibly powerful and ancient ninja clan dedicated to preserving justice and social order.

Henry Golding and Andrew Koji

To win their trust, Snake Eyes saves the life of the clan's next heir, Tommy, who invites him to join the organization. Snake Eyes overcomes a series of trials that clan members must pass or die trying. During the tests, he wins over even the greatest skeptics among the Arashikage. Unfortunately, the final one requires purity of heart, something that Snake Eyes can't claim, and though the clan spares his life, they expel him from their midst. They were right to do so: Snake Eyes betrays them, yet is overcome by guilt after realizing the cost of his betrayal and returns to defend the clan. In the heat of battle, it is Tommy who proves to be unworthy, and he is disinherited as a result, vowing to kill Snake Eyes if they ever meet again—an inevitability, given that the closing moments of the film show Tommy being recruited into Cobra as the white-clad Storm Shadow, while Snake Eyes accepts a commission in the G.I. Joe organization. The movie marked the first time two Asian actors had been cast as the leads in a big-budget Hollywood action film— and based on rumored plans for the Joe franchise, it likely won't be the last.

Of all the superhero properties that imprinted themselves onto my childhood brain, *G.I. Joe: A Real American Hero* may have had the biggest impact. Born from the mind of longtime Marvel editor Larry Hama, who not only authored the characters' comic book adventures but imbued each of Hasbro's action figures with personality and backstory, the most popular of the team was a black-clad ninja commando named Snake Eyes. He was easily my favorite. Because he wore a full-face mask and had a mysterious and classified backstory meant anyone could be under the mask. So, it was disappointing when, like so many comic characters at the time, it was revealed that Snake, the Joes' expert martial artist, was just another super white guy. It may have taken four decades, but one of comics' greatest wrongs was finally rectified when Henry Golding was cast as the cinematic Snake Eyes for a new generation.

—KEITH CHOW ON *SNAKE EYES*

Shang-Chi and the Legend of the Ten Rings

2021, PG-13, 132 MINUTES, WALT DISNEY STUDIOS, USA

DIRECTOR: Destin Daniel Cretton

STARRING: Simu Liu, Awkwafina, Meng'er Zhang, Fala Chen, Florian Munteanu, Benedict Wong, Michelle Yeoh, Ben Kingsley, Tony Leung Chiu-Wai

WRITERS: Dave Callaham, Destin Daniel Cretton, Andrew Lanham

The year 2021 brought a dual infusion of new diversity into the Marvel Cinematic Universe. There was *The Eternals*, with its multiracial coalition of world-saving demigods. But first there was *Shang-Chi*, which represented the introduction of Marvel's first Asian superhero, anchored in both traditional Chinese ideas and the larger issues surrounding Asian diasporic identity—cultural disconnects, generational divides, social and peer pressures—in a way that was organic, authentic, and for superhero movies, wholly unique.

The casting was also unprecedented: After a search of essentially every Asian male actor of a certain age and physicality to play the lead role of Shang-Chi, Marvel landed on Simu Liu, an Asian Canadian actor best known for his work on the beloved family sitcom *Kim's Convenience*. And for the almost equally critical role of Shang-Chi's father and nemesis, Marvel cast veteran Hong Kong actor Tony Leung Chiu-Wai—the star of dozens of modern Chinese classics, including Wong Kar-Wai's *In the Mood for Love* (2000) and *Chungking Express* (1994). Between the two, and with the addition of Awkwafina as Shang-Chi's best friend, Katy, and Michelle Yeoh as his long-lost aunt, Shang-Chi found its magic—and scored nearly half a billion at the global box office despite being released in the thick of pandemic restrictions.

Leung plays Wenwu, an immortal warlord sustained and made superhuman by a set of ten mystical arm rings, the original Mandarin villain from the comics (and made into an ineffective punchline by Ben Kingsley's portrayal in *Iron Man 3*). Over the centuries, Wenwu's vast criminal organization has expanded around the globe and shaped history, but his mystical tools are evidence that the world is beyond human, and he is inspired to seek them out, eventually discovering the path to a transdimensional village called Ta Lo, guarded by a powerful female warrior named Ying Li (Chen). After days of dueling, as Wenwu seeks entry into Ta Lo and Ying Li bars his path, the two fall in love and eventually leave the village to marry and create a life together. Wenwu locks away his rings and disperses his organization, and he and Ying Li have two children, Shang-Chi and Xialing (as an adult, Zhang).

Michelle Yeoh and Simu Liu

> **M**y favorite moment in *Shang-Chi* was how his finale-winning power came from combining his father's hard strength and his mother's soft resilience—underscoring that he couldn't just wield the rings by taking them, but by accepting them. That duality feels uniquely Asian American: We are employed, but too rarely promoted; citizens, but too often unwelcome.
>
> **—BING CHEN ON *SHANG-CHI AND THE LEGEND OF THE TEN RINGS***

> **T**his was the first film I went to see with my kids during the pandemic. We went to a drive-in—our first ever—and I marveled at how many Asian American and non–Asian American families and couples had fought through the challenges of quarantine to join us in watching. I kept looking at my kids whenever a character spoke Mandarin, my native tongue, though I wasn't sure how much they understood. And it was exciting for me to have them see two movie icons I grew up watching, Michelle Yeoh and Tony Leung. Movies are about connecting families across generations, and for me and my kids, this was a special moment.
>
> **—MOMO CHANG ON *SHANG-CHI AND THE LEGEND OF THE TEN RINGS***

But Wenwu's past comes back to haunt their happy family life: The Iron Gang, a rival gang that the Ten Rings organization had harshly suppressed, gets its revenge on Wenwu by attacking his home and killing Ying Li. That prompts Wenwu to bring the rings out of storage, then hunt down and slaughter members of the Iron Gang, while forging his young son as a human weapon to assassinate the Iron Gang's escaped leader. Still a teen, Shang-Chi obeys his father and accomplishes his goal, but rather than returning to Wenwu's side, he flees to the US, where he submerges his identity under the guise of Asian American immigrant "Shaun."

Of course, it's only a matter of time before Wenwu reels his wayward offspring back in, both Shang-Chi and his sister, Xialing, who has become a martial arts master herself and operates an underground fight club in Macau with herself as the final boss, seeking to release their dead mother from what Shang-Chi imagines to be captivity in Ta Lo. But the mysterious voice calling to him is not Ying Li, and the creature that is mimicking her has dark designs on Wenwu, his children, Ta Lo, and all of humanity.

If there was ever concern over whether Marvel could create a movie featuring legitimate martial arts, director Destin Daniel Cretton erases it—nostalgically paying homage to everything from classic wuxia works to legendary Jackie Chan stunts (that bus fight!) while serving up action that feels more real and less green screen than anything else in superhero comics. It didn't hurt that star Liu had the charisma, stuntman experience, and legitimate martial arts training to pull that action off.

RRR (Rise Roar Revolt)

2022, PG-13, 187 MINUTES, RAFTAR CREATIONS, INDIA

DIRECTOR/WRITER: S. S. Rajamouli

STARRING: N. T. Rama Rao Jr., Ram Charan, Ajay Devgn, Alia Bhatt, Shriya Saran, Samuthirakani, Ray Stevenson, Alison Doody, Olivia Morris, Twinkle Sharma

> **T**he term "epic" gets thrown around willy-nilly these days, but it's an accurate descriptor for *RRR*. The three-hour-plus runtime initially dissuaded me from watching, but I was a damn fool to have denied myself the pleasure. I found myself hooting, hollering, and on my feet for much of the film. Imagine the The Fast and the Furious franchise, but instead of cars suspending logic and physics, it's two dudes doing incredible feats with their bodies . . . and sometimes motorcycles, horses, CGI animal predators, and enraged deer. This is a lavish bromance for the ages. If only I too could be so lucky as to have a friend break me out of solitary confinement and put me upon his shoulders, to form an unstoppable force of vengeance!
>
> **—KULAP VILAYSACK ON *RRR***

As a movie, S. S. Rajamouli's historical fantasy extravaganza *RRR* is like an overinflated balloon—a bit too big, a bit too full of itself, and always on the cusp of eruption, but also colorful, soaring, a breeze-blown whirling dervish whose reckless story arc flies in continuously unexpected directions. As a piece of pure entertainment, it's breathtaking—an announcement by the world's most prolific film industry that it has arrived on the global stage as a source of polished, crowd-pumping action cinema at a Hollywood scale and expense (*RRR* cost $70 million, making it the most expensive Indian movie ever).

It's not like S. S. Rajamouli had anything to prove; his two prior works, the *Baahubali* period fantasy duology, are the second- and tenth-highest grossing Indian movies in history. But *RRR* is an act of escalation, a masterpiece of excess. Its fight sequences borrow the heavy integration of CGI, dynamic camerawork, and use of slow motion as a visual accent that have become the signature of big-budget Hollywood action, as exemplified by Marvel movies, and infuse them with ideas quoted from Hong Kong cinema—physics-breaking wirework, projectile point-of-view shots, and pregnant pauses that highlight the consequences of finishing blows—all while preserving the intrinsically Indian flavor of the resulting hybrid.

Rama Rao Jr. plays Komaram Bheem, a muscular, woolly-chested tribal guardian of the rural Gond tribe, who sets off to the city of Hyderabad to recover Malli (Sharma), a young girl who's been kidnapped to serve as a domestic by the region's sadistic governor, Scott Buxton (Stevenson), and his wife, Catherine (Doody). To protect them from Bheem's wrath, Catherine brings in a police officer, A. S. Raju (Charan), as security. But a chance encounter between the two, in which the pair collaborate to save a boy falling from a high bridge, soon blossoms into friendship, and eventually, blood brotherhood. Becoming partners in war against the grotesque excesses of the British occupation, Bheem and Raju save Malli while dual-handedly destroying what appears to be the entire contingent of British soldiers in Hyderabad, before capturing and executing Buxton in appropriate fashion: with an English-made rifle and British bullets imported from England. But the most captivating combat sequence in the movie doesn't involve weapons or martial arts whatsoever. Angered by mockery from a white aristocrat suggesting that Indians are too crude and lacking in finesse to dance, Bheem and Raju challenge the entire assembled party crowd to an epic dance-off while taunting their aggressor with song lyrics that include the line "Come on, white guy!" Truly a sight to behold.

"Anything worth doing is kung fu."

A Talk with **Ronny Chieng** and **Daniel Wu**

Sometimes it seems like everyone's kung fu fighting, at least when it comes to Asian characters on screen—and that's a testament to both the rich elasticity and enduring popularity of the martial arts genre and to the reality that Hollywood is most comfortable with Asian characters when they're punching people. In this Q&A, actor and comedian Ronny Chieng (*Crazy Rich Asians*) and actor and producer Daniel Wu (*Tomb Raider, New Police Story*) discuss their love of cinematic fisticuffs, their desire to see Asians reappropriate the genre, and their mutual admiration for the guy who in many ways started it all: the man they called the Dragon.

In a lot of ways, this modern era of Asian American Hollywood we're in began with one guy: Bruce Lee.

RONNY CHIENG: Oh yeah, absolutely! I actually have a vintage original Bruce Lee movie poster for the Australia release of *The Big Boss* on the wall right behind me right now. I've always felt a connection with him, but ever since I've started working in American show business, it's given me another level of appreciation for what he did.

DANIEL WU: Bruce was my first introduction to seeing a cool Asian guy on-screen, ever. I became obsessed with him. I remember when I found out *Enter the Dragon* was going to be on late-night television, my parents wouldn't let me stay up to watch it, so I took this tiny black-and-white portable TV we had in the basement, snuck it up to my room, and watched it in my closet, just to be able to watch it again. Just to soak in his aura. Yes, the kung fu was great, but ultimately it was him, his personality, his charisma, his presence. No one's been able to replicate that ever again.

At a time when Hollywood couldn't give a damn about Asian Americans, Bruce kicked in the door with this unique skill that no one else in the industry had. Martial arts was the one thing studios couldn't duplicate.

RONNY: Well, yes, definitely. And the reason why martial arts films ended up becoming one of the first ways that the rest of the world saw Asians on-screen is because they were the easiest to translate for the rest of the world. They're physical, they're dynamic. They don't require a lot of dialogue. They're Charlie Chaplin. And a lot of the films that were coming out of Asia or that were being made in Hollywood with Asian themes tended to be ones where Asians were being subjected to misery and suffering. So if you wanted to present a protagonist who could occupy the screen in a more positive way, the easiest way was to assign him these unique physical skills. It was a way to make the Asian main character a hero instead of a victim.

DANIEL: Given who Bruce Lee was, he believed he was going to succeed somehow, no matter what. When racism held him back in the US, he went to Hong Kong, where he was finally allowed to be himself, became a huge star, and threw it back in the faces of those who doubted him. Some people may have found him arrogant, but the truth is, Asians needed someone who was going to stand up and say, "There's nothing I can't do if I want to, and there's nothing you can make me do if I *don't* want to." We had to relearn a sense of warrior spirit. That's what Bruce, and what martial arts screen heroes after him, helped us to do.

People forget, martial arts movies aren't just about fighting. There's a whole spectrum of other stories that martial arts gives you the license to tell.

RONNY: Absolutely. Bruce's movies are actually very political, you know? *Fist of Fury* is really about colonialism—the Japanese occupation of China. And *Enter the Dragon* and *The Way of the Dragon* both have subtexts about race. But nobody wants to see a movie about Asians fighting colonialism with strongly worded arguments. Martial arts were an eye-candy way to get people to engage with these stories. White people would be like, "Why is this guy so mad? What is he fighting for? Oh, he's fighting for this stuff." And we're drawn to seeing people fighting. It's in our genetics—seeing people fight with skill just pulls us in. So it ended up being the easiest access point for Asians to tell stories to people who are not Asian, and to get them to empathize with the protagonist: "Hey, if someone compared me to a dog, I'd be angry too. I'd kick that guy in the face." All of a sudden, you're inside that character's head.

DANIEL: Still, martial arts stories tell you something about the fundamental differences between Western and Asian ideas of heroism. Western hero fantasies tend to be about people who have some innate talent, or who magically or scientifically become superhuman. You find a ring, you wear some armor, you get bitten by a spider, whatever. It's instant gratification: You see the end result, but not the work you put in to get there. Well, martial arts movies are not that. In martial arts movies, you lose nine times, each time you go back and train harder, and the tenth time you're the one still standing. If you're watching a martial arts movie and there isn't a sequence where the hero is learning, training, growing, you're not watching the right movies. That kind of narrative can work in stories that aren't about fighting too. You could just as easily make a martial arts movie that's about succeeding in business. Or romance.

Martial arts are something that allowed Asians to take up space. Literally and figuratively.

RONNY: I think about Jack Nicholson in *A Few Good Men*. He's so good in that—his presence, all these intangible things he's doing with his voice and his expressions to establish he's in command. He is the absolute authority. Well, given all the social stereotypes, it's a lot harder for Asians to do that on

Western screens. Obviously, martial arts cuts out the middleman, because you can show your authority by literally busting a foot off in somebody's butt.

DANIEL: Well, yeah. Martial arts films were so successful that Hollywood started ripping them off, right? Look at *Star Wars*: At its heart, it's a martial arts story that Hollywood took from us and wrapped a whole cosmos and culture around, filled almost entirely with white people. Meanwhile, how often do we do that as Asian Americans? Why don't we borrow from this cultural tradition and make our own cool things? Most of the time we're trying to build off of white culture, when we could be building off our own.

Well, I think in part it's because martial arts movies made us victims of our own success, right?

DANIEL: It bugs me when I hear that, man—the whole "being a martial artist is just a stereotype" thing. When I see people in our own community who reject martial arts stories, I want to tell them, "You're pushing away your own culture." It's like Chinese Americans who say, "I don't eat Chinese food" or "I don't use chopsticks." These are things that have been part of our civilization for thousands of years. I'm not saying that you have to put martial arts into everything, but they're something we should be embracing as part of our heritage.

RONNY: Even martial arts genres evolved over time. After Bruce, you had Jackie Chan bringing comedy to kung fu. And if you do comedy really well, you have a license for self-expression. You have a way to get across social, political, philosophical, or personal messages in a way that gets people to listen. When Bruce saw a sign that said NO DOGS OR CHINAMEN, his approach was, "I'm going to break that sign." As a comedian, mine might be to make a joke that forces people to think about it. You know that in Chinese, the phrase "kung fu" simply means "skill gained through hard work"? It's not just fighting. Comedy is also kung fu. Anything worth doing is kung fu.

4

Masculine Feminine

THE TOLL OF THE SEA · THE HOUSE WITHOUT A KEY · DAUGHTER OF SHANGHAI · THE WORLD OF SUZIE WONG · SIXTEEN CANDLES · THE KILLER · MULAN · ROMEO MUST DIE · MEMOIRS OF A GEISHA · THE MOTEL · THE FAST AND THE FURIOUS: TOKYO DRIFT · LINSANITY · ADVANTAGEOUS · STAR WARS: EPISODE VIII—THE LAST JEDI · RAYA AND THE LAST DRAGON · LOVE HARD

Not "conventionally attractive."
A Talk with **Daniel Dae Kim** and **Kelly Marie Tran**

ILLUSTRATION (OPPOSITE) BY TOMA NGUYEN

When stereotypical attributes associated with Asians—foreignness, stoicism, inscrutability—are passed through equally stereotypical prisms of gender, we see a divergent new set of stereotypes emerge. Asian men are depicted as neutered and undesirable, whether they're lethal killers, as in films like *Romeo Must Die*, or ineffectual clowns, as in films like *Sixteen Candles*. Meanwhile, Asian women are presented as sexually available objects of pursuit, whether as slyly seductive vixens, as in *Daughter of Shanghai* and *The World of Suzie Wong*, or delicate, self-sacrificing blossoms to be plucked, as in *The Toll of the Sea* and *Memoirs of a Geisha*.

By turning Asian characters into gendered caricatures, it makes it easier for cinematic narratives to sideline them, dispose of them, or use them—as human shields, as spoils of conquest, as noble sacrifices and teachable moments. And yet, plenty of counterexamples exist: effortlessly charismatic and sexually appealing men, in movies like *The Killer* and *The Fast and the Furious: Tokyo Drift*; and strong and independent women, as in *Mulan, Star Wars: Episode VIII—The Last Jedi*, and *Raya and the Last Dragon*.

As Asian Americans are empowered to tell our own stories, not only are we creating roles that avoid these stereotypes—we're actually embracing and subverting them, transforming them from paper-thin grotesques into three-dimensional characters, as in *The Motel* and *Love Hard*. Because the most powerful antidote to stereotyping isn't to substitute cartoonishly offensive depictions with idealized ones—it's to replace them with ones that are complex and human.

Anna May Wong (center)

The Toll of the Sea

1922, NOT RATED, 54 MINUTES, METRO PICTURES CORPORATION, USA

DIRECTOR: Chester M. Franklin

STARRING: Anna May Wong, Kenneth Harlan, Beatrice Bentley

WRITER: Frances Marion

This silent film provided pioneering Asian American actress Anna May Wong with her first leading role at just seventeen years old. It also made history as Hollywood's first Technicolor feature, a marvel of the modern age, drawing viewers into theaters simply to bask in the glory of a feature-length movie shot entirely in natural color.

In a story adapted from Puccini's opera *Madama Butterfly*, Wong plays Lotus Flower, a young Chinese maiden who happens upon a near-drowned American sailor, Allen Carver (Harlan). She falls in love with him and bears his child, only for him to leave them when his home country calls him back. Years later, he returns with his white wife, Barbara, and Lotus Flower realizes that he will never, as he had promised, take her to his world. She gives their son, also named Allen, to Barbara and tells him that Barbara is his true mother, and that she has only been his Chinese nurse all along. The Carvers leave with the boy, and as intertitles suggest at the end, Lotus Flower "returns the sea's gift," drowning herself in Carver's place. (If the abundant racism and misogyny in this story line makes you clench your fists, remember that this story is so resilient that it has been remade and adapted dozens of times since, most famously as the Broadway musical *Miss Saigon*.)

Wong's performance as the self-sacrificing Lotus Flower is extraordinary—the *New York Times* praised her turn as "completely unconscious of the camera, with a fine sense of proportion and remarkable panto-mimic accuracy" and said, "She should be seen again and often on the screen." Between the wonder of color and Wong's performance, this film should've made Wong a star. Alas, it did not: Hollywood's gatekeep-ers failed to offer her another leading part to build on the notice she'd received, throwing her back into small bits as exotic backdrop. (It was in one of these ornamental roles that she finally won the mass atten-tion she deserved—though her part in the Douglas Fairbanks 1924 mega-hit *The Thief of Bagdad* was small, her beauty and expressiveness captivated crit-ics and audiences.)

For years, this film was thought to be lost, until a nearly complete print was discovered and restored, preserving a key milestone in Hollywood history, and a milestone in Wong's legacy. The cultural legacy of the film, on the other hand, survived even in the absence of its celluloid document—the term "lotus flower" or "lotus blossom" quickly became shorthand for demure, submissive, and self-sacrificing Asian female characters, a term that persists today.

The House Without a Key

1926, NOT RATED, TEN SERIAL EPISODES (EACH 15–24 MINUTES), PATHÉ EXCHANGE, USA

DIRECTOR: Spencer Gordon Bennet

STARRING: Allene Ray, Walter Miller, E. H. Calvert, Betty Caldwell, Natalie Warfield, Jack Pratt, William Norton Bailey, George Kuwa

WRITER: Frank Leon Smith

BASED ON THE NOVEL BY EARL DERR BIGGERS

This "movie"—a ten-episode silent film serial—was the very first work to bring British pulp author Earl Derr Biggers's "Oriental detective" Charlie Chan to filmed entertainment. Like so many early works, it is now considered "lost," with no complete copies of it surviving. Nevertheless, descriptions and posters of it highlight how unique it was when it was first released.

Set in Hawaii, it portrayed a younger Charlie Chan who was still a plainclothesman for the Honolulu Police Department. Even more shocking given what would come next: This very first filmed depiction of the brilliant Chan was played by Japanese American actor George Kuwa. Naturally, the serial back-benched Detective Chan, focusing primarily on the white lead characters, John Quincy Winterclip (Miller) and Carry Egan (Ray), second-generation inheritors of a bitter feud between brothers.

Detective Chan doesn't appear until the fourth episode and has little to do until the tenth and final chapter, when he pops up out of nowhere to save the hero's life. *The House Without a Key*'s version of Chan is hardly the inscrutable fortune cookie–spouting sleuth he's known as today—a gun-toting man of action. He's considered the best and sharpest investigator on the Island, treated as a talented peer by the movie's white characters, even if he doesn't have much to do. The next two

Charlie Chan movies also featured Asian actors as Chan but portrayed him in increasingly diminished fashion. In *The Chinese Parrot* (1927), Chan (Sojin Komiyama) spends most of the movie disguised as a pidgin-speaking houseboy, directed to hunch over as low to the ground as possible and comically waddle from scene to scene; *Behind That Curtain* (1929) doesn't even introduce Chan (E. L. Park) until a single scene in its final ten minutes.

The first time Charlie Chan was allowed to occupy center screen came in *Charlie Chan Carries On* (1931), after the role was taken over by Swedish actor Warner Oland, playing the part in eye tape and thick yellowface makeup. Chan would never again be played on-screen by an Asian; Oland's humble, bowing, proverb-quoting version of Chan proved to be a hit, and he would go on to portray Chan in fifteen subsequent movies, before being replaced by other white actors. The saving grace: Chan's "Number One Son" Lee, embodied with athletic swagger in ten films in the long-running series by classic Chinese American actor Keye Luke—who would decades later voice an *animated* version of Detective Chan in the Hanna-Barbera cartoon series *The Amazing Chan and the Chan Clan*, in which Chan and his ten kids perform pop music as the Chan Clan band and solve mysteries, while driving around in the Chan Clan van (sixteen episodes, 1972).

Ever dapper in his white suit, Charlie Chan was the first positive depiction of an Asian man on film, puncturing the overinflated balloon of Fu Manchu and Yellow Peril stereotypes. He created a whole new stereotype, however: that of Chinese men spouting bastardized Confucianism, dispensed in whispery singsong, and acting deferential to their white counterparts. As played by Swedish actor Warner Oland in later—and much more successful—adaptations, Chan became a global sensation and kept Fox Studios afloat during the tumultuous thirties. What few now remember is that Chan's first on-screen appearance was in this 1926 film, where he was portrayed by Japanese actor George Kuwa as a hard-nosed man of action. This classic two-reeler is now considered a lost film, and I often wonder if it were lost on purpose. I'll never know, but as a writer, I'm obsessed with the truth behind the myth. And to me, the truth is that Kuwa's version of Charlie Chan was simply too authentic and too ahead of his time.

—JAMIE FORD ON *THE HOUSE WITHOUT A KEY*

Daughter of Shanghai

1937, NOT RATED, 62 MINUTES, PARAMOUNT PICTURES, USA

DIRECTOR: Robert Florey

STARRING: Anna May Wong, Charles Bickford, Buster Crabbe, Cecil Cunningham, J. Carrol Naish, Anthony Quinn, John Patterson, Phillip Ahn, Ching Wah Lee

WRITERS: Gladys Unger, Garnett Weston

A film vehicle created as an explicit showcase for established star Anna May Wong, *Daughter of Shanghai* is a remarkably progressive film by the standards of the 1930s. Wong, as Lan Yang Lin, and the rest of the movie's Asian characters speak English sans accents. The plot features Chinese Americans busting a human-smuggling ring run by ruthless Caucasians, and amazingly, Wong's love interest is played by Korean American actor Philip Ahn, marking perhaps the first movie in Hollywood's talkie era to feature Asian American romantic leads who end up together, happily ever after. (Wong and Ahn would later play a couple in 1939's unrelated melodrama *King of Chinatown*.)

After the murder of Lin's father (Lee), she goes on the hunt for those responsible, a gang of thugs who bring immigrants into the US illegally. She's assisted in her hunt by Ahn as FBI agent Kim Lee in a rare leading role—like many Asian American male actors of the era, Ahn's career was largely composed of memorable supporting parts. But the chemistry between them is real, given that the two had been friends since high school and remained so as professionals. At the movie's end, after busting the crooks—who shockingly turn out to be led by Wong's wealthy dowager friend, Mrs. Mary Hunt (Cunningham)—Agent Lee turns to Lin and asks her how she'd "like to live in Washington," where he's based. She replies to him that a change of scenery might be just what she needs, and then clarifies, "Does this mean you're asking me to marry you?" The two then exchange their final lines of dialogue in Chinese (the Taishanese dialect specifically, reflecting Wong's own family origins): "Do you want to?" "I'm happy that you love me." Remarkable.

Philip Ahn and Anna May Wong

The World of Suzie Wong

1960, NOT RATED, 126 MINUTES, PARAMOUNT PICTURES, USA

DIRECTOR: Richard Quine

STARRING: William Holden, Nancy Kwan, Sylvia Syms, Michael Wilding, Jacqueline Chan, Laurence Naismith, Yvonne Shima, Andy Ho, Lier Hwang, Bernard Cribbins, Edwina Carroll

WRITER: John Patrick

BASED ON THE PLAY BY PAUL OSBORN

This romantic drama, which was Kwan's debut as an actress, proved to be a breakout role, with her performance receiving universal critical acclaim and winning her a Golden Globe for Most Promising Female Newcomer. Yet it also established pop-cultural archetypes that have lingered into the present day—framing Asian women as sexually available objects for inspiration, validation, and exploitation by white men, and turning the traditional Chinese dress (the qipao or cheongsam) into a slinky, body-hugging outfit associated with prostitution.

Kwan plays Wong, a lovely young woman who catches the eye of American architect Robert Lomax (Holden), who has moved to Hong Kong to pursue his dream of painting. Wong initially introduces herself as Mei Ling, the daughter of a wealthy tycoon, but soon after, Lomax encounters her in her real element, as the most popular bar girl in Hong Kong's red-light district, dressed in her trademark high-slit, tight-fitting red cheongsam. Lomax remains entranced by her, and when Lomax tells her he loves her, she moves in with him. But Wong has further secrets, notably an infant son she's been hiding in a small house on a hillside, and Lomax's jealousy and sense of pride won't let him accept her for who she is. Though the two still end up together, it's only after the darkest of tragedies has ensued.

In some ways, the Suzie Wong story is the inverse of the Madame Butterfly tale—instead of an innocent Asian girl sacrificing herself to give her baby a better life with its white father, Wong is a world-wise Asian woman who sacrifices her baby for a better life with her white lover. But both paradigms turn Asian women into an object of exotic fascination and make their sacrifice the hinge for white male fantasy fulfillment.

The backstory of Kwan's casting in the movie is fascinating: Born the daughter of a wealthy Hong

Nancy Kwan

Kong tycoon and a European model, Kwan was a trained ballet dancer with no acting experience, until producer Ray Stark ran across her application in an open call and instantly decided that she was his Suzie Wong. The studio preferred France Nuyen, who had gotten critical acclaim for playing the role in the stage play, but Stark persisted, even having Kwan fly to the US for acting lessons. Nuyen was cast and fired before production, and replaced with

Kwan after Nuyen's volatile breakup with Marlon Brando prompted a nervous breakdown. One of Stark's key arguments in favor of Kwan was that she had a sexier figure than Nuyen, and director Quine was conscious of making sure it was seen as much as possible: In a scene where Lomax rips off Wong's Western clothing, demanding that she wear the garb of her own people, Kwan was revealed to be wearing a full slip underneath. Quine demanded she switch

How do you solve a problem like Suzie Wong? For many, the name alone requires a a trigger warning. Like Madame Butterfly before her and Miss Saigon after, she's the midcentury celluloid fantasy of an Asian woman subjected to sexual exploitation and violence, her cheongsam-clad body used in this case as the forum for an ideological contest between British colonial manners and Cold War liberalism. Creaky melodrama aside, I still can't get over its utterly unforgivable conflation of patriarchal abuse with cultural superiority and—gulp—"love." But the magnetism of Nancy Kwan's on-screen presence is undeniable. One can only wonder what cinematic magic and mischief Kwan could have achieved had she had better roles.

—ANTHONY KIM ON *THE WORLD OF SUZIE WONG*

to a revealing bra and half-slip and threatened to fire her—as the production had done with Nuyen—if she refused.

The movie and Kwan's follow-up, *Flower Drum Song* (1961), made her a star, gracing the covers of magazines and having her later signature asymmetrical bob hairdo become an iconic look for the mod generation, who would ask hairstylists to give them "the Kwan." But as she grew older, roles dried up. By the nineties, her role as the spokeswoman for a skin-care product dubbed "Oriental Pearl Cream"—a cream with actual pearls ground into the mix, whose late-night infomercials offered women the secret to "perfect oriental skin"—had eclipsed her status as a legendary Hollywood pioneer.

Sixteen Candles

1984, PG, 93 MINUTES, UNIVERSAL PICTURES, USA

DIRECTOR/WRITER: John Hughes

STARRING: Molly Ringwald, Anthony Michael Hall, Michael Schoeffling, Haviland Morris, Gedde Watanabe, Paul Dooley, Carlin Glynn, Blanche Baker, Justin Henry, John Cusack, Joan Cusack, Billie Bird, Liane Curtis

It's no exaggeration to say *Sixteen Candles* shaped a generation of white youth—girls who saw themselves in wistful wallflower Sam Baker, boys who aspired to be handsome Jake Ryan (or triumphant nerd Farmer Ted)—and a generation of Asian youth, especially Asian men, through its depiction of Long Duk Dong (Watanabe). Dong, an exchange student from an unspecified Asian country, ultimately serves as the slapstick butt of many of the film's most cringeworthy and deeply racist jokes.

Gedde Watanabe and Deborah Pollack

Dong, who proudly refers to himself "the Donger," is a guest at the home of the Bakers, a white suburban family whose elder daughter, Ginny (Baker), is getting married the next day, an event whose imminent arrival has eclipsed the sixteenth birthday of younger daughter Sam (Ringwald). Sam feels unloved and ignored, and pines for attention—the right *kind* of attention from hunky Jake Ryan (Schoeffling), not desperate nerds like Dong and Ted Farmer (Hall). While Ted attempts to impress Sam, and Sam sulks over Jake's seemingly idyllic relationship with his girlfriend, Caroline (Morris), Dong manages to find his own "sexy American girlfriend" in the form of much larger jock girl Marlene (Pollack), derided by the other cast as "the Lumberjack."

By the end of a remarkably sordid series of exchanges, Jake and Sam are together, Ted and Caroline have somehow hooked up after spending the night in Jake's father's car, and Dong is discovered passed out alone on a neighbor's lawn, having overdone it at the party the night before. What follows is a relentlessly racist scene that begins with the neighbor pointing out to Sam's father that "Hey, there's your Chinaman," and concludes with Sam's grandmother kicking Dong in the crotch for losing Sam's grandfather's car.

Dong's purpose in the film would seem to be comic relief, but there's more at play here. With Jake serving as the aspirational romantic lead, and Ted—the initial comic relief—being "promoted" over the course of the film to unlikely lothario, there's a need to establish someone as occupying the permanent bottom rung of social status and sexual appeal in the film's imagined white society. Dong, as an eternal foreigner and temporary guest, is assigned that position. Yes, he finds a "sexy American girlfriend," but the movie's joke is that the girlfriend, though white and American, is not perceived as sexy. And the unlikeliness of the pairing is accentuated by Sam herself, who complains that Dong has been in the US for just hours and already has someone (albeit someone

intended to be a visual gag, towering over him while slow dancing).

But Dong isn't even allowed to ride off into the sunset with his giant queen. After being reviled by Sam and her siblings and treated like a houseboy by Grandpa Baker, who forces him to mow the lawn, he is publicly humiliated and physically abused, and then left at home to nurse his wounds as the rest of the family attends the wedding. The lack of any saving grace for Dong's character arc combines with the movie's continued microaggressions (constant jokes about Dong's name, the gong sound heard whenever he enters a room, the radio playing "Turning Japanese" by the Vapors when he drives) to make this an extremely uncomfortable watch for many Asians.

Though a generation of eighties kids see *Sixteen Candles* as a seminal classic, the role of Long Duk Dong is one of the most memorably racist in Hollywood history. But what if it wasn't? Here (opposite) **barbarian flower** imagines a teen-com makeover, with Long Duk Dong at its center.

In 1988, legendary Asian American actor Sab Shimono and I originated the starring roles in Philip Kan Gotanda's seminal play about Asian representation in Hollywood, *Yankee Dawg You Die*. A journalist covering the production asked me for an example of a demeaning and racist character in a Hollywood movie. Of course my answer was the most glaringly offensive Asian character of that decade, Long Duk Dong. I railed on about the accented, emasculating portrayal, and how I would never take a role like that. Sab read the published article back to me in our dressing room, then invited me to his house for a get-together after the show: "There's someone you simply must meet," he said. That night I went to his house, where a party was raging with all of Asian American Hollywood in attendance—every Asian actor you've ever seen on TV and in movies. He greeted me, then pushed me toward a shy, unassuming man standing by the punch bowl—"Kelvin, meet Gedde Watanabe!"—before leaving me alone with the person I'd just dragged in the newspaper. He turned out to be the sweetest, most vulnerable person I'd ever met. I mumbled an apology; he waved it away and said, "No need." I spent the evening getting to know him and quickly realized that nearly every other Asian American actor in that room had auditioned for the same part. Many Asian American men have unquestionably suffered because of Long Duk Dong. But Gedde is a good guy and a generous soul who continues to give back to the Asian American community. He didn't deserve the rage; John Hughes and Hollywood did. And that night, my mentor Sab had given me a lesson about empathy and respect. Because being part of a mutually supportive community makes our art better. It makes our world better.

—KELVIN HAN YEE ON *SIXTEEN CANDLES*

Sixteen Candles

CULTURAL EXCHANGE CAN BE A REAL TRIP. Jeong Deok-won is turning sixteen, and instead of partying it up with his pals in Seoul, he's stuck on a school-sponsored "sister-city immersion" trip to the most boring part of America imaginable: Some cow-town called Shermer, Illinois, where he's expected to spend two weeks living with the Bakers—a family that puts butter on their rice and still uses dial-up Internet. K-pop-loving middle daughter Sam has a massive crush on him. Her older sis Ginny is intent on shooting his experience as a documentary for her college film class. And their MMA-loving kid brother Mike keeps on testing his hand-to-hand combat skills with surprise flying kicks. But a chance meeting with Jacinda Ryan, star center for Shermer High's championship women's hoops team, might make the whole trip worthwhile. Will the tall queen of Deok-won's dreams make his birthday wishes come true?

The Killer

1989, R, 111 MINUTES, CIRCLE FILMS, HONG KONG/CHINA

DIRECTOR/WRITER: John Woo

STARRING: Chow Yun-Fat, Danny Lee, Sally Yeh, Chu Kong, Kenneth Tsang, Shing Fui-On

Although it arrived after director Woo laid the foundations for the heroic bloodshed genre in *A Better Tomorrow* (1986) and its sequel *A Better Tomorrow II* (1987), most Western audiences saw *The Killer* first, since unlike its predecessors, it made film festival rounds in North America (Toronto, Palm Springs, Sundance) and Europe (Cannes), then rode the critical acclaim from those showings to a limited American arthouse release, followed by a wider release in the UK.

Among keen action viewers, *The Killer* quickly established itself as a litmus test: If you had seen it, you understood—John Woo was the greatest action filmmaker on the planet. If you had not, you became irrelevant to all future conversation until you did.

The film's story was equal parts absurd and brilliant: Chow Yun-Fat plays Ah Jong (subtitled as "Jeffrey"), a retiring hit man who accidentally burns the corneas of a nightclub singer named Jennie (Yeh) during a shoot-out. Remorseful, Ah Jong decides to serve as her guardian angel, attending her shows and defending against street predators. After he saves her from potential assault, the two begin a romantic relationship—made bitter by their discovery that Jennie needs expensive eye surgery immediately or her blindness will be permanent. To pay for the operation, Ah Jong decides to secretly take on one last job, assassinating a high-ranking Triad boss.

When crossfire in another shoot-out hits a young child, Ah Jong races the bystander to the hospital, followed all the way by a maverick cop, Li (Lee), who is astounded to see a cold-blooded killer risk his own getaway for the life of an innocent. As a result, Li becomes obsessed with understanding Ah Jong, and the two develop a deepening sense of mutual respect as cop investigates killer.

Meanwhile, Ah Jong's attempts to procure the money he's owed to save Jennie's sight result in his being repeatedly betrayed and having to fight his way out of ambushes again and again. Rather than arresting Ah Jong, Li ends up saving his life, and the two form a tight bond, with Ah Jong even forcing Li to vow that he'll follow through on getting Jennie her operation should the embattled hit man finally catch a bullet. Li ends up being forced to break his promise:

John Woo's *A Better Tomorrow* served as my gateway drug for binges of bromantic bullet-ballets by Ringo Lam, Tsui Hark, and many others at my local Chinatown video store. But even so, I was shocked to see *The Killer* at my local Blockbuster Video, in an official American release on VHS. Watching it made me realize why: It was the apex of Woo, with all the classic Woo tropes—white doves, Catholic imagery, balletic gun choreography, and Chow Yun-Fat being effortlessly cool in a performance that readily rivaled any by James Dean or Steve McQueen. *The Killer* didn't just awaken America to a golden age of Hong Kong cinema. It also opened the door for Woo-mania in Hollywood, where he unleashed Hong Kong–flavored hybrids like *Hard Target*, *Broken Arrow*—my fave of his American efforts—and the cult classic *Face/Off*.

—ANDERSON LE ON *THE KILLER*

Chow Yun-Fat

An apocalyptic final shoot-out at a church ends with Ah Jong blinded and bleeding out; Jennie, equally sightless, crawling across shattered stained glass trying to find him as he dies; and Li executing Ah Jong's murderer in front of his former HKPD colleagues, leading them to arrest him as he collapses to the ground in tears over the death of his friend.

Embedded within the explosions and angst are masterful comic sequences, such as the one where Ah Jong and Li run into each other at Jennie's apartment and pretend to be old childhood friends who call each other by the nicknames "Mickey Mouse" and "Dumbo," even as they hold guns to each other's faces, right under blind Jennie's nose.

This movie is also where the tropes that have become Woo's directorial signatures achieve full resolution: sliding backward on the floor while shooting two pistols simultaneously, gunfire that startles flocks of doves into flight, explosive acts of bloody violence on sacred ground, and of course, matched rivals on opposite sides of the law who find their way to an uneasy but unbreakable friendship. Woo's ambition in *The Killer* and his subsequent works in the genre is to present violence and self-sacrifice as a forge for manhood and, even more importantly,

brotherhood. His success is apparent in the many who've adopted his aesthetics and narrative themes across global cinema, including fans like France's Luc Besson and Hollywood's Quentin Tarantino and Robert Rodriguez.

Mulan

**1998, G, 88 MINUTES,
BUENA VISTA PICTURES, USA**

DIRECTORS: Tony Bancroft, Barry Cook

STARRING: Ming-Na Wen, Eddie Murphy, B. D. Wong, Miguel Ferrer, June Foray, James Hong, Pat Morita, George Takei, James Shigeta, Gedde Watanabe

WRITERS: Rita Hsiao, Chris Sanders

The nineties were a period of reflection and reinvention for Disney's once-unstoppable feature animation juggernaut. The prior decade had seen the studio release a series of disappointments and middling successes, with its standout hit being the musical adaptation of the Hans Christian Andersen fairy tale *The Little Mermaid* (1989). On cue, the studio began investing effort and attention toward replicating that success, releasing *Beauty and the Beast* in 1991 and then expanding into non-European folklore with *Aladdin* (1992), *Pocahontas* (1995), and in 1998, *Mulan*—a story inspired by the Chinese legend of a brave and dutiful young woman who, to save her ailing father's life, dresses in men's clothing and goes to war in his stead.

Fa Mulan

But while Disney likely saw *Mulan* as an opportunity to expand the relevance of the "Disney Princess" brand to include the oldest culture and most populous nation on Earth, the story presented unique and disruptive challenges. First, Mulan wasn't a princess, strictly speaking. And the story wasn't, at its core, a love story, as prior "Princess" tales had been. And the protagonist was . . . a cross-dressing warrior who eschewed the glittery gowns and hair ornaments that made the Princess brand so lucrative in favor of swords and armor. Disney, to its credit, forged ahead anyway, and brought Mulan to the screen, creating an idiosyncratic classic that raised a generation of Asian Americans and remains both beloved and groundbreaking today.

As in the original legend, Fa Mulan (Wen) answers the call of the emperor to go to battle in her father's stead, dressing as a man and taking his

F a Mulan saved China with a lucky cricket, a dragon spirit, and a hard-ass training regimen from a hunky warrior, but along the way she dealt with imposter syndrome and parental pressure and trying to balance professional and personal fulfillment. That's a distinctly Asian American deal, and frankly, a distinctly "me" deal. So when her dad tells her at the end, "The greatest gift and honor is having you for a daughter," it's such an emotional release that I cry just thinking about it. Generational therapy for the price of a movie ticket: Thank you, Disney. You brought catharsis to us all.

—CYNTHIA WANG ON *MULAN*

sword and his horse to enlist. Disney added a quirk of rebellion and feminism to the mix, depicting Mulan as unable and unwilling to be the stereotypical "good Chinese girl"—and eventually, obedient wife—that is her expected lot in life, making her choice to join the military a means of escape as well as an act of heroic self-sacrifice. (They also devised a comic sidekick for Mulan in the form of Mushu, a miniature dragon who ends up becoming Mulan's guardian spirit, played by Eddie Murphy as a dragon.)

The nature of the original story means that the thematic core of the movie is gender and the expectations that go along with being male and female; there's even a whole musical anthem called "I'll Make a Man Out of You," delivered by Imperial Army Captain Li Shang (Wong) to Mulan and her miserable lot of fellow army trainees. "Did they send me daughters, when I asked for sons?" sings Shang in one line from the song, triggering a full-body cringe from the human answer to that question. Suffice it to say that by the movie's end, not only has Mulan successfully passed through basic training and bonded with her fellow army men, but she has also saved the emperor himself from the ravaging Huns, by sneaking her infantry unit into the Imperial Palace dressed as . . . women. The brilliantly disruptive nature of this film could be seen in how many boys *and* girls engaged in mock sword fights on the way out of the theater, with kids of both genders clamoring for the right to play the movie's hero.

Romeo Must Die

2000, R, 115 MINUTES, WARNER BROS., USA

DIRECTOR: Andrzej Bartkowiak

STARRING: Jet Li, Aaliyah, Isaiah Washington, Russell Wong, DMX, Delroy Lindo, Henry O, Jon Kit Lee

WRITERS: Eric Bernt, John Jarrell

It's easy to forget that in 2000, Aaliyah and Jet Li were rising stars with limitless ceilings—the former a hip-hop and R&B phenom, the latter a global action star who'd just broken into the American consciousness as the sole reason to watch the fourth chapter of the fading Mel Gibson and Danny Glover *Lethal Weapon* franchise. The notion of pairing them in a movie inspired by Shakespeare's classic play of star-crossed lovers made all the sense in the world on paper (if you just overlooked the awkward fact that Li, at thirty-seven, was just about old enough to be

As a preexisting fan of both Aaliyah and Jet Li, my high school self could not believe I was getting the two together in a major Hollywood movie. Jet as the lead, opposite my favorite R&B singer? That was a fantasy dream collab come true. Add on an amazing soundtrack featuring my favorite hip-hop and R&B artists and the fact that it took place in Oakland, just thirty minutes away from my hometown, and this movie seemed like it was purpose-built for my teenage self. I watched it in theaters, bought the DVD, had its poster on my wall, even taped the "Try Again" music video off the TV onto VHS. It was not until years later that I learned how the final kiss we'd all expected between Jet and Aaliyah was edited out due to negative test audience reactions, making this film truly a textbook example of what Asian male actors experienced in Hollywood—until more recently than any of us like to think.

—PHILIP WANG ON *ROMEO MUST DIE*

Aaliyah and Jet Li

twenty-one-year-old Aaliyah's father). But *Romeo Must Die* ended up light on the "Romeo" and heavy on the "Must Die," serving up little romance and substantial quantities of violent action.

The sole love scene that had been scripted for the two leads, a kiss intended for the film's conclusion, ended up on the cutting-room floor after it apparently "tested poorly" with audiences. It's fair to reason it tested poorly because the audiences of the early 2000s—white, Black, and even Asian—weren't ready for the depiction of an Asian man and Black woman as romantic partners, or perhaps for an Asian man to be a romantic lead at all. Given the movie's success ($91 million on a $25 million budget), perhaps their relationship could have evolved in a sequel. But the tragic passing of Aaliyah in a plane crash the following year made that impossible.

Memoirs of a Geisha

2005, PG-13, 145 MINUTES, COLUMBIA PICTURES, USA

DIRECTOR: Rob Marshall

STARRING: Zhang Ziyi, Ken Watanabe, Michelle Yeoh, Koji Yakusho, Youki Kudoh, Kaori Momoi, Gong Li, Samantha Futerman, Mako, Elizabeth Sung, Tsai Chin, Eugenia Yuan, Karl Yune, Ted Levine

WRITER: Robin Swicord

BASED ON THE NOVEL BY ARTHUR GOLDEN

In this period melodrama, a young girl named Chiyo (Zhang) is sold by her father to procurers, who deliver her to a drinking house to be schooled as a future geisha—to the resentment of the establishment's existing geisha, Hatsumomo (Li). She rejects her new lot and attempts to escape, until she encounters a wealthy patron, "the Chairman" (Watanabe). The Chairman treats her with kindness, prompting her to vow to become a top geisha in order to gain his attention.

Renamed Sayuri as a newly made maiko, or trainee, she quickly attracts attention from the older men around her, who end up bidding an extraordinary amount for the right to take her virginity. After the end of the war, Sayuri uses her skills to help influence an American military officer (Levine) while using the officer's infatuation with her as leverage to fend off other suitors and win the heart of the Chairman. By the film's conclusion, she is finally able to confess her love for him and learns that she had always been in his heart—in fact, he was the one who arranged for her grooming as a geisha.

Though it was a qualified hit and earned three Oscar nominations, the film received mediocre reviews and generated angry backlash in Japan. Looking back at the context of the film's creation, it's easy to see why. *Memoirs* was based on a book of the same name by Arthur Sulzberger Golden, scion of the family that owns the *New York Times*. After graduating from Harvard with a degree in Japanese

Michelle Yeoh and Zhang Ziyi

art, he spent a few years traveling in Beijing and Tokyo, where he was ultimately inspired to write the book. Golden interviewed a number of retired geishas as background, and even obtained an audience with the most famous geiko of the modern era, Mineko Iwasaki, under the strict condition he depict the profession accurately and respectfully, and not breach her personal privacy.

Despite his promise, his book leaned heavily into sensation, portraying geisha as elevated prostitutes while weaving loosely disguised events, people, and

Memoirs of a Geisha was the first film to make me realize that a good book sometimes makes for a terrible movie. In a novel, especially one with a first-person perspective, the world is seen through the eyes of the characters—novels are all about interiority. But movies are visual and ultimately have to focus on external conflict; they're about action and reaction. Even setting all of the other controversies aside, this just ended up being very sumptuous and very, very slow.

—JENNIFER 8. LEE ON *MEMOIRS OF A GEISHA*

anecdotes from Iwasaki's life—ones that close friends and family would easily recognize—into his fictionalized narrative. The book became an international bestseller, selling four million copies and staying on the bestseller lists for two years. Iwasaki, who earned nothing from the book's success and was aghast at the lurid view of geisha it presented, sued him for defamation, with Golden settling out of court. Despite all this, Spielberg moved ahead in developing an $85 million prestige adaptation of the book, setting Rob Marshall—best known for his opulent film versions of Broadway musicals—as its director.

In short, this cinematic extravaganza about a historically unique and deeply revered subculture of Japanese women was entirely conceived and created by white men, which is likely why the decision was made to cast Zhang Ziyi as protagonist Chiyo and, opposite her, Gong Li as her bitter rival Hatsumomo. The casting of Chinese actors in the movie's lead roles generated massive backlash in Japan while also leading to the movie getting banned in China. Meanwhile, Asian American women had to contend with the resurgence of stereotypes that colored how they were perceived and treated, of being submissive, exotic, available, and in need of saving by patriarchal men.

The Motel

2005, NOT RATED, 75 MINUTES, IMAGINASIAN PICTURES, USA

DIRECTOR/WRITER: Michael Kang

STARRING: Jeffrey Chyau, Sung Kang, Jade Wu, Samantha Futerman, Alexis Kapp Chang, Stephen Chen, Conor J. White

BASED ON THE NOVEL *WAYLAID* BY ED LIN

The feature debut of Michael Kang is an earnest coming-of-age film, following thirteen-year-old Ernest Chin (Chyau), whose family (minus his father, who abandoned them long ago) owns a dilapidated motel with a primary clientele of sex workers and their clients. Though he spends his days cleaning after-coitus detritus from the motel's run-down rooms, his aspiration is to eventually become a writer. He receives an honorable mention, which his bitter mother (Wu) dismisses as a sign of his also-ran talent. Meanwhile, Ernest must contend with the demands of his bratty younger sister (Chang) and doddering grandpa (Chen) while dodging the attention of the only kid his age living in the motel—a racist bully named Roy (White) who tries his best to make Ernest's life miserable.

The only bright spot in this Upstate New York hell: Christine (Futerman), the cool older girl who works in her parents' neighboring Chinese restaurant and the amused object of Ernest's affections. But Ernest's life is upended by the arrival of Sam (Kang), a hard-living, hard-partying ne'er-do-well who arrives at the hotel after being kicked out by his long-suffering girlfriend. Sam steps instantly into Ernest's seedy, empty reality as the father figure he never had, teaching him how to drive, hitting golf balls on the highway, and giving him terrible advice about women.

Sam's example leads Ernest to begin to act out against his mother's oppressive rules. In a desperate attempt to win Christine's love, he steals his mom's car for an illicit drive, then confesses to Christine, and after being instantly rejected, he tosses the car keys into the woods in a fit of pique. The incident prompts Ernest to confront Sam and recognize that he's not a role model for how to be a man, but instead a worst-case scenario. The lesson doesn't quite offer hope, but offers at least a degree of self-awareness that suggests he may find his way out of Poughkeepsie after all. Few Asian American indie films have had as deft a touch as *The Motel* in navigating the awkward nuances of adolescence (the movie even promoted itself at a website with the URL "PubertySucks.com"), or as authentic a critique of the pathway to toxic masculinity.

The Fast and the Furious: Tokyo Drift

2006, PG-13, 104 MINUTES, UNIVERSAL PICTURES, USA

DIRECTOR: Justin Lin

STARRING: Lucas Black, Bow Wow, Sung Kang, Brian Tee, Nathalie Kelley, Sonny Chiba, Leonardo Nam, Brian Goodman

WRITER: Chris Morgan

The Fast and the Furious (2001) was a breath of fresh air tinged with the smell of burning nitrous—a sleek multiplex-friendly thriller about street racing, car

Sung Kang and Brian Tee

chases, and breathtaking automotive stunts. After it made over $200 million, a sequel, *2 Fast 2 Furious* (2003), was quickly greenlit (missing the original's breakout star Vin Diesel, who passed after reading the script). While that movie earned even more than its predecessor, critical reaction was abysmal, and the concern at Universal was that the budding franchise had driven down a blind alley. They took a huge risk by deciding to do a soft reboot of the series, breathing new life into its theme of street racing by transplanting the action to Japan and the world of "drifting," a balletic move that skilled drivers can pull off using overpowered rear-drive cars with manual transmissions, essentially causing the back wheels to lose traction and spin out of line in order to allow much tighter and quicker turns than otherwise possible.

Doubling down on the theme of novelty, the studio decided to put the $85 million film in the hands of a relatively unknown director, Justin Lin, who'd caught Hollywood's attention with his breakout indie film *Better Luck Tomorrow* (2002) and who pitched a take on the movie that emphasized Japan's postmodern aesthetics rather than the exotic orientalism the studio had originally envisioned. He brought in his longtime collaborator, actor Sung Kang, for a major role, Han Lue, who serves as a racing mentor for delinquent high schooler Sean Boswell (Black).

Twinkie (Bow Wow) introduces Boswell to

> **G**rowing up with brown skin and a name like "Arune," I never expected to be considered cool. But then *Tokyo Drift* brought us the Drift King and Han. They were the "cool guys" of the film, playing parts that had always felt reserved in blockbuster films for white actors. Han gets the good lines, love from everyone, and the respect of his peers; DK is clearly presented as a dangerous and charismatic antagonist who might not be as bad as some think. Watching *Tokyo Drift* was the first time I felt like someone who looked like me could be the cool guy in a Hollywood story, and even my own story.
> —ARUNE SINGH ON *THE FAST AND THE FURIOUS: TOKYO DRIFT*

Tokyo's underground racing scene, dominated by Takashi (Tee), a.k.a. the Drift King. Sean borrows a car from Han for the race but wrecks it and loses, due to his unfamiliarity with drifting—a necessary skill for Tokyo's narrow and winding roads. To pay Han back, Sean works for him at his garage while learning drift techniques to rechallenge Takashi. Later, Takashi, Sean, and Han engage in a wild high-speed demolition derby on the crowded streets of Tokyo, leading to Han's apparent death in a fiery explosion. To avenge Han, Sean challenges Takashi to one last race on an extremely difficult mountain track. Naturally, Sean wins, becoming the new Drift King—at least until an unannounced Dom Toretto (Diesel) shows up in the final moments of the film in a surprise cameo, challenging him to a race for the crown. The return of Diesel sets up a lane shift back to the main *Fast and Furious* story line in *Tokyo Drift*'s sequels, also helmed in large part by Lin, who is generally acknowledged as having saved the franchise.

Over the course of the series, even the untimely passing of Han is unwound, with his backstory explored in the fifth and sixth films and—after a viral social media campaign demanding #JusticeForHan—his shocking survival of the crash revealed in *F9*, courtesy of a hoax engineered by the mysterious government operative "Mr. Nobody," allowing Sung Kang to fully return to the series' main continuity. Han, a fan favorite for being an island of easygoing sensitivity and compassion amid the franchise's surging sea of testosterone, is apparently hiding another secret: As Lin has explained in

interviews, he's not just named the same as Kang's character in Lin's *Better Luck Tomorrow*—he's the *same* person, which makes *BLT* the *Fast and Furious* films' secret prequel.

Linsanity

2013, PG, 89 MINUTES, ARC ENTERTAINMENT, USA

DIRECTOR: Evan Jackson Leong

STARRING: Jeremy Lin

NARRATION: Daniel Dae Kim

In early 2012, an undrafted, unknown, and unheralded NBA player named Jeremy Lin caught the attention of the entire sports world—and most of the world beyond sports too. Picked up by the New York Knicks to fill out their injury-depleted roster, Lin was expected to, at most, eat minutes as point guard. What Lin did next stunned the sports world, and Lin himself, as he admits in this thoroughly engrossing documentary.

Put on the court in a desperate shake-up by coach Mike D'Antoni after the team had lost eleven of their last thirteen games, Lin scored twenty-five

When I moved to New York City in 2008, I adopted the Knicks as my second team. (Spurs for life, okay?) Sadly, the Knicks weren't good, and wouldn't be for years . . . except for one brief, shining period dubbed Linsanity, one of the most exciting and unexpected moments in modern basketball. Yet it was one with racist undertones: What made Jeremy Lin's meteoric rise "special" was how few people could imagine a player of Asian descent succeeding at the highest level of the sport. In charting one of my favorite sports stories of this century, Linsanity manages to shine a light on some of our cultural biases, both implicit and explicit.

—SIMRAN JEET SINGH ON *LINSANITY*

Jeremy Lin

points in his first full game as a Knick, leading them to a resounding victory. He scored twenty-eight points in the next game, with eight assists, again sparking the team to a win, then twenty-three points with ten assists the game after. And then, on February 10, 2012, Lin delivered the performance that led to the phenomenon dubbed "Linsanity," scoring thirty-eight points on 57 percent shooting against the Lakers and the legendary late Kobe Bryant, who had told reporters ahead of the game that he didn't know who Lin was. He certainly did after that night, and so did the world, as Lin's picture graced magazine covers and his highlights saturated sports reports, night after night, turning him into a global celebrity. At the end of March, unfortunately, tragedy struck as quickly as success had. Lin injured the meniscus in his left knee, ending his season, any hopes the Knicks had to make the playoffs, and, as it turned out, his brief, shining chapter as an NBA superstar.

He made solid contributions on other good teams, even winning a championship with the Toronto Raptors, but Lin would never reach the global hype of Linsanity again. Lin's status as the first Asian American player to achieve dominant pop culture superstardom in a big-league team sport remains (a fact we're reminded of today as Japanese native Shohei Ohtani blazes his staggering two-way path across Major League Baseball).

Linsanity is documented here by director Evan Jackson Leong, who'd begun filming Lin when he was in college setting conference records on Harvard University's basketball squad. Leong persisted in covering him through his early struggles in the NBA after going undrafted and was in the miraculous position to cover the behind-the-scenes reality of Lin's ascent during the months of Linsanity, showing his faith, humility, and passion for the game. (Lin was so sure his dream would tumble back to earth that he didn't even rent an apartment in New York, instead choosing to crash on his brother's living room sofa as he was making headlines.) While others in his position might have chosen to exhibit swagger and live large, Lin instead focused on honing his skills, building relationships with his teammates, and preparing for whatever might come next.

The real revelation of *Linsanity* isn't what Lin did on the court in his three months in the spotlight but how he stayed anchored in the face of persistent dismissal of his abilities (even by his own teammates, some of whom were resistant to sharing the spotlight), racist insults from rivals, degrading attacks on his manhood by pundits, and the pressures of being a role model to millions of Asian Americans. The wonder isn't how he achieved Linsanity—it's how he preserved his own personal sanity as it happened.

Advantageous

2015, NOT RATED, 90 MINUTES, FILM PRESENCE, USA

DIRECTOR: Jennifer Phang

STARRING: Jacqueline Kim, James Urbaniak, Freya Adams, Ken Jeong, Jennifer Ehle, Samantha Kim

WRITERS: Jacqueline Kim, Jennifer Phang

Science fiction offers a unique canvas for exploring social issues that are too wound into our culture for us to see clearly, and in her debut feature, *Advantageous*—adapted and expanded from her own critically acclaimed short film—director Jennifer Phang tackles a number of them all at once: the pressure society places on women to stay young, the cannibal competitiveness and gross inequality of late capitalist society, the need to erase race in order to seem "universally appealing."

Gwen (Jacqueline Kim) is a spokesperson for the Center for Advanced Health and Living, a health tech company. The center's stock in trade is procedures to enhance appearance and wind back the clock, which aren't luxuries in a future where every "advantage" is necessary to avoid becoming one of the 45 percent of the population that's unemployed, especially if you're female, as women are discouraged from work due to rapidly falling fertility rates.

Gwen has the rare fortune of having a child, a daughter named Jules (Samantha Kim), but the costs of giving her the advantages she needs to survive keep Gwen at the edge of bankruptcy. Her only professional choices are to sell her eggs for money or to undergo the new and still-experimental procedure that she'd previously been touting, a consciousness-transfer operation that will put her mind in a youthful and racially ambiguous new body that's ideal for her old spokesmodel job. Though the latter is more radical, it seems like it has a firmer future, and the results appear to be successful. The transfer, however, seems to erase a key element of Gwen's personality—her maternal love for Jules—which forces the center to reveal a dark secret about the truth behind the operation. It's rare for independent science fiction movies to have staying power, given rising audience expectations for special effects and media saturation (and our reality, for that matter) with future dystopias. Nearly a decade after its making, *Advantageous* holds up.

Star Wars: Episode VIII—The Last Jedi

2017, PG-13, 152 MINUTES, BUENA VISTA HOME ENTERTAINMENT, USA

DIRECTOR/WRITER: Rian Johnson

STARRING: Mark Hamill, Carrie Fisher, Adam Driver, Daisy Ridley, John Boyega, Oscar Isaac, Andy Serkis, Lupita Nyong'o, Domhnall Gleeson, Anthony Daniels, Gwendoline Christie, Kelly Marie Tran, Laura Dern, Benicio del Toro

A year after *Rogue One* (2016), Disney released the second film of the *Star Wars* Skywalker saga, handing the franchise's reins to Rian Johnson, who introduced ideas, events, and characters that could have transformed *Star Wars* continuity. The good guys are a young white woman, a Black man, a woman of Asian descent, and a Latino man! Force sensitivity isn't limited to certain "elite" bloodlines! Luke Skywalker dies! Porgs! These all-new elements in the *Star Wars* tapestry proved to be too different for old-guard fans, who then engineered a massive, toxic social media campaign targeting Johnson and one of the fresh-faced stars, Kelly Marie Tran.

As Rose Tico, Tran plays a Resistance mechanic who discovers Finn (Boyega) attempting to go AWOL in the wake of a deadly First Order ambush. Finn explains to her that the First Order can now track Resistance ships through hyperspace, potentially dooming the Rebel fleet. So, Rose joins Finn in his quest to find a way to disable the new First Order tracking device. Meanwhile, ace pilot Poe Dameron (Isaac) readies the surviving Resistance fighters for an inevitable final confrontation with the First Order, while Rey (Ridley) attempts to convince the great Jedi hero Luke Skywalker to come out of self-imposed retirement, both to teach her how to use the Force and, ultimately, to join the Resistance.

She's successful: Skywalker mentors her in the way of the Jedi and, in an extraordinary feat, fights his corrupted former student, Kylo Ren (Driver), using a Force ghost projected from across the galaxy.

John Boyega and Kelly Marie Tran

Sadly, the enormous effort required to project himself light-years away is too much for even Skywalker to survive—except as the subject of legends, whispered across the galaxy among those seeking inspiration and hope. Within *Jedi*'s constellation of outsized characters, Tran's grounded, empathic Rose stands out as a hero. It's a tragedy that she ended up as a lightning rod for hostile fans, who attacked her race and appearance, questioning her right to even appear on-screen alongside icons like Jedi master Luke and Princess-General Leia—an ironic tragedy, as Rose seems designed as a loving proxy for fans themselves. The final movie in the trilogy, helmed once more by J. J. Abrams, featured Rose in a reduced role. Many fans feel *Star Wars* still owes us a continuation of her story, and perhaps someday we'll see one.

George Lucas has never denied how much Asian culture and aesthetics influenced the creation of *Star Wars*. The films of Akira Kurosawa are so indelible to the original trilogy that Lucas nearly cast Toshiro Mifune as Obi-Wan Kenobi. Alas, despite *Star Wars*' samurai roots, actual Asians were few and far between in that galaxy far, far away—Natalie Portman's wardrobe and a couple of racist aliens notwithstanding. That all changed in 2017, when Kelly Marie Tran brought Resistance fighter Rose Tico to life here. *The Last Jedi* is also the film that revealed how toxic the *Star Wars* fandom could be, forcing Tran off social media. But for many Asian American *Star Wars* fans, Rose was a character finally worth rallying around.

—KEITH CHOW ON *STAR WARS: EPISODE VIII—THE LAST JEDI*

Raya (Tran) and Sisu the dragon (Awkwafina)

Raya and the Last Dragon

2021, PG, 107 MINUTES, WALT DISNEY STUDIOS, USA

DIRECTORS: Don Hall, Carlos López Estrada

STARRING: Kelly Marie Tran, Awkwafina, Daniel Dae Kim, Gemma Chan, Izaac Wang, Benedict Wong, Sandra Oh

WRITERS: Qui Nguyen, Adele Lim

With *Moana* (2016), Disney proved it could tell a story that wove disparate mythic threads of the vast Pacific Islander diaspora. Over on the Marvel side of the company, *Black Panther* (2018) demonstrated that the company could invent a wholly original yet authentic Pan-African culture and bring it believably to the big screen. With *Raya*, Disney chose to create a fantasy world from the ground up, building it on a foundation rarely seen in American entertainment: the influences and aesthetics of Southeast Asian cultures.

The result feels novel but also tantalizingly familiar: The land of Kumandra is an Asian dish made in an American kitchen, by cooks whose palates and palettes have been shaped by their diasporic immigrant roots. The world of Kumandra was once overseen by the Dragons, enchanted beasts whose magic guaranteed good weather, fertile soil, and the well-being of Kumandra's human population. But the sudden invasion of the ravaging evil spirits known as the Druun ends the land's peace and bounty. Their mere touch causes living things to turn to stone, including Dragons. Facing mass petrification, the desperate guardians of Kumandra choose to transfer their spirits and magic into a gemstone and entrust it to their youngest sibling, Sisu (Awkwafina), to use in driving away the Druun and save the land. Sisu succeeds, and peace in Kumandra, for a time, is restored. Eventually, the very existence of the five gems tempts the tribes to battle for possession.

Kumandra ends up breaking apart into five kingdoms: Fang, Heart, Spine, Talon, and Tail, each named for where they sit on the river's "dragon." As the movie begins, the benevolent Heart kingdom maintains control over the gem, but the other four

> I will never forget my five-year-old niece's excitement in watching a Southeast Asian Disney Princess on-screen. Watching her, I could see the real-life impact of representation in shaping young hearts and minds. My niece felt empowered to be a strong heroine herself, and to this day, still watches *Raya* whenever she needs a pick-me-up. On top of that, seeing Kelly Marie Tran in an áo dài at the Academy Awards was just an incredible moment for the entire Vietnamese American community!
>
> **—JEREMY TRAN ON *RAYA AND THE LAST DRAGON***

> As a Lao American, I am a minority of a minority in the United States. Aside from being a surprisingly consistent *New York Times* crossword answer, Lao folks don't get to see much representation in mainstream media. (I only know about the crossword because my husband screengrabs and texts me every time he sees it.) So, for me it was huge that Disney set an animated feature in a world inspired by Laos and other Southeast Asian countries. Starving to be seen, I ate up the details of Raya's hat, the food, the darker skin tones of its characters, and the role of Boun being voiced by Lao Chinese actor Izaac Wang. *Raya* is an action-adventure with female leads with full agency, who make mistakes and do better. And as I'm writing this, I'm also setting up my daughter's nursery. I've put all the *Raya* merch that I bought for myself in there for her.
>
> **—KULAP VILAYSACK ON *RAYA AND THE LAST DRAGON***

kingdoms, led by Fang, have executed a plot to steal the gem away. The theft is a success. Escape with the gem, less so—in the chaos of the heist, the gem falls and breaks into five pieces, which are claimed in flight by the different chieftains of the tribe. As the Druun arrive, some people flee, while others decide to fight and are picked off and turned to stone one by one, including Benja (Kim), chief of the Heart tribe and father of warrior-princess Raya (Tran). Though Benja's incapacitation means that Raya is now chief, her whole clan has been petrified: Even if she felt ready to rule, she'd be leading just one surviving Heart tribe member, herself. She resolves to go on a quest to find Sisu, the last Dragon, and recover the four missing fragments of the gem.

Even in an era where Disney "Princesses" are as likely to save their princes as vice versa, Raya is a standout—a female protagonist who's a trained and intrepid fighter, explorer, guardian, and leader, facing a rival who is the same. An Asian protagonist and antagonist (like everyone else in the cast!) seems like icing on the cake.

Love Hard

2021, TV-MA, 104 MINUTES, NETFLIX, USA

DIRECTOR: Hernán Jiménez

STARRING: Jimmy O. Yang, Nina Dobrev, Darren Barnet, James Saito, Rebecca Staab, Harry Shum Jr., Althea Kaye, Mikaela Hoover

WRITERS: Danny Mackey, Rebecca Ewing

The cleverness of this Christmas rom-com begins with its title, which blends together the preferred Yuletide movies of Josh Lin (*Love Actually*) and Natalie Bauer (*Die Hard*) into a kind of cinematic ship-name. This discussion of favorite Christmas flicks is how the online flirtation between hunky, athletic Upstate New York–based Josh (Yang) and quirky, winsome Los Angeles–based Natalie (Dobrev) begins. Except, it turns out that Josh is *not* the hunky athlete his dating profile presents him as, because he's uploaded pictures of his hunky, athletic friend Tag Abbott (Barnet) instead of his own. Natalie has a secret too, though: While she's genuinely interested in "Josh"—at least

(From left) Harry Shum Jr., Jimmy O. Yang, Nina Dobrev

the Josh she sees in the pictures—she also writes a column about her dating misadventures. So, if Josh doesn't turn out to be "The One," the experience will still be fodder for her day job. At the urging of her boss, she flies out to his hometown of Lake Placid to surprise him . . . only to discover he's not only not "The One," he's not even the one in the pictures. Josh convinces her to pretend to be his girlfriend for the rest of the trip by promising to hook her up with the real Tag later. Though Natalie agrees, the more time she and Tag spend together, the more she realizes they have nothing in common. When, on the eve of her return to LA, Josh's family throws Josh and Natalie a surprise party to celebrate what they think

is going to be their engagement, they finally come clean, and Natalie leaves to try and at least salvage one column out of the debacle. As she writes, she's reminded that the things she found compelling about Tag—his personality, his sense of humor, their shared interests—were Josh all along, and she finds herself revisiting the dating app, finding Josh's new, honest profile, and realizing that he is, in fact, The One. *Love Hard* is funny and cute, but also smarter than it looks, exploring the ways that white-majority normative definitions of masculinity often exclude Asian men. And Jimmy O. Yang is a sneaky good romantic lead, and with luck he'll get more chances to show it.

Christmas movies are so exotic. As a Muslim girl raised in Southern California, our family never celebrated Christmas, but it was always on the periphery. The guy in the red suit at the mall, mistletoes on lampposts, twinkly songs about sexual assault—all so otherworldly. Naturally, I am obsessed with the Christmas movie genre for this reason. It's like science fiction or fantasy—a complete immersion into a fantastical land with their own mythos and miracles wrapped with a happy-ending red ribbon. I will watch over fifty movies between Thanksgiving and New Year's. They all usually have an all-white cast where a single, independent woman falls for a small-town hunk with a dead wife. In *Love Hard*, though, the protagonist has to choose between the average-looking, good-hearted Asian American boy and the athletic but basic Asian American boy. It's not a political movie, by any means, but the movie is disruptive—inserting Asian American men as love interests, and telling the viewers that Asian Americans belong in fairy-tale holiday-themed romances too.

—TAZ AHMED ON *LOVE HARD*

Not "conventionally attractive."

A Talk with **Daniel Dae Kim** and **Kelly Marie Tran**

Historically, it's been nearly impossible to watch Asian screen images without the filters of race and gender; until very recently, most Asian cinematic roles have been deeply coded with tropes and stereotypes that framed Asian men as either brutal and stoic or weak and passive, and Asian women as either aggressively exotic and sexual or demure and servile. Things have changed, but as actor and producer Daniel Dae Kim (*Raya and the Last Dragon, Always Be My Maybe*) and actor Kelly Marie Tran (*Raya and the Last Dragon, Star Wars: Episode VIII—The Last Jedi*) note in this Q&A, the changes are just beginning.

I wanted to begin by talking a little bit about your own personal experiences growing up.

DANIEL DAE KIM: My upbringing was a tale of two childhoods. When my parents immigrated to America, we moved to a small town in Pennsylvania called Easton. Easton was filled with Taiwanese, Korean, Jewish, African American families. We were all friends, and we'd all go around and play at each other's houses. I never felt like an outsider. But in sixth grade, my parents bought a big new house; they wanted to live the American Dream. We moved five miles from that little town to another one—a different school district—right in the middle of a school year. That small geographical move changed my world entirely. Suddenly, I was seen as a nerd. A martial artist. A kid who was quiet. A kid who was good at math. And none of those things applied to me! It was the first time I heard racial slurs with regular frequency. That really showed me America at its best, and America at its worst.

KELLY MARIE TRAN: That absolutely resonates with me. I grew up in San Diego. And when I encountered racial slurs and microaggressions, all I wanted to do was fit in. I don't like admitting it, but sometimes I'd play along—"Yeah, I'm a *really* bad driver!"—because I wanted to feel like I was part of the jokes, instead of the butt of them. My American upbringing was shaped by the fact that, other than those stereotypes, there wasn't much out there in popular culture about what it means to be an Asian American.

For a long time, pop culture really was a wasteland for us.

KELLY: Yeah. I remember it was so rare to see Asians in the media that every depiction I saw, I held on to for dear life: Lucy Liu in the *Charlie's Angels* movie. Brenda Song on that Disney show, *The Suite Life of Zack and Cody.* The Yellow Power Ranger, Trini. And even in the animated world: *Mulan.* I was too young to verbalize it, but every time I saw an Asian face, I had an out-of-body experience, because I was so used to *not* seeing them.

DANIEL: And if you did see Asians, it tended to be in very narrow contexts! When I entered the business, if you were an Asian actor, you had a mental checklist in your head. Are they looking for an accent? Are they looking for a martial artist? Are they looking for a dutiful son who's going to sacrifice himself for the family? Is he the tech guy? We all had these presuppositions of any role specified as Asian. Plus, every Asian actor of a given gender would be called out for all the same roles. It would be like: "Oh, we're going to do a Chinatown episode! Let's send out a cattle call for every Asian male actor, regardless of age, size, shape, and appearance."

And yet for lead roles, there are types that are expected, right? The *Action Hero* must look a certain way. The *Romantic Lead* must look a certain way. And Asian male actors don't necessarily have that look.

DANIEL: No, but there's definitely room for us to be the comic buffoon, the stoic gang leader, the probable wife beater. But for Asian actors, the first part is just getting jobs. If you're lucky enough to get a job, it's really about what you can do with it. If it's underwritten on the page, usually the case for Asian roles, is there a way you can bring it to life so it's more than what you were given? If there are stereotypes associated with the role, how could you get those stereotypes changed? With our own experiences, we have a much richer, fuller idea of a character's potential than the writers who wrote it, you know, who were mostly non-Asian. And sometimes that process goes well, and sometimes it does not.

KELLY: Wow. Hearing you say this is both wonderful and sad. It's wonderful because I don't feel as crazy and alone for having had these experiences, and sad this is a battle you've been fighting for so long, and one that actors who are just starting out today continue to fight. Everything you're saying I greatly, greatly relate to. The very first thing we have to do is get over this hump of having to feel so grateful just to be employed. Like, before *Star Wars*, I had done nothing, and no Asian had had a speaking role in *Star Wars* before. So, my immediate default reaction was "Oh my God, I'm so grateful to be here." And in some ways, that gratitude silenced me. But I think you reach a certain awareness to know that yes, being grateful is an important, wonderful part of life, but not to the point where you feel like you don't have a say in the people you're portraying, the roles you're lending your voice and your body and your face to.

I'm better at having these conversations, because it's important not just for myself and my self-respect but for the community at large. I'm hoping in twenty years, Daniel and I won't be having this conversation because the roles will be so numerous and so fully formed!

DANIEL: It took twenty years for us to get to Kelly. Twenty years of us asking, "Um . . . where are the Asian-looking people in *Star Wars*?" And not just *Star Wars*: Where are the Asian-looking people in *Lord of the Rings*? We were excluded from so many of the biggest franchises in cinema, simply because people could not imagine us on those canvases. And when you're excluded from those spaces, it means you're locked out of the hearts of all the millions who consume those experiences.

It's amazing that for so long, these blockbuster epics couldn't imagine a star-spanning future or mythic past that included Asian people: "Space is full of aliens, but not a single Asian! Middle-earth can have orcs and hobbits, but no Asians!"

KELLY: The change to include us doesn't even require that much work. Rose Tico wasn't specifically Asian in the breakdown. They were auditioning many different types of women—all it said was "character, quirky, female." I think their goal was to challenge a certain projection of this laser-blasting, Spandex-clad science fiction heroine people were used to from the past. I adore Rian Johnson more than anyone in the world. I think he's a genius. His ideas of casting this character that isn't a white, conventionally attractive woman, or someone created and dressed for the male gaze, let her exist in a different light than past female science fiction characters. She's someone we never got to see in movies, not just because she looks Asian, but also because she's not a Jedi. She's not a princess. She's just a normal everyday person who got to become a hero.

And that was exactly what my personal journey felt like. My parents are both refugees from the Vietnam War. My dad worked at Burger King my whole life. Even as a kid, I think I knew I wanted to perform, but it seemed too impossible for me. I didn't see enough people who looked like me doing it. And we didn't have enough money to go on vacations, much less to take headshots. So, Rose's journey for me was very personal, and I am so happy that I got to be her and that she exists in the world.

DANIEL: On the note about "conventional attractiveness": Well, you know, I was never considered attractive in high school. And I think that's in many ways liberating. When I got named to *People*'s "Sexiest Man Alive" list, my mom said to me, "Really, they picked you?" in this incredulous voice. I don't think that was meant to be an insult! My mom always thought of me as handsome, in the way only a mother would think of her son. But she's in America, and she was acknowledging that this wasn't a typical response to someone who looks like us in America. She knew that there's a whole segment of the population who will dismiss me without even looking at me—that to them, just by virtue of my race, I will be invisible and unseen.

Do you feel like you've each had a particular burden to change that? To make Asians more visible in the world?

DANIEL: Well, when you become an actor, you're not necessarily thinking you want to do so because you want to represent all Asian people. That is not part of most of our dreams, creatively or artistically. But it's something that comes along with being a person of color in this industry, and equipped to do so or not, that responsibility is placed upon us. It's not something we seek out. Either way, we are artists first. It's not something that should be incumbent on all of us, just because we happen to be Asian.

KELLY: And yet, there are still things we deal with that non-POC actors often don't. As Asian Americans, you equip yourself with the ability to have conversations in the moment, even when you're a young actor and all you care about is working and getting a job and getting hired. That means potentially putting yourself at odds with someone like a casting director or a producer. I had coffee with a young Vietnamese actor, and he told me he auditioned for a lead role, and he "had to unlearn all of the things he learned about how to be a funny sidekick." And it broke my heart because I was thinking, "Wow, this is still happening consistently." It's sad to say that this is progress, but it is.

So that burden isn't just political, it's personal. Which makes sense.

KELLY: Well, you don't get to choose whether to experience the hard things about your life. You only get to choose how you react. I think I've become a better person because of them, and prouder of who I am and the community I come from, because with *Star Wars* and *Raya and the Last Dragon*, I feel like my first two experiences in Hollywood were ones where the representation conversation was just so at the forefront. It feels good, though, to be in a position where I feel like I'm able to be part of the positive change.

DANIEL: Agreed. And as for *Raya*, it was wonderful to play a kind, paternal Asian dad character, supporting an Asian woman hero, because things are not often portrayed that way. How many stories of Asian fathers and Asian daughters do we see? I'm getting to the age where I'm playing a lot more dads, and our culture is starting to see more women in lead roles pushing the action forward, independent of any male figure. I know it's loaded to talk about honor as an Asian American, but it was such an honor to play your dad, Kelly.

KELLY: You know, so many Disney stories are about romance, but the story of *Raya* is really about a daughter trying to save and reconnect with her father, and I couldn't imagine a better person to be that father than you, Daniel. The honor is all mine.

5

Social Studies

THE GOOD EARTH · CHAN IS MISSING · GANDHI ·
MY BEAUTIFUL LAUNDRETTE · GUNG HO · THE LAST
EMPEROR · WHO KILLED VINCENT CHIN? · CHILDREN OF
INVENTION · SLUMDOG MILLIONAIRE · TWINSTERS ·
GOOK · CRAZY RICH ASIANS · MINDING THE GAP ·
AMERICAN FACTORY · PARASITE · YELLOW ROSE · MINARI

"You have to trace the scars."
A Talk with **Justin Chon** and **Renee Tajima-Peña**

ILLUSTRATION (OPPOSITE) BY TOMA NGUYEN

Movies give us front-row seats to the grand shudders of history and allow us to watch the flow of sociological change as it ripples through communities. As Asian American history is largely untold in classrooms, cinema takes on a more meaningful role to shed light on past and current issues and events.

Films like *Chan Is Missing, My Beautiful Laundrette, Children of Invention, Slumdog Millionaire,* and *Yellow Rose* give shape to absence, demanding that we confront the reality of what—and who—we overlook in our day-to-day routines. *Gandhi, The Last Emperor,* and *Who Killed Vincent Chin?* offer us essential windows into the lives of leaders, dinosaurs, and martyrs. Apparent is the impact of globalism on economic change in *Gung Ho* and *American Factory,* the staggering breadth of the wealth divide in *Crazy Rich Asians, Minding the Gap,* and *Parasite,* and the desperation of the inner-city core and the rural expanse in *Gook* and *Minari.* We see others, and in those others, we see ourselves.

Luise Rainer (center) and Paul Muni (pointing)

The Good Earth

1937, NOT RATED, 138 MINUTES, MGM, USA

DIRECTOR: Sidney Franklin

STARRING: Paul Muni, Luise Rainer, Walter Connolly, Tilly Losch, Charley Grapewin, Jessie Ralph, Soo Yong, Keye Luke, Roland Lui, Suzanna Kim, Ching Wah Lee

WRITERS: Talbot Jennings, Tess Slesinger, Claudine West

BASED ON THE NOVEL BY PEARL S. BUCK

The Good Earth was the nation's top bestseller in 1931 and 1932; the advance paid to option the book for cinematic adaptation was the highest in Hollywood history. It wasn't just incredibly successful, it was also widely celebrated: The book was awarded the Pulitzer Prize, and the film received Oscar nods for Best Picture, Best Director (Sidney Franklin), and Best Film Editing (Basil Wrangell), and won Oscars for Best Actress (Luise Rainer) and Best Cinematography (Karl Freund).

History hasn't been as kind to Buck's novel or film. The white daughter of US missionaries, Buck wrote The Good Earth while living in Nanjing with her parents, in hopes, she said, of providing Westerners with a more realistic and sympathetic portrait of Chinese people and culture than offered by most popular texts—for example, Sax Rohmer's Fu Manchu novels. Though the story eschewed some egregious stereotypes of China, it leaned into others, depicting Chinese men as capricious, lustful, and abusive, and presenting Chinese women as conniving temptresses (Lotus) or self-sacrificing drudges (O-Lan). The film commits the all-too-common sin of casting white actors with taped eyelids and brown makeup in the Chinese roles, with the handful of Asian supporting actors making the prostheses and face paint of the leads even more obvious.

Rainer plays O-Lan, who is enslaved by a wealthy merchant. The family gives her to a farmer, Wang Lung (Muni), as a wife, telling him that she has a strong body and works hard. O-Lan toils away at his farm, while also giving birth to two sons and a daughter. With her at his side, Wang's fortunes rise, even as the family that had owned O-Lan collapses under its own decadence. But the Wangs are dragged under when China experiences drought and famine, with O-Lan choosing to murder her newborn daughter so she doesn't suffer from starvation. When the city is invaded by revolutionaries, O-Lan joins a mob looting the homes of the wealthy, using her knowledge of how rich people hide their treasures to steal a bag of gems, which she turns over to her husband. All O-Lan asks from the hoard is two pearls; the rest is used to bring the family home and invest in rebuilding their farm.

As years go by, Wang's fortune grows, and he purchases the mansion of O-Lan's former enslavers. He has also become obsessed with Lotus (Losch), a beautiful "singsong girl"—even taking away O-Lan's pearls to give to her. But the arrival of a deadly swarm of locusts brings Wang back to earth, and the family manages to save their crops through the ingenuity of their elder son (Luke), and Wang makes

peace with the younger one, giving his blessing for him to marry Lotus.

Wang takes the pearls and gives them back to O-Lan—too late. A life of hard work, disappointment, and ill-use has finally driven O-Lan to death from exhaustion. Wang does not inform the rest of the family, but merely considers the peach tree that grew from his first gift to her: a peach, whose pit she planted on their wedding day rather than tossed away. Perhaps O-Lan herself was the true goodness of the earth.

Rainer's Oscar-winning performance meant that for years, there were as many white women who'd won Academy Awards for playing Asian characters as there were Asians. Things could have been different: Anna May Wong was considered for the role and campaigned for it, but the studio decided that the rules of the Production Code of the Motion Picture Producers and Distributors of America (the "Hays Code") against depicting "miscegenation" on-screen meant Muni's wife would also have to be played by a white woman. Naturally, the option of replacing Muni never came up. Wong was offered the role of Lotus but noted that MGM wanted to cast her, an actual Chinese American actor, in the only unsympathetic role in the movie, and told them where they could put their offer.

If only Anna May Wong, the greatest Chinese American actress of her era, had won the role of O-Lan in *The Good Earth*. Here (opposite) **Zi Xu** reimagines the film with the leading actors it always deserved.

Wood Moy and Marc Hayashi

Chan Is Missing

1982, NOT RATED, 76 MINUTES, KOCH LORBER FILMS, USA

DIRECTOR: Wayne Wang

STARRING: Wood Moy, Marc Hayashi, Laureen Chew, Peter Wang, Presco Tabios, Frankie Alarcon, Judi Nihei, Ellen Yeung, George Woo, Emily Woo Yamasaki, Virginia Cerenio, Roy Chan, Leong Pui Chee

WRITERS: Isaac Cronin, Wayne Wang

Shot in San Francisco's Chinatown with an all–Asian American cast for just $22,000, Wayne Wang's feature debut *Chan Is Missing* received rave critic reviews and is considered by many to be the first Asian American independent feature.

Jo (Moy) is a cab driver looking to start a taxi company of his own with his nephew Steve (Hayashi). To do so, he's trusted an old friend, Chan Hung, to take some money and facilitate acquiring a cab license. Chan has disappeared and Jo and Steve have no choice but to search for him as best they can by interviewing Chan's friends, family, and most recent acquaintances. But as they explore Chan's life, they receive an increasingly confusing and complex portrait of the man, full of enigmas and contradictions. Was he killed because of political activism—waving the wrong flag in a confrontation between supporters of mainland China and Taiwan? Did he run away with Jo and Steve's cash? Did he even exist at all?

The film doesn't answer these questions, ending with Jo staring at a picture of his old friend that has his face unrecognizably covered by shadow, and then a montage of the many facets of Chinatown, suggesting the goal of the film wasn't to solve a mystery but to complicate the way audience members might imagine Chinese people and cultural legacies. Like Chan, the narrative points to much that's missing and untaught in our schools by Americans. But the movie makes it clear that, as in hunting down Chan, the journey, not the objective, may be the real point.

Gandhi

1982, PG, 191 MINUTES, COLUMBIA PICTURES, UK/INDIA

DIRECTOR: Richard Attenborough

STARRING: Candice Bergen, Edward Fox, John Gielgud, Trevor Howard, John Mills, Martin Sheen, Ben Kingsley

WRITER: John Briley

This epic biopic of the leader who made modern India begins with his end: The shooting murder of the elderly Mohandas Gandhi (Kingsley) by Hindu nationalist Nathuram Godse; the great man's final words, "Oh God!"; his state funeral, which was attended by millions from every class, caste, and background. By establishing the enormous impact of his passing, director Richard Attenborough puts an exclamation point on his importance for the few audience members who might not be fully aware of his legacy.

Attenborough covers Gandhi's much humbler beginnings, as a twenty-three-year-old lawyer being kicked off a train in South Africa for daring to be a colored man in a first-class whites-only seat. The incident led the young Gandhi to launch a vast campaign to demand civil rights for Indians—a campaign founded on nonviolent protest. The success of his efforts led Indian resistance leaders to urge him to return to his homeland and join the fight for the colony's independence from the British Empire. He accepts the invitation and inspires millions of Indians to embrace his principles of passive resistance, which is met with brutal suppression by British forces, including the horrific Jallianwala Bagh Massacre of 1919, where soldiers were instructed to shoot directly into crowds of unarmed, nonviolent protestors, with as many as 1,500 being killed and thousands more wounded.

Gandhi, despite frequent stints in jail, including one that lasted nearly all of World War II, calmly

Mohandas Gandhi (left) and Ben Kingsley

urged his people to stay the course. After the war, India is finally given its independence, but on terms heavily opposed by Gandhi and others, notably the partition of India into three countries, with Muslim regions in the northwest and east becoming Pakistan and Bangladesh, respectively. The news triggers widespread violence between Hindus and Muslims, and Gandhi declares he will not eat until the rioting ends. His hunger strike calms the street violence, but his efforts to bring the new nations to peace prove less successful; the murder of the father of India comes just weeks after he breaks his fast.

In 1982, my father surprised us with thrilling news: we were going to our first movie! *Gandhi* was premiering in San Francisco. It was so momentous, my sister and I put on matching frocks and stood in long lines to see a film neither of us was really mature enough to view. That inconvenient detail was irrelevant: My father's two eldest brothers had been jailed during India's struggle for independence and he was immensely proud of them, so what better way to convey our uncles' sacrifices than to watch them on the biggest screen we'd ever seen? We were quiet and attentive as we sat between our father, emotional as he relived history, and our mother, exhausted in her sari. We entered that theater as young Americans and emerged with nascent hyphens. While we were Malayalee before, now we felt Indian too. And that epiphany was important, and good.

—ANNA JOHN ON *GANDHI*

Gandhi was a stunning success, both critically and at the box office, earning $128 million and winning eight of the eleven Oscars for which it was nominated, including Best Picture, Best Director for Attenborough, and Best Actor for Ben Kingsley in a star-making movie turn—and notably, one of the first acting performances in which the veteran stage actor portrayed an Indian character. (Born Krishna Pandit Bhanji, the half-Indian Kingsley changed his professional name in the 1960s out of concern that his "foreign" name was preventing him from getting parts.)

My Beautiful Laundrette

1985, R, 97 MINUTES, KLV-TV, UK

DIRECTOR: Stephen Frears

STARRING: Saeed Jaffrey, Roshan Seth, Daniel Day-Lewis, Gordon Warnecke, Shirley Anne Field, Derrick Branche

WRITER: Hanif Kureishi

Written by playwright Hanif Kureishi, this slice-of-life journey into the intersectional world of the London underclass dissects a range of different categories of marginalization while telling a star-crossed love story that ends, somewhat unexpectedly, in a happy ending.

Omar (Warnecke) is a British Pakistani man living with and caring for his father, Hussein (Seth), a former journalist. Hussein's brother Nasser, meanwhile, is a successful businessman who lives life to the fullest, supports both his family and his white mistress Rachel (Field), and indulges his love of the finer things. Nasser employs Omar as a car wash attendant, until Omar convinces him to let him take over one of his less successful businesses, a failing laundrette, instead. Through Nasser, Omar also meets Salim (Branche), who has made his fortune by selling drugs. While driving Salim home from the airport, they encounter a gang of neo-Nazi skinheads, whose leader turns out to be an old childhood friend of Omar's named Johnny (Day-Lewis)—or, as it turns out, more than a friend.

As Omar and Johnny rekindle their old romance, Omar convinces him to leave his street-punk gang to join him in renovating the laundrette. Johnny accepts, but the pair soon realize that their vision for the laundrette requires money they don't have. They agree to take a job delivering drugs for Salim but instead sell the drugs themselves, using the money to launch the aptly named "Powders." The laundrette is a success,

T**hanks to AIDS, coming out as a teen in the eighties was the absolute worst. Everything was all about death and doom; I really thought I wouldn't live beyond the age of thirty. Then I had the fortune of watching the story of Omar and Johnny in *My Beautiful Laundrette*. There was so much I could relate to in Omar. I was growing up on the streets of Detroit, and he was in a similar neighborhood in South London. I was trying to navigate my identity in a working-class immigrant family that owned a restaurant. His family was also Asian, but they worked in the laundry business. I was a young Republican (though I'm not anymore). He was an aspiring businessman, a popular ambition during that era when "greed was good." Watching Omar and Johnny fall in love gave me hope that there was a future for me, one that included love and a happy ending.**

—CURTIS CHIN ON *MY BEAUTIFUL LAUNDRETTE*

but Salim, Omar, and Johnny once again encounter trouble when they run into Johnny's old gang.

The film's empathic and sexual portrayal of Omar and Johnny shocked some viewers, but it became an international success, establishing Frears as a first-tier British director and serving as Day-Lewis's platform to stardom; many Asian American gay men cite this film as a pivotal one in their journey to self-affirmation and coming out.

Gordon Warnecke and Daniel Day-Lewis

Gung Ho

1986, PG-13, 111 MINUTES, NBC, USA

DIRECTOR: Ron Howard

STARRING: Michael Keaton, Gedde Watanabe, George Wendt, John Turturro, Mimi Rogers, Soh Yamamura, Sab Shimono, Rick Overton, Clint Howard, Jihmi Kennedy, Michelle Johnson, Rodney Kageyama, Rance Howard, Patti Yasutake, Jerry Tondo

WRITERS: Edwin Blum, Lowell Ganz, Babaloo Mandel

A media-savvy Republican president energizes his base with sound bites celebrating a muscular America while amplifying xenophobic hostility toward military and economic rivals. That aptly describes the presidency of Donald Trump, but it applies equally well to the era of Ronald Reagan, whose populist messaging had similarly dire consequences for Asian Americans and others perceived as "foreign": targeted harassment, cultural isolation, and even physical attack.

Ron Howard's *Gung Ho* was, in its own way, a movie made to moderate American anti-Japanese sentiment, in sharp contrast to works like 1993's *Rising Sun*. But while trying to tell a story of building bridges between cultures, *Gung Ho* ended up leaning into easy stereotypes and gags based on Japanese customs, beliefs, and physical appearances (though Americans don't come off looking too great in this film either). Michael Keaton plays Hunt Stevenson, former foreman of a shut-down car factory who convinces a major Japanese auto manufacturer, Assan Motors, to take over and reopen it. Assan Motors agrees on their own terms, reducing salaries, demanding impossible benchmarks for quality and productivity, and forcing workers to participate in morning calisthenics to encourage team building. Kaz Kazihiro (Watanabe) is the English-speaking

Gedde Watanabe and Michael Keaton

Japanese executive who's been sent to America to run the factory, knowing that it's his last chance after a career full of failure.

Hunt and Kaz strike a deal: If the American workers can match the output of the company's Japanese plants (fifteen thousand cars a month), Kaz will give them all raises and hire back still-unemployed workers from the former company. The team gets to work but gives up when they hit thirteen thousand, deciding it's "good enough," at which point Hunt reveals that it isn't: If they're even one car short of fifteen thousand, they get nothing. In response, the workers walk out. Desperate, Hunt and Kaz go to work assembling cars by themselves, trying

I was sixteen years old when I saw *Gung Ho*. In 1986, a movie featuring not just one but several main Asian characters was a rarity. Unfortunately, seeing a movie featuring Asian characters depicted in a racist manner was not. *Gung Ho* made me cringe with its over-the-top "clash of cultures" and broad stereotypes: Model minority Japanese auto workers, sacrificing family and health to meet factory quotas, versus the rugged individualism and union swagger of their white American colleagues. And don't get me started on the puerile pun of naming the Japanese/American auto plant "Assan Motors." Yet despite these clunky and exasperating images, I was delighted by the Asian American actors who gave their limited roles depth and dignity, stealing scenes with their comedic chops and timing. They inspired me to feel that perhaps one day we would have more movies in which people who looked like me were no longer the punch line, but the heart of the story.

—PAULA YOO ON *GUNG HO*

to meet the quota—but they fall just short, leading Hunt to create a hopeful ruse, which is quickly discovered. Rather than shutting down the plant as threatened, the CEO (Yamamura) praises the workers' resourcefulness and negotiates a compromise with his American employees.

The happy ending seems dubious but is in line with Howard's goals of showing the benefits of mutual respect and cross-cultural collaboration. Unfortunately, whoever marketed the movie didn't get the memo: *Gung Ho*'s ludicrous trailer begins with Keaton invoking World War II in front of Assan's board and ends with the sound of a gong. The trailer was also set to the tune of the Vapors' "Turning Japanese," apparently a legal requirement for eighties media focusing on Japan.

The Last Emperor

1987, PG-13, 163 MINUTES, COLUMBIA PICTURES, USA

DIRECTOR: Bernardo Bertolucci

STARRING: John Lone, Joan Chen, Peter O'Toole, Ying Ruocheng, Victor Wong, Dennis Dun, Vivian Wu, Ryuichi Sakamoto, Lisa Lu, Fan Guang

WRITERS: Enzo Ungari, Mark Peploe, Bernardo Bertolucci

The eighties were a prime decade for a certain kind of spectacle—opulent Oscar-bait period pieces that brought history to life on an epic scale, shot in real locations with lush production values and teeming casts. Bernardo Bertolucci negotiated the full cooperation of the Chinese government in the production—for the first time in history, the Forbidden City was made available as a shooting location. Bertolucci took good advantage of the unique opportunity, hiring thousands of extras to fill the Imperial Palace and bring it back to its heyday. (The film ultimately needed nineteen thousand background players, a number so large that Bertolucci conscripted the People's Liberation Army to fill in crowds.)

Despite the grandeur of his vision, or because of it, Bertolucci couldn't find a studio willing to finance it, given that he intended to cast mostly unknown Asian and Asian American actors (although veteran British actor Peter O'Toole was given a small role as Emperor Puyi's childhood tutor, Reginald Johnston). Even Columbia Pictures, who had seen success with its prior biopic, *Gandhi*, was reluctant to back Bertolucci. Ultimately, producer Jeremy Thomas raised the entire $25 million budget independently, which proved to be a windfall for those investors after the film earned $80 million theatrically in one of the oddest trajectories of any modern movie. It didn't break into the box office top ten for twelve weeks, bubbling under the radar until it was nominated for nine (and won all nine) Academy Awards, completing a rare sweep of the Best Adapted Screenplay, Best Director, and Best Picture Oscars.

The Last Emperor tells the story of Puyi, the final occupant of the imperial throne after thousands of years of dynastic rule in China. Beginning with his 1950 capture by the Red Army and imprisonment under charges of collaborating with the Japanese, the film flashes back to Puyi at age two, being crowned after the sudden death of the previous emperor, his half uncle. Despite nominally ruling China, Puyi grows up a sheltered prisoner in the palace, so disconnected from reality that his younger brother, Pujie (Fan), is the one who tells him the Qing dynasty has fallen and China has become a republic. Rather than eliminating Puyi, the new republic assigns a British tutor to give him a Western-style education.

As Puyi learns more about the world, he is advised that the best way to assert his status is to marry. Puyi subsequently takes two wives—Wanrong

Puyi as a child, played by Richard Vuu

(Chen) as empress and first wife, and Wenxiu (Wu) as imperial concubine. Puyi subsequently begins to flex his power, expelling eunuchs from the Forbidden City and cracking down on palace corruption. But in 1924, a coup leads to the imperial family being expelled from Beijing and fleeing to Tientsin, where Puyi leads a life of indolence. When the Communists take power in China, they arrest Puyi and demand he confess he was a Japanese collaborator. He is released nearly a decade later, taking up a quiet private existence as a gardener. The movie ends with Puyi visiting his old home, the Forbidden City, and demonstrating to

The first time I watched *The Last Emperor*, as the end credits rolled I immediately went to the bathroom and bawled my eyes out. At the time, I didn't understand and was somewhat embarrassed by my response; I couldn't express why Emperor Puyi's story struck my emotional core so deeply. And then it hit me: Here was a film celebrating a culture that I was mostly running from as a young American kid, yet it also precisely marked how the passage of time made that ancestry seem obsolete. As an adoptee with roots in my mother country yet living a new life abroad, the feeling of powerlessness at being overrun by circumstances beyond your control was gut-wrenching. This was the film that made me want to become a filmmaker, and the one that opened my eyes to the power of cinema as a cross-cultural experience.

—MICHELLE KRUSIEC ON *THE LAST EMPEROR*

Lily Chin

a young boy that he was the emperor by finding a hidden cricket cage that was given to him as a gift on the day of his coronation. He gives the cage to the boy and disappears into history.

The Last Emperor's critical acclaim and commercial success should have established the careers of John Lone and Joan Chen, its marquee stars, but Lone found few leading-man opportunities after receiving a Golden Globe nomination for his performance. A handful of movies later, including the movie adaptation of David Henry Hwang's *M. Butterfly*, Lone was mostly working in Chinese television, and by 2007 had retired from acting. Chen, meanwhile, had a memorable role in the 1990 television series *Twin Peaks* and was also offered a few big-screen roles of note by Hollywood—co-starring in action movies with Rutger Hauer and Steven Seagal—but eventually she found more interesting roles in indie productions like 2004's *Saving Face*.

Who Killed Vincent Chin?

1987, NOT RATED, 88 MINUTES, PBS, USA

DIRECTORS: Christine Choy, Renee Tajima-Peña

On June 19, 1982, a twenty-seven-year-old Chinese American draftsman named Vincent Chin was out with friends celebrating his last few days as a bachelor when he got into an altercation with a pair of white autoworkers—Ron Ebens and his son Mike

Nitz. The fight began at a Detroit strip club, where Ebens, mistaking Chin as Japanese, allegedly used racial slurs in accusing him of being part of the reason the US auto industry was going downhill. By the end of the evening, Chin was unconscious in a McDonald's parking lot, his skull crushed in by Ebens with a baseball bat. An EMT responding to the scene noted "there were brains on the floor." Chin would never awaken from his coma—and Ebens and Nitz would never serve a day in jail for the crime, receiving instead a three-year probation and a $3,780 fine.

The incredible injustice prompted a broad outcry from Asian Americans and a multicultural array of supporters, both in Detroit, Michigan, and across the nation. This Academy Award–nominated documentary brought together archival news footage, interviews with key witnesses, and organizers of the protests against the verdict. Vincent's mother, Lily Chin, eventually won a civil suit against Ebens and Nitz for over $1.5 million but passed away with most of the penalty unpaid. The fight for Vincent Chin galvanized a generation of Asians toward political and social involvement and has been cited as the origin of the national Asian American movement. The movie, a landmark in Asian American independent filmmaking, has served to continuously recharge later generations of activists. With the rise in anti-Asian violence in the early 2020s prompted by COVID anti-China rhetoric, Chin's story is more relevant than ever.

Crystal Chiu and Michael Chen

Children of Invention

2009, NOT RATED, 86 MINUTES, ASIAN CRUSH, USA

DIRECTOR/WRITER: Tze Chun

STARRING: Cindy Cheung, Michael Chen, Crystal Chiu, Jackson Ning, Lynn Mastio Rice, Kathleen Kwan, Han Tang, Takeo Lee Wong

There are shades of Hirokazu Kore-eda's starkly horrifying *Nobody Knows* (2004) in *Children of Invention*, this impressive indie debut from director Tze Chun. *Invention* follows a family that represents the opposite end of the model minority—surviving on the tenuous goodwill of friends and family, always looking for an opportunity to climb above the bottom rung of society, even if the means feel shady.

Elaine Cheng (Cheung) is an immigrant single mother doing her best to care for her two children, Raymond (Chen), mature beyond his years, and Tina (Chiu), precocious but needy. With no resources, Elaine is repeatedly sucked into various marketing schemes that all promise a fast and easy path to wealth. Her efforts to succeed in this shady world leave ten-year-old Raymond and six-year-old Tina to their own devices. To amuse themselves, they make their own get-rich-quick scheme, related to an invention Raymond is sure will earn a million dollars, more money than the kids can imagine. The invention? A self-spinning fork, to use with spaghetti and noodles.

When Elaine unexpectedly fails to come home one night—she's been arrested by the feds in the latest scam—Raymond decides saving the family and their mom is up to them, and they leave to find help. Though the family reunites by the film's end, there's the bitter sense that the story isn't over, and neither are the trio's troubles. Loosely based on Chun's own childhood experiences and even more loosely inspired by his acclaimed Sundance short film *Windowbreaker* (2006), *Children of Invention* boasts terrific performances by both the kids and Cheung and shows a unique perspective on lower-class immigrant life.

Slumdog Millionaire

2008, R, 120 MINUTES, SEARCHLIGHT PICTURES, UK

DIRECTOR: Danny Boyle

STARRING: Dev Patel, Freida Pinto, Madhur Mittal, Anil Kapoor, Irrfan Khan

WRITER: Simon Beaufoy

BASED ON THE NOVEL Q&A BY VIKAS SWARUP

Dev Patel and Freida Pinto

Based on the novel *Q&A* by Indian author Vikas Swarup, the narrative of *Slumdog Millionaire* hinges on a series of incredibly unlikely events that bring it into the world of magical realism—yet brilliant performances by young actors Dev Patel and Freida Pinto and the cleverness of its central conceit make it an addictive and compelling watch.

Jamal (Patel), a teen who grew up in Mumbai's Juhu slum, has somehow found his way to becoming a contestant on the Indian version of *Who Wants to Be a Millionaire?* and, despite his lack of formal education, has made it to the show's penultimate question. The implausibility of Jamal's impending victory isn't lost on the police, who drag him offstage and savagely interrogate him, seeking a confession to cheating on the show. As he explains how he knows the answers, he flashes back into his memories. A wonderful dive into magical realism, these recollections cover Jamal's life from five years old (a memorable moment when he got an autograph from iconic Bollywood actor Amitabh Bachchan) to the present and show how he's encountered the show answers throughout his lifetime.

Jamal's decision to become a contestant on *Who Wants to Be a Millionaire?* is a noble one, driven not by greed but because he knows the girl he loves, Latika (Pinto), like everyone else in India, is watching the show, the sole means in which he might find and communicate with her—a brilliant, modern-media conceit that makes the movie's final romantic reunion feel just plausible.

Slumdog was nominated for ten Academy Awards and won eight of them, also earning $380 million at the box office on a budget of just $15 million—a stunning success. The movie launched the careers of Patel and Pinto, while confirming Boyle as one of the UK's leading directors. It received criticism, however, within India from those who referred to it as "poverty porn" and questioned Boyle's intentions to make a film about India's slum children. It also led to an investigation of the casting of the young children. When it was discovered that the amateur performers, recruited from Mumbai's actual slums, were paid just a few hundred dollars for their work despite the film's massive earnings, Boyle reached out and gave them additional compensation, including purchasing houses for their families and setting aside an education trust fund. Still, the ethics debate on whether the production exploited its Indian cast and crew continued to shadow the film long after its release.

Twinsters

2015, PG-13, 99 MINUTES, IGNITE CHANNEL, USA

DIRECTORS: Samantha Futerman, Ryan Miyamoto

STARRING: Anaïs Bordier, Samantha Futerman, Kanoa Goo

WRITER: Samantha Futerman

The circumstances that surround this documentary's creation are amazing: Futerman, an actor who received acclaim for her work in Michael Kang's indie feature debut *The Motel* and in *Memoirs of a Geisha*, received a Facebook friend request out of the blue from a French woman who looked like her doppelgänger. The woman, Anaïs Bordier, who shares her

The twins, Anaïs Bordier and Samantha Futerman

I remember watching the opening moments of *Twinsters* with dread and delight. Dread for the unfolding of her unknown, for the watching-through-fingers anxiety of a discovery so fundamental to an adoptee's experience. And delight for her chance to meet the person who had shared the territory of the primordial motherland—the womb. As a fellow Korean adoptee, watching Samantha leap into the uncharted upon discovering the existence of a twin sister left me breathless at her courage and vulnerability. Korean adoptees were the first organized group of children to be lifted from their country and scattered across the world, and that trauma has continued to unfold in me. Adoption can hold beauty and love within it, but always, profound loss. *Twinsters* is a quiet love song for that particular pain, and a revelation.

—JOY OSMANSKI ON *TWINSTERS*

I fell in love with this documentary as soon as I saw its trailer, not only from an adoptee perspective, but as someone who just enjoys great storytelling. It was heartwarming and refreshing to see a story of adoptees reuniting with someone other than their birth parents; watching the story of identical twins meeting for the first time was mind-blowing. Truthfully, I felt a little twinge of envy, because as an adoptee, we all kind of hope for a Sam and Anaïs story. This was just a slice of their lives, but it offered so much joy and hope for adoptees who constantly wonder who else might still be out there.

—MICHELLE LI ON *TWINSTERS*

birthday and her status as a transracial adoptee from Korea, had been alerted to Futerman's existence after being forwarded a YouTube video in which Futerman appeared alongside popular Asian American influencer Kevin "KevJumba" Wu. The interaction set two things in motion: a desire by the two women to research whether they're related—and, as Bordier suspects, long-lost twin sisters—and this documentary capturing their journey toward the truth and meeting each other for the first time. The film captures their international Skype sessions as they take DNA tests and learn that yes, lo and behold, they are identical twins. We then follow their journey of mutual rediscovery and their quest to connect with their birth mother—who ultimately refuses to acknowledge them. But even without her, they found something they didn't have before the movie began: one another.

Gook

2017, NOT RATED, 94 MINUTES, SAMUEL GOLDWYN FILMS, USA

DIRECTOR/WRITER: Justin Chon

STARRING: Justin Chon, Simone Baker, David So, Sang Chon, Ben Munoz, Curtiss Cook Jr.

With *Gook*, Justin Chon—a gifted and underutilized comic and dramatic actor, best known for his role as Bella's classmate in Stephenie Meyer's *Twilight* movies—firmly established himself as a filmmaker to watch, winning the Audience Award at Sundance with this thoughtful, uncomfortable exploration of the interactions between ethnic communities in diverse yet culturally segregated Los Angeles.

Eli (Chon) and Daniel (So) are brothers struggling to stay afloat as they operate a shoe store they inherited from their late father. They face abuse from their predominantly Black and Latin customers; they observe members of their own community, like liquor store owner Mr. Kim (Justin's father, Sang Chon) exercising his prejudices toward their friend Kamilla (Baker), an eleven-year-old who uses their store as an oasis from the troubles in her family life. The whole stew of microaggressions, misunderstandings, and barely restrained rage is at the edge of boiling over, and the verdict of the Rodney King trial—exonerating the white cops who viciously beat him—is more than enough to send it sizzling into flames.

South Central LA erupts into riots, and Daniel, who has left the store after an argument with Eli, is assaulted and robbed. Chaos and tragedy unfold throughout the day as the lives of Eli, Daniel, and Kamilla intertwine during the riots. In the aftermath, unable to process what has happened, Eli sets the shoe store on fire, feeding the legacy of two generations of violence into the inferno. Shot for well under six figures in stark black and white, the film is an apt reminder that life is anything but.

This is one of my favorite Asian American films, in part because it focused on connections and interactions across race during a fraught and terrifying time that many of us experienced through the lenses of cameras. I lived in LA County in 1992; I was in junior high, and I still couldn't understand what had happened after watching hours of footage of burning Koreatown buildings. Years later, through this fictionalized account, Chon's film helped me to understand that history isn't the stories of places or events, but of people.

—MOMO CHANG ON GOOK

Justin Chon (left) with his father (in *Gook* and in real life), Sang Chon

Crazy Rich Asians

2018, PG-13, 120 MINUTES, WARNER BROS., USA

DIRECTOR: Jon M. Chu

STARRING: Constance Wu, Henry Golding, Gemma Chan, Lisa Lu, Awkwafina, Ken Jeong, Michelle Yeoh, Chris Pang, Ronny Chieng, Jimmy O. Yang, Nico Santos, Remy Hii, Tan Kheng Hua, Pierre Png, Harry Shum Jr.

WRITERS: Peter Chiarelli, Adele Lim

BASED ON THE NOVEL BY KEVIN KWAN

No single movie has changed the metrics of how Asian Americans are seen in Hollywood than *Crazy Rich Asians*, Jon M. Chu's adaptation of the book by Singaporean author Kevin Kwan. A rom-com with an all-Asian cast in an era when rom-coms and all-Asian casts were seen as box office poison, *Crazy Rich Asians* ended up rallying unprecedented support from the Asian American community, who bought out theaters; saw the movie two, three, or more times; evangelized it to parents and grandparents; and kept the film buzzing on social media via endless layers of discourse, from the film's food and fashion to the intricate symbolism of a single game of mahjong.

First-time film actor Henry Golding plays Nick Young, a ridiculously handsome history professor at New York University; Constance Wu, breakout star of TV's *Fresh Off the Boat*, plays Rachel Chu, a fellow professor (of game theory!) and Nick's girlfriend, though he's kept at least one big secret from her—he's the heir to a vast fortune in his native Singapore. When summoned back home for his best friend's wedding, Nick invites Rachel to join him. As their journey progresses, it becomes evident that Young's family is not

Henry Golding and Constance Wu

just rich but—as Rachel's Singaporean college roommate Peik Lin (Awkwafina) informs her—*crazy* rich.

As the Asian American daughter of a poor Chinese immigrant, Rachel is seen as an unacceptable match and a gold-digging threat to Nick and, by extension, the entire Young family. The biggest threat to their relationship is Nick's mother, Eleanor (Yeoh), who strongly disapproves of Rachel and tells her as much during a family dumpling-making party. The blow doesn't stop Rachel and Nick's optimism, with Nick admitting to Colin (Pang) that he intends to propose to her after Colin's wedding. At the reception, however, Eleanor and Nick's grandmother (Lu), the matriarch of the Young family, reveal to Rachel that

they've used private investigators to dig up her family skeletons. They tell Nick they cannot accept their family being linked to someone of such scandalous background, and Rachel leaves the party in tears.

Away from home and unaccepted, she's surprised by an unexpected visitor—her mother, Kerry Chu (Tan), flown in by Nick. Kerry explains that she didn't flee China out of shame but out of fear because her husband had been violent and abusive. After learning this, Rachel makes an appointment to meet Eleanor at a mahjong parlor. As they play, Rachel tells Eleanor that Nick proposed, and she turned him down. Eleanor tells her that's ridiculous—no one would give away such a perfect hand. But when the

To me, *Crazy Rich Asians* wasn't just about money. It was about entitlement, in a good way. Before I walked into the theater, I'd never seen an American movie featuring kueh, Singaporean Auntie Bible study, and texting the term "Alamak!" I'd never imagined that my Malaysian upbringing could be recognized, and in such a huge, big-budget production. I cried in wonder at seeing myself and in recognition that I had never realized that I, that we, deserved to take up so much space. Rachel's ultimate entitled act is fully owning her complex Asian American identity and prioritizing that over love and money. She is fierce, loud, and unabashedly proud of her chimeric identity. This movie, with its scenes of chili crab and mahjong, allowed me to feel the same.

—STEPHANIE FOO ON *CRAZY RICH ASIANS*

game ends, Eleanor realizes that her victory was out of her control, as Rachel purposefully gave Eleanor the tile that would have produced victory for Rachel as well, metaphorically underscoring what she's done in saying no to Nick. For those familiar with the rules of mahjong, this was a gasp-in-the-theater moment. As Rachel and Kerry board their flight back to New York, Nick suddenly shows up on the plane, bearing a ring box in hand. He proposes to her again—this time not with the ring he'd purchased but with Eleanor's emerald ring, a sign from her that she finally accepts Rachel as Nick's match.

Given that *Crazy Rich Asians* made $240 million on a $30 million budget, the sequel is inevitable—though the pandemic and dispersal of the suddenly super-hot cast to other projects have pushed it back. Though some criticized the movie's focus on the hyper wealthy, by contrasting the Young extended family with mother and daughter, Chu underscored the wide array of circumstances behind the Asian diaspora—from transnational elite to opportunity seekers to refugees fleeing from personal or political danger.

Minding the Gap

2018, NOT RATED, 93 MINUTES, HULU, USA

DIRECTOR: Bing Liu

STARRING: Keire Johnson, Zack Mulligan, Bing Liu

This documentary by Bing Liu—winner of a Peabody Award, Oscar-nominated for best documentary feature, and a favorite of former president Barack Obama—offers a blended first- and third-person perspective of growing up in middle America, focusing on three friends (one white, one Black, and director Liu himself) as they grow through adolescence and into adulthood.

Skateboarding provides a necessary way of life in *Minding the Gap*.

Zack Mulligan, Keire Johnson, and Liu grew up in a blue-collar suburb in Rockford, Illinois. All three, we learn during the film, grew up physically abused by their fathers (in Liu's case, his stepfather), and have carried the scars into their adult lives. Their primary mode of recreation is skateboarding, both a figurative escape from the limitations of bleak existence and perhaps a literal one. Mulligan tries to launch an indoor skate park and fails. Johnson hopes to become a professional skater (and, we learn in a postscript, eventually succeeds). But along the way, Mulligan struggles with his tumultuous marriage and alcoholism, and Johnson contends with the white town's ambient racism while working as a dishwasher. The three end up in a somewhat positive place by the film's end, which seems like a miracle, but the documentary makes clear that the issues the men faced growing up—toxic masculinity, lack of mobility, and racial discrimination—are real, pervasive, and a present threat to the social fabric of this nation.

American Factory

2019, TV-14, 110 MINUTES, NETFLIX, USA

DIRECTORS: Steven Bognar, Julia Reichert

STARRING: Junming "Jimmy" Wang, Robert Allen, Sherrod Brown, Dave Burrows, Dawnetta Cantrell, Lori Cochran, Austin Cole, John Crane, John Gauthier, Cynthia Harper, Wong He, Rob Haerr, Timi Jernigan, Betty Jones, Jill Lamantia, Jeff Daochuan Liu

This Oscar-winning film from Barack and Michelle Obama's Higher Ground Productions is a devastating

勤劳 DILIGENCE　朴实 SIMPLICITY　学习 LEARNING　创新 INNOVATION

The Fuyao factory in Fuqing, China

portrait about the future of American labor in a global economy—treating a topic huge in scope with intimate detail and, in many cases, disarmingly awkward humor. Directors Bognar and Reichert, who had made a 2009 short documentary about the closing of a General Motors plant in Moraine, Ohio, titled *The Last Truck: Closing of a GM Plant*, found themselves in the unique position of being invited as the factory

reopened under very new management: Fuyao Glass Industry Group, a publicly traded Chinese company founded by Cao Dewang that has become the fifth-largest maker of automotive glass in the world over the past twenty-five years. The acquisition of the Moraine plant was both a pragmatic move (Fuyao is a major supplier to GM) and an exercise in soft power, demonstrating that a Chinese company could

My favorite line in this film is when one of the Chinese workers tells another, "Oh, Americans aren't good at this because they have fat fingers." The bluntness with which they describe Americans is oftentimes hysterical, providing a fresh look at America from the outside. It reminds me that one of the classes that I took in my study abroad at Beijing University was called "America." At first, people would ask me, "Why would you do that? You're *from* America." But it was interesting to see how the *Chinese* look at America. There was one lecture where the professor said, "Okay, Americans are really individualistic, and you can see this in three ways: 1. When they go to restaurants, they split the check. 2. When kids are done with school, they leave the house. And 3. When parents are old, they put them in old-age homes." That's what watching *American Factory* was like for me.

—JENNIFER 8. LEE ON *AMERICAN FACTORY*

successfully operate at scale in the US, as Japanese and Korean manufacturers have already shown they could do, while saving thousands of American blue-collar jobs.

As *American Factory* shows, neither Fuyao nor its US employees quite knew what they were getting into, with the venture quickly stumbling into cultural and political obstacles. American workers are unable to meet production standards, in part because they resist the dangerous practices and grueling hours embraced by Chinese peers and demanded by Fuyao. They threaten to unionize, which prompts Chairman Cao to threaten shutting the whole venture down. And yet, beneath surface-level discontinuities and drama, differences are bridged across the widest divides, as friendships between Chinese and American team members develop, holidays are celebrated communally, and even the linguistic boundary begins to be crossed by a handful of intrepid individuals. The end of the documentary leaves open questions about the future of the plant and of Chinese/American relations in general and reinforces the basic shared humanity of working people, while raising the specter of growing automation, a phenomenon that threatens blue-collar jobs on both sides of the Pacific.

Parasite

2019, R, 132 MINUTES, NEON, SOUTH KOREA

DIRECTOR: Bong Joon-ho

STARRING: Song Kang-ho, Lee Sun-kyun, Cho Yeo-jeong, Choi Woo-shik, Park So-dam, Lee Jung-eun, Jang Hye-jin, Jung Ji-so, Park Myung-hoon, Jung Hyeon-jun

WRITERS: Bong Joon-ho, Han Jin-won

Jubilee spread across Korea and Asian American communities when director Bong Joon-ho's searing black-comedy horror-satire *Parasite* won a quartet of major Oscars: Best Original Screenplay, Best International Feature Film, Best Director, and Best Picture, becoming the first non-English-language film in history to win the night's biggest prize. For anyone who'd seen the film, its success was hardly surprising: Funny, smart, heartbreaking, intimate, and scathingly political, *Parasite* is both uniquely of its culture and place but wholly accessible to those with no knowledge of Korean society. It's also incredibly well acted, with Park So-dam as daughter Kim Ki-jung and Song Kang-ho as patriarch Kim Ki-taek receiving particular acclaim for their performances. Unfortunately, as is all too common, acting in a non-English language led to the nuance and depth of the cast's work being mostly overlooked by American critics and award shows. (Director Bong famously called out the awkward truth of how fear of foreign language limits American tastes in his Oscar acceptance speech, telling viewers, "Once you overcome the one-inch-tall barrier of subtitles, you will be introduced to so many more amazing films.")

The Kims are a family at the lowest stratum of Korean society, literally living underground in a cramped basement apartment where they steal Wi-Fi from upstairs tenants and pay the rent with menial work like folding pizza boxes. Their lives change when a friend of son Ki-woo (Choi) pays him a visit, giving him an ornamental "scholar's rock" said to draw fortune to its owner, while recommending he take over his job as an English teacher for the wealthy Park family's daughter, Da-hye (Jung). Ki-woo, a college dropout, convinces the Parks he's qualified for the position, aided by Da-hye's instant crush on him. He quickly finds job opportunities for the rest of his family within the Park household, installing his sister Ki-jung (the glorious Park So-dam) as an art therapist to Da-hye's troubled brother, his father as Mr. Park's chauffeur, and finally, his mother as the Parks' housekeeper, after getting rid of the Parks' longtime housekeeper Gook Moon-gwang (Lee Jung-eun).

But this happy arrangement soon spins into chaos as the Kims discover a deeper embedded

Bong Joon-ho

When *Parasite* won the 2020 Oscar for Best Picture, I literally rolled on the living room carpet and screamed. To me, the significance of this was fathomless. As a fan and scholar of Asian cinema, I deeply enjoyed seeing a South Korean film get love from the biggest movie awards show in the US. I also loved Bong Joon-ho shading the Oscars by referring to it as "very local," calling out the provincial nature of the Academy. Recognition in the West is by no means the ultimate goal for Asian entertainment, but it was still nice to finally see Hollywood acknowledging what much of the world has known for decades: That Asian cinema rocks, and it's about time America opened our eyes and caught up.

—VALERIE SOE ON *PARASITE*

"parasite" in the form of Geun-sae (Park Myung-hoon), the former housekeeper's half-crazed husband, whom she has been caring for in an underground bunker beneath the Park home. Geun-sae's release unleashes a bloodbath in the film's exhilarating third act, leading to major consequences for all.

The title of the movie may be read in two ways—the Kims, as well as Moon-gwang and Geun-sae, are parasites of the wealthy Parks, living among and feeding off them. The Parks, however, are shown to be reliant on lower-class people to perform basic functions of living. Who are the true parasites after all?

Yellow Rose

**2019, PG-13, 94 MINUTES,
SONY PICTURES WORLDWIDE, USA**

DIRECTOR: Diane Paragas

STARRING: Eva Noblezada, Dale Watson, Princess Punzalan, Lea Salonga

WRITERS: Diane Paragas, Annie J. Howell, Celena Cipriaso

Diane Paragas's music-infused feature directorial debut is the story of a dreamer who happens to be a DREAMer—an undocumented Filipina American teenager named Rose (Noblezada), who'd been brought to the United States as a small child and never left. After her mother is arrested in an immigration sweep, Rose must accept either deportation with her mom to an overseas ancestral land she's never seen or pursuing her heart's goal of becoming a country-western singer in the only place she knows as home: Texas. After evading a squadron of militarized ICE agents, Rose bounces from shelter to shelter—including a stint at her estranged aunt Gail's (Salonga) home, who's married to country icon Dale Watson (himself). Watson's kindness doesn't mean he's offering her a home either, and Rose must choose between following her passion and following her mom. We see her choice by the end of the film, with Rose and Watson singing a duet titled "I Ain't Going Down" to a live audience with her mom watching via livestream.

Noblezada's performance is a revelation, both as an actress and the singer of the soundtrack's reliably catchy honky-tonk ballad. Her charisma and raw authenticity sell us on the film's subtext: that America owes much of its color, culture, and economic infrastructure to immigrants, including those without papers, and if the will of nativists was enacted, we'd lose it all.

Watching *Yellow Rose*, I knew I was witnessing something special. It not only starred two of my Pinay sisters who'd also starred in *Miss Saigon*, both of whom I deeply admired—the original Kim, Lea Salonga, and rising star Eva Nobelazada—but at the film's helm was Filipina American filmmaker Diane Paragas. And the story she was telling was about the gut-punching experience of undocumented families in our own Filipino American communities, even as news outlets were airing endless stories on the thousands of children being detained in cages by US border patrol. The film's most striking scene is when its heroine comes face-to-face with an ICE officer, his gun drawn. Rather than report her, he chooses to spare her. That scene continues to stay with me—it's a beacon of hope, reminding us of our shared humanity.

—JENNIFER PAZ ON *YELLOW ROSE*

Eva Noblezada

Minari

2020, PG-13, 115 MINUTES, A24, USA

DIRECTOR/WRITER: Lee Isaac Chung

STARRING: Steven Yeun, Han Ye-ri, Alan Kim, Noel Kate Cho, Youn Yuh-jung, Will Patton

---

This deeply evocative film from director Lee Isaac Chung, loosely based on his own childhood memories, stops just short of being an elegy. Nevertheless, it delivers a remarkable payload of broken dreams and bitter resilience in the tale of a Korean immigrant family moving from California to deep-country Arkansas in the early eighties. Led by the dream of owning a vegetable farm, Jacob Yi (Yeun) and his wife, Monica (Han), tend the farm by day and take on additional work sexing chicks in the evenings.

The Yis fly Monica's mother, Soon-ja (Youn), from South Korea to help take care of their two children, adolescent Anne (Cho) and six-year-old David (Kim). David, a charming rascal, initially dislikes Soon-ja, rebelling against her demands and playing a stomach-churning prank on her involving Mountain Dew that isn't Mountain Dew. But eventually, they bond over Soon-ja's own agricultural hobby—she has brought the seeds of a Korean leafy herb called minari with her to the States and enlists David to help find a good location to plant them. Meanwhile, the farm encounters a string of small disasters, fraying the Yis' marriage due to Monica's belief that Jacob values his business over the family. Against all expectations, a gut-wrenching fire brings the family together and anchors them in their new land—like Soon-ja's minari, which proves it can grow just as lushly in Arkansas as in Korea.

(From left) Steven Yeun, Alan Kim, Youn Yuh-jung, Han Ye-ri, Noel Kate Cho

Minari won the Grand Jury Prize and the Audience Award at Sundance, and scored six Academy Award nominations, winning for Youn Yuh-jung's supporting performance—just the second Asian woman to win an acting Oscar, and the first in fifty-three years. Yeun's Oscar-nominated performance, equally powerful in a competitive category, and child actors Noel Kate Cho and Alan Kim received well-deserved critical praise for their work.

When most people think about the "quintessential Asian American story," chances are that story takes place on one of the coasts—San Francisco Chinatown or a Korean enclave in New York. Set in rural Arkansas of the eighties, *Minari* showed there are more dimensions to the Asian American story, and as someone who similarly came of age in the rural American South, *Minari* was the first time I felt truly represented in the canon of Asian American cinema. The film also subverted expectations for what an Asian American story could be. Ultimately, like the eponymous plant that takes root in the creek near the Yi family farm, *Minari* proved our stories can thrive in any environment.

—KEITH CHOW ON *MINARI*

"You have to trace the scars."

A Talk with **Justin Chon** and **Renee Tajima-Peña**

It's not easy to make movies based on life, especially the most turbulent, controversial, or unsettling aspects of it, but without such contemplations, we literally can't reflect. The cinema of social issues weaves Asian stories into historical narratives while forcing both those within the community and beyond it to confront choices they make—taking action or remaining passive. In this Q&A, Academy Award–nominated documentarian Renee Tajima-Peña (*Who Killed Vincent Chin?*) and actor and filmmaker Justin Chon (*Blue Bayou, Gook*) discuss the importance of shining a spotlight on the tides of change sweeping across our communities.

What led you to want to tell stories that focused on social issues?

JUSTIN CHON: I started acting around 2000. I'd gone to USC to study business and decided that's not what I wanted to do, so I enrolled in an acting school. And I looked around and asked, "Okay, what is a possible career trajectory within this arena?" And at that time, the only Asian American role without an accent that most people might recognize was John Cho as the "MILF guy" in *American Pie*. What was allotted to me as an Asian American guy was comedy. It didn't help I was twenty-one but looked fifteen. I started out doing kids' television and then ended up doing these lighthearted comedic roles. I'd studied the Meisner technique and foundational elements of acting, but these were the only gigs I could get. Meanwhile, the films I grew up with and loved were all really truth-based: family dramas, workplace stories, social investigations. And they were all about white people. So basically, I was quickly taught that that was not the place for me. Then I discovered the Asian American indie space, Wayne Wang's work—*Chan Is Missing!*—and I was blown away. I said to myself, *If I can't get cast in these kinds of stories, I need to tell them for myself*—stories I can really be passionate about and believe in.

RENEE TAJIMA-PEÑA: When I went to college at Harvard, I wanted to be a civil rights lawyer. And then I dated a couple guys who were first-year law students, and I thought, *No, I don't wanna be around guys like this. And I don't want to do that*

reading. And all they do is argue. Forget it. Instead, I found myself drawn into a group of students of color who'd formed a creators collective, and we confiscated this video equipment from the School of Public Health and started to do our own videos. That's how I got interested in making films, despite never having seen any Asian Americans on-screen when I was growing up, unless you count Mickey Rooney as Yunioshi on *Breakfast at Tiffany's*, which was an abomination. I even got some grant money and went down to Grenada, which had just had a socialist revolution, and interviewed the head of the movement, Maurice Bishop. It was me and a friend interviewing the new prime minister of Grenada, who was then assassinated by US troops a few years later. Of course, those tapes are now gone, and it's part of why I sometimes feel like I'm just making up for what I lost as a college student who just didn't know any better.

Do you think cinema has a unique power to make the world a better place?

JUSTIN: I feel like, to a certain extent, we change the world just by being on-screen. I mean, representation matters. Seeing diverse performers in diverse stories just makes things feel more possible. Then when you take that additional step and say, "Hey, I'm going to try to put a dent in the universe with this film, in whatever small way I can," that takes some chutzpah. But that's the kind of boldness and ambition that's required to make this kind of a film. In *Gook*, we were exploring the LA Riots and race relations among Blacks and Asians, which are gigantic issues in the Asian American, and especially the Korean American, community, and we were doing it on a micro budget. I wouldn't even have tackled it if there were another filmmaker working on a similar project from a similar perspective—given that the twenty-fifth anniversary of the Riots were coming up.

RENEE: People often talk about how cinema can change the world, and I tend to think that no, films don't change the world on their own; when they do, it's because they're a part of movements that are changing the world. Our documentary *Who Killed Vincent Chin?*—the reason it has had staying power is because it has been shown, year after year and decade after decade, by the ethnic studies programs and community groups that make up the Asian American movement. Vincent was killed in June 1982, and in the spring of 1983, a friend of ours sent us a clipping from Detroit, Michigan, about the case. The killing itself had been mostly ignored, but after the courts handed down that sentence—it was like paying off a car, "a $3,000 fine, and you have three years to pay it off"—the community there was outraged, and they started to reach out to other communities. So we originally went down to Detroit just to do a short organizing video for American Citizens for Justice, the group fighting on the Chins' behalf. But once we got some seed money from PBS, the project started to grow. I went down with our associate producer, Nancy Tong, for three months to record interviews. The very night we got there, we were mugged at gunpoint. But we dug in and were fortunate to be there to tell the story as this whole political transformation spread from Detroit across to the wider Asian American community. We were in the right place at the right time.

A big part of what these socially focused films do is fill in holes in the broader narrative.

JUSTIN: Yeah. When it came to the LA Riots, I knew that our community had not ever been portrayed in an accurate or even humane way. We were treated like a superficial prop or the source of the problem, as if we didn't have our own POV. And I was like, it's been twenty-five years and we have not moved. How long are we going to have to wait?

RENEE: The goal of a social-issue documentary is to help people who aren't living these moments firsthand to understand what happened, and how things are changing as a result. The upshot is that, within the DNA of a documentary, you have to take into account the context of how your work is going to be received and what role it'll play in the lives of its audience. You're capturing facts on the ground and bringing them into a whole new context. Our film came out right as the civil suits against Vincent's attackers, Ronald Ebens and Michael Nitz, were being settled, and it was one of the first times there was a hard-news film by Asian Americans about Asian Americans—most of the documentaries that people were funding at the time were softer, more human-interest stories. So that's part of the reason it had such an impact: For a lot of people, it felt like breaking news and a call to action. To be honest, I don't think it was a very special film—I think there was just so little else like it at the time. It's different now. If something as urgent as that case happened today, there'd be many different voices all over the story.

There are a lot of stories that urgently need to be told; how do you know that you're the one who has the right perspective to tell them?

RENEE: I wonder about this a lot these days. I mean, in the documentary space you have white filmmakers with resources and infrastructure and relationships with big funders, and they're seen as "generalists." They don't necessarily have any knowledge about a subject, but because they're seen as occupying our society's universalist, normative position, they can do anything. Like, Ken Burns can make a movie about anything. And meanwhile, we're trying to make films just to trace the edges of our own culture and identity. When I made *My America . . . or Honk If You Love Buddha*, I remember talking to a Laotian woman who had lost eight children during the war. And here I was, a middle-class third-generation Japanese American whose experience was so removed from her life experience. But there were parts of her story that were parts of my family's story. And both of our stories fit into something larger—this emerging portrait of Asian America. Telling each other stories and listening to them are a part of that process of self-definition and self-determination, right? A lot of times, the question isn't about appropriation—it's about whether you give empathy and respect.

JUSTIN: I know through making *Blue Bayou* that a lot of people felt like it wasn't my story to tell. Because I'm not an adoptee—I didn't have that experience. And I can accept that. But I do wonder: If you see a crisis happening, or you see the memory of a tragic event being lost, and you have the resources to tell that story, how long do you wait before you step in? That feeling of urgency can lead to some bad choices, but if you see something that you emotionally resonate with, that breaks your heart, it's hard not to feel like you need to do something. And frankly, we do need to tell stories outside of our own worlds—that's how we break down walls, by going outside of our narrow boundaries. Still, the lesson I've taken away from that is that the answer is empathy, first and foremost. Empathy and specificity. Our diaspora has stories within stories, and we need to do whatever we can to help make sure those specific stories are being told, in as true a fashion as we can.

Even if it's hard and painful to tell them, or if we run into resistance.

JUSTIN: Yeah. It can mean airing out our dirty laundry. It can mean disagreeing with one another. We're all fucked up in one or another way, and we all fuck up at one or another time. But when we shine a light and aim a camera at these darker, more painful parts of our lives and histories, it helps us to really understand where our place is in this country—how beautiful the experience of being here can be, and how ugly. You have to trace the scars even if it splits them open, because you can't really heal until you've let out that blood. I think we've gotten to the point now where people are willing to listen to us and ask, "What is your Asian American story?" And what we need to tell them is, "You're not gonna necessarily like what I tell you. It may sound obscure and uncommercial and difficult, but it's a story that urgently needs to be told, and it has never been told before."

RENEE: When I talk about why images matter, I say it's because they define the difference between who is us and who is them—who belongs and who doesn't belong. Who's in the picture, and who's outside of the frame? Images have been used as a bludgeon against people of color, against Asian Americans. They've been used to say, "No, you're not a part of *us*." Encoded in images are markers that tag us as subjects or objects, heroes or demons or faceless background. And when we control the ability to capture images, to tell stories with them, we can make sure that what's put on the screen is human. The hardest part of the process is figuring out how to preserve nuance, to keep things complex and human, while also compressing them into a couple dozen rectangular frames racing past your eyes every second.

6

The Dark Side

DAUGHTER OF THE DRAGON · PHANTOM OF CHINATOWN · LITTLE TOKYO, USA · GODZILLA · BREAKFAST AT TIFFANY'S · INDIANA JONES AND THE TEMPLE OF DOOM · YEAR OF THE DRAGON · BIG TROUBLE IN LITTLE CHINA · FULL METAL JACKET · AKIRA · THE CROW · SHOPPING FOR FANGS · RINGU · SPIRITED AWAY · BETTER LUCK TOMORROW · OLDBOY · THE LAST AIRBENDER · REVENGE OF THE GREEN DRAGONS · UMMA

"Chaos [with] deliberate intent."
A Talk with **Ken Jeong** and **John Cho**

ILLUSTRATION (OPPOSITE) BY TOMA NGUYEN

Movies bring dreams to life—but also nightmares. From the earliest days of the motion picture industry, the camera has been used to expose ugly things we'd rather keep hidden, and to distort the normal into the monstrous. Studio libraries are full of films that were made as tools of war, designed to frame Asian peoples as savage, treacherous, and deserving of destruction, like *Little Tokyo, USA*, a movie intended to build support for the incarceration of Japanese Americans during World War II. But this image-twisting hasn't been limited to the battlefield: In films like *Daughter of the Dragon*, *Year of the Dragon*, and *Revenge of the Green Dragons*, the lurking specter of Asian criminality is depicted in every dark alley and behind each ordinary storefront. (This is satirized, to some extent, in John Carpenter's *Big Trouble in Little China*, a movie that turns the tunnels beneath Chinatown into a literal gateway to hell.)

In *Breakfast at Tiffany's* and *Indiana Jones and the Temple of Doom*, Asians are presented as repulsive creatures—leering and lecherous, with disgusting dietary habits and religious practices. Though *Full Metal Jacket* seeks to interrogate the moral underpinnings of the Vietnam War, it uses the Vietnamese as pawns and pantomime objects, most infamously in the scene where a Da Nang streetwalker tells its protagonist, "Me love you long time."

There are better uses of cinema's ability to stare into the abyss. Through horror and the uncanny, movies like *Godzilla*, *Ringu*, and *The Crow* and animated classics *Akira* and *Spirited Away* illuminate the darkness of human souls and human civilization. *Better Luck Tomorrow*, *Oldboy*, and *Umma* explore the corrupting power of greed, thirst for revenge, and desire for control. Darkness can be frightening and foul, but without it, we can't see the light.

Anna May Wong

Daughter of the Dragon

1931, NOT RATED, 70 MINUTES, PARAMOUNT PICTURES, USA

DIRECTOR: Lloyd Corrigan

STARRING: Anna May Wong, Warner Oland, Sessue Hayakawa, Bramwell Fletcher

WRITERS: Lloyd Corrigan, Monte M. Katterjohn

BASED ON THE NOVEL *DAUGHTER OF FU MANCHU* BY SAX ROHMER

It's unfortunate that this movie is awful, a bad idea badly executed, because it represents several unique moments in cinematic history. Not only does the movie co-star the iconic Anna May Wong and her fellow silent screen great Sessue Hayakawa in their only on-screen pairing, but the story also makes them romantic partners. The film was the very first "talkie" role for both actors and represented Hayakawa's Hollywood comeback after retreating to overseas work due to rising anti-Japanese sentiment.

The film belongs to the Fu Manchu franchise—with Wong playing the daughter of the "devil doctor," referred to in Sax Rohmer's pulp novels as "the Yellow Peril incarnate in one man." As in all the Fu Manchu films, he plays a grotesquely racist caricature by a white man in yellowface (Swedish American actor Warner Oland would also debut his other yellowface role, as "Oriental detective" Charlie Chan, the very same year).

Ling Moy (Wong), a London-based dancer seeking the father she never knew, discovers he is none other than the notorious Dr. Fu Manchu (Oland). He subsequently manipulates her into helping him get revenge on the descendants of a British general named Petrie, whom he blames for the death of his family during the Boxer Rebellion. Ah Kee (Hayakawa), Fu Manchu's nemesis, seeks to thwart the doctor's murderous plans but hesitates when he realizes the instrument of those plans is Ling Moy, with whom he has fallen in love. Ling Moy, meanwhile, uses her wiles to seduce Ronald (Fletcher), the engaged grandson of General Petrie, to try to kill him. Her efforts are thwarted by Ah Kee, who shoots her just as she is about to stab a hapless Ronald in the back and then falls dead, attesting to his eternal love for her.

It's almost unwatchable because of what it does to two incredibly talented Asian American stars—casting them as second and third banana to a preening white actor in yellowface, and then having them kill each other on-screen. Hayakawa must've felt similarly, because after *Daughter of the Dragon*, he returned to films in Japan and Europe, not appearing in another Hollywood film for nearly two decades.

Phantom of Chinatown

1940, NOT RATED, 62 MINUTES, MONOGRAM PICTURES, USA

DIRECTOR: Phil Rosen

STARRING: Keye Luke, Lotus Long, Grant Withers, Charles Miller, Huntley Gordon, Virginia Carpenter, John Dilson, Paul McVey, John Holland, Lee Tong Foo, Willly Castello

WRITERS: George Waggner, Ralph Gilbert Bettison

The thirties and forties saw the proliferation of "Oriental detective" film franchises: the original Asian supersleuth, Charlie Chan, who ultimately appeared in forty-seven movies; Japanese secret agent Mr. Moto, who starred in nine; and Mr. Wong, an urbane Chinese American investigator solving crimes in San Francisco Chinatown, who was featured in six films for mini studio Monogram Pictures.

(From left) Willy Castello, Grant Withers, Keye Luke, and Paul McVey

In this Poverty Row programmer—the sixth and last of the Mr. Wong detective series—Boris Karloff steps down from his yellowface duties and is replaced by genial and mustachioed Keye Luke, the Number One Son of Charlie Chan promoted to a rare leading role. The clash of civilizations boils down to that age-old quandary of what's for lunch—chop suey or apple pie and coffee? As for Jimmy: "My sympathies follow my heritage, but after all, I am an American." Teamed with a brash police captain and languid ingenue Lotus Long, our Chinese American sleuth maneuvers through a backlot SF Chinatown and does his best to demystify "oriental hocus-pocus." Look for a plot point involving the Chinese Telephone Exchange, where female operators once helmed the switchboards while speaking multiple dialects and committing over a thousand numbers to memory, before the rise of dial telephones shut its doors in 1949.

—ANTHONY KIM ON *PHANTOM OF CHINATOWN*

White actors in yellowface makeup played the protagonists in all but three of these sixty-two films—two of the Chan films (both shot without sound) and this final film in the Mr. Wong series, a franchise reboot with a fresh face. The new man on the spot: none other than Keye Luke, who rose to fame playing "Number One Son" to Charlie Chan.

In *Phantom*, he gets the rare chance of a lead role, portraying a younger, hipper, and clearly Chinese American version of James Lee Wong—called "Jimmy Wong" here—becoming the first actual Asian to headline an Asian detective film in the talkie era. The first of four planned Mr. Wong movies starring Luke, *Phantom* focuses on the sudden death of an American archaeologist, Dr. John Benton, after his triumphant return from a dig in the Mongolian desert, where he uncovered the lost tomb of an ancient Ming dynasty emperor.

In the tomb, his team found a scroll detailing a place called the Temple of Eternal Fire, which the team believes marks the location of a vast oil reserve that would make them immensely wealthy. The scroll, however, is supposed to be cursed; earlier, an expedition member named Mason (Holland) is killed at the dig by a mysterious force. Right before Benton details more about the temple, he takes a sip of water, chokes, and dies. In the chaos, the scroll is lost, prompting one of Benton's favorite students, Jimmy Wong (Luke), to take the investigation and the scroll's disappearance into his own hands.

Theaters and audiences showed little interest in a Mr. Wong film, unfortunately, with the title role vacated by monster maestro Boris Karloff. This is, of course, the dark truth of yellowface: It wasn't done out of practicality—even then there was plenty of talent around—but because viewers preferred watching a white actor in, often, quite ghastly yellow makeup to an actual Asian person.

Little Tokyo, USA

1942, NOT RATED, 64 MINUTES, TWENTIETH CENTURY FOX, USA

DIRECTOR: Otto Brower

STARRING: Preston Foster, Harold Huber, June Duprez, Abner Biberman, Brenda Joyce, Don Douglas, George E. Stone, Charles Tannen, Frank Orth, Edward Soo Hoo, Beal Wong, Emory Parnell

WRITER: George Bricker

Though largely forgotten, this monstrosity from World War II has to be considered one of the most notorious films Hollywood has ever made. My mother and her entire family were forced into Japanese American concentration camps, and this movie perfectly captures the twisted Yellow Peril logic that swayed mass sentiment in those years, with a white male detective making QAnon-level accusations that Japanese Americans were spies and saboteurs only pretending to be loyal, hard-working citizens. (He could have been quoting the actual mayor of Los Angeles at the time.) Of course, this racist protagonist turns out to be the hero that uncovers a widespread plot by Nisei to aid the Japanese invasion of the West Coast. Propaganda like this helps explain why Trump and many other Republicans refuse to categorically state that Japanese American incarceration was wrong.

—SCOTT KURASHIGE ON *LITTLE TOKYO*

Victor Sen Yung (left) and Harold Huber

A horrendous piece of propaganda that attempts to excuse and rationalize the Japanese American incarcerations during World War II, this brief film invents a US-born Japanese American businessman named Takimura (Huber), who's recruited by spies in Tokyo to join the Black Dragon Society, a global group of pro-Japan extremists, and soon organizes a network of fifth columnists within LA's Little Tokyo community. A cop, Michael Steele (Foster), is assigned to investigate odd activities in Little Tokyo, which he traces back to Takimura's gang. With the help of his radio-reporter girlfriend, Maris (Joyce), he discovers the Black Dragons have been relaying vital US intelligence to the Japanese Imperial Navy. While in jail for a framed crime, Steele eventually learns about the bombing of Pearl Harbor and concludes that Takimura's group must have been involved. He

escapes, tracks them down, and with Maris's assistance, gets Takimura and his accomplices to confess to their crimes with his fellow cops listening in.

The film ends with Maris's report on the "evacuation" of Japanese Americans—using real footage of actual Little Tokyo residents being rousted from their homes—and proclaiming that even innocent Japanese Americans needed to make a sacrifice, because "in a time of war, the loyal must suffer inconvenience with the disloyal." Maris reads lines from Robert Nathan's hypernationalistic poem "Watch, America":

> *God who gave our fathers freedom*
> *God who made our fathers brave*
> *What they built with love and anguish*
> *Let our children watch and save.*

Little Tokyo, USA was screened as a double feature with Charlie Chaplin's classic *The Gold Rush*, of the need to "Be vigilant, America!" It is now a reminder that no person of Japanese ancestry living in the US was ever convicted of serious acts of espionage or sabotage during the war. Decades later, President Ronald Reagan issued a formal apology to Japanese Americans for the incarceration and authorized reparations of $20,000 to every surviving internee. Meanwhile, this film is now a prime example of studio collaboration in creating racist disinformation—a lingering mark of shame on both the government and Hollywood.

Godzilla

Godzilla's debut in 1954

1954, NOT RATED, 96 MINUTES, VESTRON VIDEO, JAPAN

DIRECTOR: Ishiro Honda

STARRING: Akira Takarada, Momoki Kochi, Akihiko Hirata, Takashi Shimura

WRITERS: Takeo Murata, Ishiro Honda

Godzilla didn't just launch one of the most beloved and iconic cinematic monsters of all time—it created a cottage industry, laying the foundation for a franchise that includes thirty-six films and counting (the longest-running film series in history!). With a host of spin-offs, imitations, and adaptations, this movie is arguably responsible for the entire cinematic category known as tokusatsu, the uniquely Japanese live-action genre that utilizes miniatures, stop-motion, fanciful costumes, rubber suits, and a gleefully camp aesthetic.

Godzilla begins with the sudden destruction of a series of Japanese ships at sea, which a villager blames on an ancient ocean-living titan named

Gojira. Reporters converge on Odo Island to cover the story, but a huge storm, and something using the storm for cover, devastates Odo. Survivors head to Tokyo for aid, and the government enlists Dr. Kyohei Yamane (Shimura) to investigate if a living being was responsible. Yamane finds weird things on the island—such as living examples of long-extinct creatures and enormous radiation-laced footprints. And then he encounters the source of those footprints: the titanic radioactive dinosaur Godzilla.

While Yamane wants to study the monster, the government wants it gone and sends out navy ships to kill Godzilla. But a creature that can withstand abyssal depths and survive an atomic explosion isn't killable with conventional weapons. Even a giant electrified fence proves to be no barrier—Godzilla blows it away with his atomic breath and stomps onward into Japan's capital.

Finally, secret research is shared with the anti-Godzilla forces: the Oxygen Destroyer, which causes oxygen atoms to disintegrate in its presence. Serizawa (Hirata) volunteers to use the prototype

Sure, I can write about how the original *Godzilla* brilliantly wove political themes related to the atomic bomb into a familiar sci-fi monster genre. But if I'm being honest, what made the film significant to me was simply seeing the most badass kaiju ever shooting fire out of its mouth and destroying everything in its path. We'd had "giant monster" movies before—*King Kong* set a high bar for that in 1933—but *Godzilla* took things to another level. Not just because of its social commentary, not just because of the innovative creature design that suggested something both prehistorically primal and futuristically sleek, but because it was a cool monster flick that featured people who looked like me. In a time when it was almost impossible to find interesting Asian heroes, villains, or monsters, Godzilla was all three.

—PHILIP W. CHUNG ON *GODZILLA*

against Godzilla and is delivered by ship. On the ocean floor, Serizawa unleashes the machine and then cuts off his own relief line, ensuring both he and Godzilla will die in the one and only test of his invention. The threat of the monster lizard is over—but, Yamane warns, if humanity continues to use nuclear weapons, the future may see another Godzilla rise.

Over the course of the film, the radioactive reptile is unquestionably used as a metaphor for the atomic bomb, lending a sharp poignance and immediate relevance to what would otherwise be hokey science fiction (less than a decade after the US dropped atomic bombs on Hiroshima and Nagasaki). But the version that crashed into US theaters in 1956, *Godzilla, King of the Monsters!*, was different. The American version featured twenty-one minutes of entirely new footage, used to clumsily insert actor Raymond Burr, playing reporter Steve Martin, into various scenes to serve as a narrator and proxy POV for white Western audiences. It also removed all mention of radioactivity, the atomic bomb, and nuclear energy from the narrative, putting the onus for the rise of Godzilla on nature rather than people, and purposely omitting any suggestion that the US was in any way to blame.

King of the Monsters earned $2 million at the US box office in its 1956 release, making it the first Japanese film to be a commercial hit in the United States, and opened the door to toys, video games, animated TV series, and multiple Hollywood remakes. Godzilla is here to stay, even if his real message, about the dangers of unfettered technology and the need to unite in peace with other humans around the world, has been shunted to the side.

Breakfast at Tiffany's

1961, NOT RATED, 115 MINUTES, PARAMOUNT PICTURES, USA

DIRECTOR: Blake Edwards

STARRING: Audrey Hepburn, George Peppard, Patricia Neal, Buddy Ebsen, Martin Balsam, José Luis de Vilallonga, John McGiver, Dorothy Whitney, Stanley Adams, Elvia Allman, Alan Reed, Miss Beverly Hills, Claude Stroud, Mickey Rooney

WRITER: George Axelrod

BASED ON THE NOVELLA BY TRUMAN CAPOTE

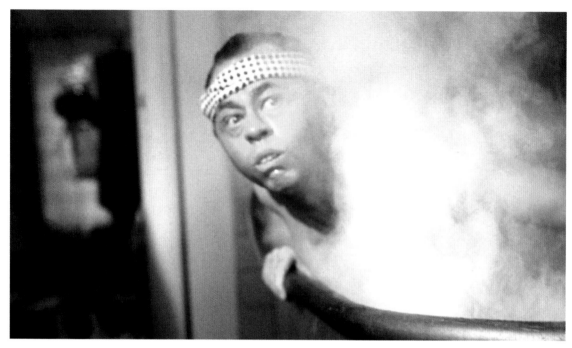

Mickey Rooney

A handful of classic films can produce polarizing reactions and leave audiences torn between their cinematic importance and the reality of outright offensive depictions and content: *Gone with the Wind* (1939) is one, beloved but harshly criticized for its rose-tinted depiction of slavery and cartoonishly drawn Black characters. *Breakfast at Tiffany's* is another—a huge box office success that scored five Academy Award nominations, winning two.

Breakfast is frequently cited as an all-time favorite film, in large part due to the indelible performance of the great Audrey Hepburn as

In 2017, the Brooklyn Historical Society presented a film series called "Capote on Screen." I was honored to be asked to help introduce each of the four films in the series. But I was also torn about the film that would kick off the first night, *Breakfast at Tiffany's*. I obviously couldn't ignore the existence of Mr. Yunioshi, one of the most offensive depictions of an Asian American on-screen—in a long history of racist depictions of Asian Americans. Was I supposed to scold white audiences for enjoying the movie? Should I have said, "I really wish these Yunioshi scenes weren't in the film"? In the end, I brought in historical context about Yellow Peril, and reminded the audience that the Japanese internment had occurred just a decade and a half before *Breakfast at Tiffany's* began production. I talked about the history of yellowface and blackface. I tried my best to frame the film as something to be learned from, as well as a historic artifact that reflected our changing awareness and values as Americans. I said, "I think we know better now, or at least, many of us want to do better, and I think we can."

—KRISTEN MEINZER ON *BREAKFAST AT TIFFANY'S*

country-girl-turned-socialite Holly Golightly. But *Breakfast* is a definitively problematic fave: The Holly Golightly who's depicted as a starry-eyed sweetheart in the movie is clearly a grifter and hustler in the gritty Truman Capote novella. (Marilyn Monroe turned the part down after hearing Golightly was a "lady of the evening.") And of course, there's bucktoothed, squinty-eyed Mr. Yunioshi, played in broadly racist yellowface caricature by Mickey Rooney.

Holly is a failed actress and professional partygoer who somehow survives on cocktails and the danishes and coffees she eats out of a paper bag each morning while staring at the jewelry display at Tiffany's. She pays her landlord Yunioshi rent out of the "tips" she receives from admirers, and the $100 she gets weekly from the imprisoned Mafia don, Sally Tomato (Reed).

A new resident in the building catches her eye—Paul Varjak (Peppard), a struggling writer, his living expenses paid by a wealthy older lover (Neal). They hit it off immediately, but Holly isn't interested in hooking herself to a poor wordsmith—she wants to marry rich so she can support herself and her brother once he's discharged from the army. The men she has her eyes on, however—a millionaire named Rusty Trawler (Adams) and a Brazilian politician named José da Silva Pereira (Vilallonga)—prove elusive. Meanwhile, Holly and Paul get closer, but as their romance seems like a foregone conclusion, Holly receives terrible news. She chooses to leave for Brazil in pursuit of José, but her affiliation with the Mafia ends up getting her arrested and José breaking their relationship off. After some time, Holly realizes Paul is the one for her, and they embrace as the strains of "Moon River" build up on the soundtrack.

The performance by Hepburn is startlingly good, a revelation even to her existing fans. But everyone associated with the movie regretted the decision to cast Rooney as Yunioshi after the film was released. Both Rooney and director Blake Edwards say they would've gone back and unmade the choice if they could have, but Rooney's leering, screeching performance is part of *Breakfast* forever.

Indiana Jones and the Temple of Doom

1984, PG, 118 MINUTES, PARAMOUNT PICTURES, USA

DIRECTOR: Steven Spielberg

STARRING: Harrison Ford, Kate Capshaw, Ke Huy Quan, Amrish Puri, Roshan Seth, Philip Stone, Roy Chiao, Raj Singh

WRITERS: Willard Huyck, Gloria Katz

The sound of a gong opens the second installment in the blockbuster adventure franchise starring Harrison Ford as the titular whip-wielding, fedora-wearing archaeologist. Besequinned lounge singer Willie Scott, played by Kate Capshaw, performs a show-stopping rendition of Cole Porter's "Anything Goes" in surprisingly good Chinese.

After a full-on Broadway chorus number by dancers with fans, rice-paddy hats, and side-slit miniskirts, the action shifts to the nightclub ("Club Obi-Wan," for the Easter egg fans). Indy negotiates with Chinese gangster Lao Che (Chiao), offering the grave-robbed cremated remains of Qing emperor Nurhachi for a diamond the size of a baby's fist. Things go downhill from there, as Lao poisons Indy's drink, leading to a physical scramble for guns, the diamond, and the poison antidote. Thanks to the timely arrival of friend and sidekick Short Round (Quan), Indy and Willie survive. What follows is a dark and preposterous ride that takes the trio from an exotic and racist depiction of China to an exotic and even more racist depiction of India—where a

Ke Huy Quan and Harrison Ford

religious leader named Mola Ram (Puri) is collecting the Sankara Stones.

Stones given to humanity by the gods to fight evil, these artifacts will bestow his cult of Kali worshippers (Thuggees) the power to take over the world. The Thuggees practice human sacrifice and child enslavement and are generally presented as barbaric and subhuman. So are the "civilized" Indians—a

As a baby Chinese tomboy in the eighties I remember the excitement of finally getting to see a movie sequel that I was pretty sure would include both Nazi-punching and a hard-hitting lady sidekick who could drink the male hero under the table. I remember being confused when the film started with a Shanghai fantasy nightclub musical number. Dancers masked in a kind of halfhearted yellowface simpered around a blond white woman singing "Anything Goes" in Mandarin, my mother tongue. As an eight-year-old child, I was consciously thinking, *What is happening? Why is she the star? A Chinese woman should be singing this and then punching Indiana Jones.*

Then the movie degraded my parents' Singaporean-Malaysian community even more, presenting the culture of my beloved Indian aunties as gruesome, demonic, cannibalistic, and utterly terrifying. But at least there was that kid Short Round, who cracked wise and had a cool nickname, who was streetwise, spunky, and called Indy out for cheating at cards. He was the star of this movie, the only thing I remember apart from the grisly racism and depressing sexism. In the eighties you took what you could get, treasure from the trash. You wiped it off and you held it close.

—TZE MING MOK ON *INDIANA JONES AND THE TEMPLE OF DOOM*

boy Maharajah (Singh) welcomes the three white Westerners with a feast that includes giant beetles, eyeball soup, living snake, and as a pièce de résistance, chilled monkey brains for dessert.

The final conflict between Indiana and Mola Ram, in which Indiana is saved by calling upon the power of Shiva, feels like a culturally appropriate version of the ending of *Raiders of the Lost Ark* (1981). The conclusion of the film, in which British Indian Army soldiers fire rifles into a crowd of remaining cultists, feels like a grotesque mirror of the historical Jallianwala Bagh Massacre. All in all, a dark installment of the Indiana Jones franchise—whose saving grace is the incredible performance of a young Ke Huy Quan as Short Round in his screen and acting debut.

Year of the Dragon

1985, R, 134 MINUTES, MGM/UA ENTERTAINMENT COMPANY, USA

DIRECTOR: Michael Cimino

STARRING: Mickey Rourke, John Lone, Ariane, Dennis Dun, Raymond J. Barry, Leonard Termo, Caroline Kava, Eddie Jones, Victor Wong, Jack Kehler, Tony Lip, Roza Ng

WRITERS: Oliver Stone, Michael Cimino

BASED ON THE NOVEL BY ROBERT DALEY

Like so many other war movies to be modeled after (or not), *Year of the Dragon* takes a very real threat to the lives, safety, and human rights of Asians and turns it into a test of the soul of a . . . Caucasian man. Not entirely surprising given that its director, Michael

Cimino, made his name with the excruciatingly over-the-top Vietnam War melodrama *The Deer Hunter* (1978). But *Year of the Dragon*'s war isn't on a battlefield in an Asian country; it's on the streets of the highest-density Chinese immigrant enclave in the Western hemisphere, Manhattan's Chinatown—though as the movie's ad campaign blared, "It isn't the Bronx or Brooklyn. It isn't even New York. It's Chinatown, and it's about to explode."

Why is it about to explode? A Vietnam vet turned maverick cop, whose name underscores the blunt-object nature of this film: Captain Stanley White. Upon being assigned to police Chinatown, White, played by Rourke, declares war on the Chinese Triads, recruiting a promising Chinese American cop, Herbert Kwong (Dun), to be his undercover "inside man" in the Chinatown gang world. He also tries to convince a Chinese American news reporter, Tracy Tzu (model Ariane in her first acting role), to be his mouthpiece, promising to leak her info on the anti-gang campaign in exchange for favorable coverage. Tzu refuses, calling the proposal unethical, but somehow ends up having a torrid affair with White, even though White's seduction involves ripping off her clothes without her consent, and despite White's marriage to his wife, Connie (Kava).

White's anti-Triad campaign runs afoul of Joey Tai (Lone), a young upstart seeking to take over the Triad's drug trade, whose ruthlessness, ambition, and penchant for violence are an even match for White's. Everyone around White ends up being hurt or destroyed at Tai's hands as the two men recklessly clash. Finally, White and Tai go head-to-head, racing each other on a set of railroad tracks, shooting wildly at each other until Tai is hit and begs White for his pistol to take his own life. White obliges, in exchange for the location of Tai's heroin cargo. White attends Tai's funeral and ends up inciting a brawl, yet still manages to walk away with Tracy Tzu at his side, a happy ending that neither White nor the movie has earned.

The film was not received well, criticized as overwrought, confusing, misogynistic, and profoundly racist. It mapped the ugliest tropes

Chinatown thugs, eighties style, in *Year of the Dragon*

of Vietnam War movies onto the sidewalks of Chinatown, and the face of the enemy onto Chinese immigrants. The final line of Cimino and Stone's script, which did not make the final cut, underscored this—White, embracing Tzu, would have said, "If you fight a war long enough you end up marrying the enemy." Because, of course, all people with Asian faces are the enemy. There was room for a cinematic exploration of the Chinese criminal underworld (Hong Kong was doing plenty of them) set in Manhattan Chinatown of the eighties. But this movie was not the one.

To be exceedingly generous, Michael Cimino's *Year of the Dragon* may have had ambitions to be the next *Godfather*. If so, his best move should have been to center on John Lone's Joey Tai, the up-and-coming gangster fighting a multipronged war against other triad members, the Italian mafia, Thai drug smugglers, and the NYPD. Alas, Cimino made Mickey Rourke's Stanley White—seriously, even his name is White!—the protagonist instead. The result: a critical and commercial flop that inspired a new generation of Asian Americans to hate Hollywood's portrayals of Asians in America.

—OLIVER WANG ON *YEAR OF THE DRAGON*

(From left) Kurt Russell, Kim Cattrall, Suzee Pai, and Dennis Dun

Big Trouble in Little China

**1986, PG-13, 99 MINUTES,
TWENTIETH CENTURY FOX, USA**

DIRECTOR: John Carpenter

STARRING: Kurt Russell, Kim Cattrall, Dennis Dun, James Hong, Victor Wong, Kate Burton, Donald Li, Carter Wong, Peter Kwong, James Pax, Suzee Pai, Chao-Li Chi, Jeff Imada

WRITERS: Gary Goldman, David Z. Weinstein, W. D. Richter

The marketing for this cult favorite from genre genius John Carpenter made it seem like a schlocky orientalist, low-budget white-savior adventure, and in many ways, that's exactly what it is. But anyone who's actually watched it knows that, behind the exotic facade, *Big Trouble* is secretly a subversive breakthrough: Kurt Russell is just the tank-topped front man for a movie whose real hero is Dennis Dun and the most interesting characters are iconic Asian Americans.

Russell plays Jack Burton, a trucker seeking money owed to him by his old friend, restaurant owner Wang Chi (Dun). Wang agrees to settle, but only after a trip to the airport to pick up his fiancée, Miao Yin (Pai), who has rare green eyes "like creamy jade." When they arrive, Jack and Wang prevent a street gang from abducting a Chinese immigrant girl, the client of blond and green-eyed attorney Gracie Law (Cattrall). Thwarted from taking their original target, the Lords grab Miao Yin instead, sending Wang and Jack into San Francisco Chinatown after

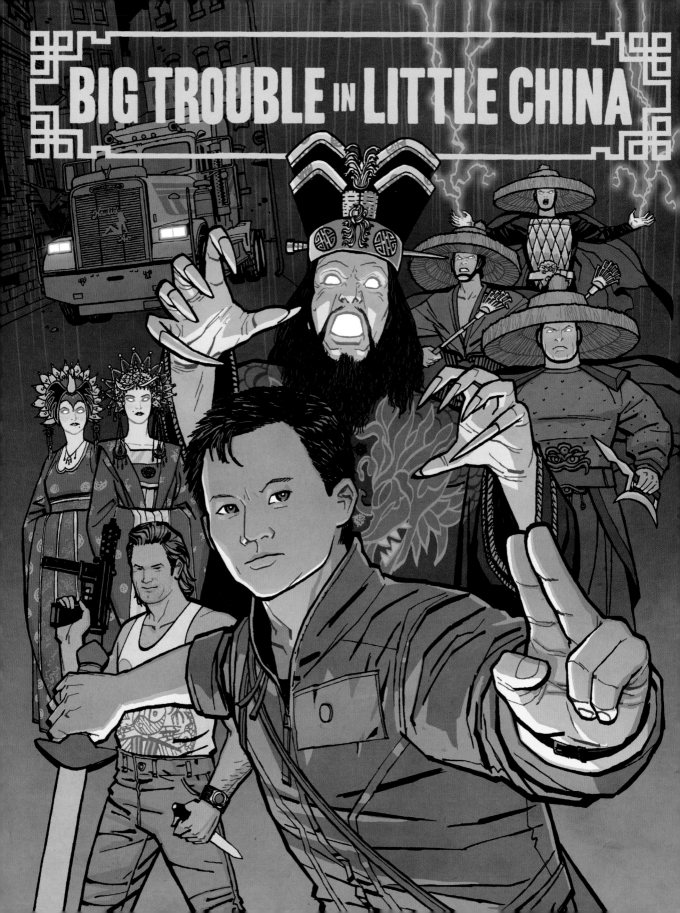

Subverting expectations of the typical white savior movie, this film is a progressive, rollicking, and hilarious action comedy that is still one of the best films of the eighties. From its synth rock soundtrack to Kim Cattrall's spunky performance, to the legendary James Hong as the immortal Lo Pan, to its amazing set design and bizarre and fantastical creature effects, *Big Trouble* embraced clichés while poking fun at them. Yet rather than laughing at the primarily Asian cast, it laughed with them. *Big Trouble in Little China* is definitely a product of its time, but also truly timeless.

—ANDERSON LE ON *BIG TROUBLE IN LITTLE CHINA*

When *Big Trouble in Little China* came out, I was in the middle of six formidable years in Hawaii, a biracial kid on my own voyage through racial identity, and this movie helped me to get through it. Dennis Dun looked and sounded just as "American" as any other hero in Hollywood movies, and yet he was an Asian man. Most importantly, he was smart, capable at fighting, and an essential part of the good-guy team. Kurt Russell's character was a goofball who didn't know the ropes, and the few things that he did know were kind of useless in the world that they were trying to navigate together. And yet they were buddies, and that just meant a lot to me for some reason. It was exactly what I wanted to see. It told me a lot about who I was.

—ERIC BYLER ON *BIG TROUBLE IN LITTLE CHINA*

the gang. As soon as they arrive, they literally run into a street battle between two rival martial arts clans, which ends with the arrival of a mysterious sorcerer, David Lo Pan (Hong), and his trio of supernatural henchmen, the Three Storms—Thunder (Carter Wong), Rain (Kwong), and Lightning (Pax).

Reinforced by Eddie Lee (Li), Chinatown tour guide and Taoist magic practitioner Egg Shen (the iconic Victor Wong), and uninvited interlopers Gracie and her reporter friend Margo (Burton), the pair form a plan to save Miao Yin. Descending into the underbelly of Chinatown, the motley rescue crew encounter Lo Pan again, who explains that millennia in the past, he was cursed by the first Chinese emperor, Qin Shi Huang. To break the curse, he must marry a green-eyed woman and then sacrifice her to the emperor,

which is the reason he kidnapped Miao Yin. Once Lo Pan realizes Gracie has green eyes too, he decides to marry them both ("The best of two worlds!"). An antic chase through the tunnels of subterranean San Francisco ensues, the bad guys are defeated, and romantic pairings are made, though not necessarily the ones you might expect.

The movie is dorky fun throughout, and even its more culturally offensive aspects are offset by the freedom Carpenter gave his Asian American ensemble. Dennis Dun, Donald Li, and Victor Wong deliver sterling performances without speaking in exaggerated Chinese accents. And Russell puts in a fun performance as bumbling blowhard Burton, whom Carpenter describes as "a sidekick who thinks he is a leading man."

Even director John Carpenter admitted it: The real hero of *Big Trouble in Little China* is Dennis Dun's Wang Chi. It was just studio racism that pushed him to be presented as Kurt Russell's "sidekick." Here (opposite) **Cliff Chiang** reimagines the movie's classic poster with a focus on its real leading man.

(From left) Kevyn Major Howard, Matthew Modine, Papillon Soo

Full Metal Jacket

1987, R, 116 MINUTES, WARNER BROS., USA

DIRECTOR: Stanley Kubrick

STARRING: Matthew Modine,
Vincent D'Onofrio, Lee Ermey, Adam Baldwin,
Arliss Howard, Kevyn Major Howard, Dorian
Harewood, Tim Colceri, Ed O'Ross,
John Terry, Bruce Boa

WRITERS: Stanley Kubrick, Michael Herr,
Gustav Hasford

Full Metal Jacket, directed by cinematic legend
Stanley Kubrick, is undoubtedly a work of art. And

art comes with a cost, often as collateral damage,
impacting those at the edges of its main audiences.
As with most American Vietnam war movies, *Jacket*
is not about the devastation experienced by the
Vietnamese but about the trauma suffered by US soldiers. Unlike similar films, the movie begins in basic
training, suggesting that the psychological damage to
enlistees was caused not just by the war but also by
the process of turning them into warriors.

The first half of the movie is set at Parris Island's
boot camp for new Marines, where drill instructor
Gunnery Sergeant Hartman (Ermey) deploys a campaign of aggressive brutality toward his raw recruits,
seeking to break them down and remold them into
fighting men. This involves nonstop verbal abuse
laced with racist, ethnic, and homophobic slurs.
POV character J. T. Davis (Modine) gets off relatively
easy, dubbed "Joker" for his penchant for wisecracking. But overweight and awkward Private Leonard
Lawrence (D'Onofrio)—nicknamed by Hartman as
"Gomer Pyle"—becomes a special target for the gun-
ny's over-the-top harassment. Hartman punishes the

entire squad for Lawrence's frequent incompetence, causing the squad to engage in a mass nighttime beating of their hapless fellow soldier, which causes a change in Lawrence: His affect flattens, he submits to Hartman's orders obediently, and he unexpectedly becomes an expert marksman. Joker worries that these aren't signs of a turnaround for Lawrence but signs of a psychological collapse, a fear proven correct when he finds a psychotic Lawrence in the barracks bathroom the night before they ship out to Vietnam. Parked on a toilet and loading live ammo into his service rifle, Lawrence recites the "Rifleman's Creed" that has been drummed into them since their arrival. Hartman arrives and orders him to stand down (with the famous line "What is your major malfunction, numbnuts?"), but Lawrence kills him before taking his own life.

The movie then switches gears and skips to 1968, when Joker has become a Da Nang–based correspondent for the military newspaper *Stars and Stripes*. A scene plays out that shows how acclimatized he has already become to the war landscape, in which he and his photographer, Rafterman (Kevyn Major Howard), negotiate with a prostitute, played by French Chinese actress and model Papillon Soo, to get her to drop her prices to ten dollars apiece. (Soo's line "Me so horny, me love you long time," popularized through samples by rappers like 2 Live Crew and Sir Mix-a-Lot, has since become a persistent, degrading catcall aimed at Asian women.)

Jacket unflinchingly shows the grotesque and corrosive elements of war, and the Vietnam War in particular. It is without question one of the greatest war movies ever made, but it's also worth remembering that its power in framing how war shapes American men depends in no small part on the dehumanization of Asian women.

Akira

**1988, R, 124 MINUTES,
STREAMLINE PICTURES, JAPAN**

DIRECTOR: Katsuhiro Otomo

STARRING: Mitsuo Iwata, Nozomu Sasaki, Mami Koyama, Taro Ishida, Mizuho Suzuki, Tessho Genda, Fukue Ito, Tatsuhiko Nakamura, Kazuhiro Kando, Yuriko Fuchizaki, Masaaki Okura, Takeshi Kusao, Hiroshi Otake

WRITERS: Katsuhiro Otomo, Izo Hashimoto

It's hard to recall a period when anime wasn't a central pillar of American pop culture. Yet in the 1980s, anime fandom was still an underground activity, and awareness of Japanese animation was mostly limited to remixed and overdubbed children's shows like *Speed Racer* and *Robotech* that did their best to disguise their overseas origins.

Katsuhiro Otomo's monumental sci-fi epic *Akira* was one of the first animated features to capture the mass attention of adult audiences through arthouse cinema showings, college campus screenings, and eventually home video, where it made over $80 million. Otomo's dystopian vision remains as compelling and vividly drawn as ever. But the movie's subversive aspect has always been Otomo's decision to make most of its primary characters children—monster children, whose exponential intellects and inhuman powers make them WMDs (weapons of mental destruction, maybe?) at the scale of nuclear arms—*Lord of the Flies* at a cataclysmic scale. While precociously mature superpowered children are common in anime, *Akira* marked the first exposure of it for many Western viewers, and many of them were shocked, inspiring a future generation of creators to reverently embrace its visuals and narratives. (How many times have we seen that killer horizontal bike slide since?)

Akira is set in Neo-Tokyo, a new city built on a set of artificial islands after the original metropolis was obliterated by a young psychic prodigy named Akira. The film opens with a motorcycle street duel between two biker gangs: the Capsules, led by a red-jacketed hothead named Kaneda (Iwata), and the Clowns. Japan's military, led by Colonel Shikishima (Ishida), captures Tetsuo (Sasaki), a junior Capsule

member, and Takashi (Nakamura), a runaway child with ESP powers. Kaneda is arrested with the other Capsule members, where he meets Kei (Koyama), a leader of a grassroots resistance that seeks to overthrow Neo-Tokyo's martial law.

Meanwhile, government researchers soon discover that Tetsuo's powers are potentially on par with the legendary Akira, prompting discussion on whether to develop his abilities as a weapon or to kill him before another city-destroying disaster. With Tetsuo's mental growth spiraling out of control, Takashi and two other army-controlled ESPers intervene, flooding his brain with debilitating hallucinations to either control or kill him. The psychic attack causes Tetsuo to discover his telekinetic powers, which he uses to smash free of his locked wardroom, indiscriminately killing hospital staff as he hunts for his adversaries. With every fear about Tetsuo now coming true, Colonel Shikishima deploys all his resources against him, hoping to stop him from connecting with Akira. Tetsuo searches for any relief for the pounding pain in his skull, and with no options seemingly left, he heads for the stadium to find Akira, only to discover that all that remains of him are a set of frozen and preserved neurological samples.

Kei, Kaneda (armed with a giant laser rifle), and the colonel (armed with an even more giant orbital space laser) try to stop Tetsuo in turn, and all of them fail as Tetsuo loses control of his physical form, ballooning into an enormous, pulsating mass of flesh that crushes everything in its vicinity. After the three ESPers beseech the dead Akira to address the Tetsuo crisis, Akira reforms himself from his remains and generates yet another singularity, erasing Neo-Tokyo as he had its original template. Swallowed by the singularity, Kaneda has visions of the origins of Akira and the psychic children, and nostalgic memories of his time with Tetsuo. The movie ends with Tetsuo apparently introducing himself to whomever is on the other side of Akira's singularity, with the line "I am . . . Tetsuo."

The Crow

1994, R, 102 MINUTES, MIRAMAX, USA

DIRECTOR: Alex Proyas

STARRING: Brandon Lee, Rochelle Davis, Ernie Hudson, Michael Wincott, Bai Ling, Sofia Shinas, Anna Levine, David Patrick Kelly, Angel David, Laurence Mason, Michael Massee, Tony Todd, Jon Polito, Bill Raymond, Marco Rodríguez

WRITERS: David J. Schow, John Shirley

BASED ON THE COMIC BY JAMES O'BARR

A brooding, visually stunning, supernatural revenge drama and beyond-the-grave love story, *The Crow* was buzzed as Brandon Lee's breakthrough even before production began. The buzz proved true, but Lee would never see his triumph, losing his life to a horrific misadventure during the last few days of shooting: A dummy shell was mistakenly left in the firing chamber of a prop gun loaded with blanks, and when fired, the combination of the gunpowder and the shell created a live bullet that shot him. Media swarmed to compare Lee's death to that of his father, Bruce, a tragic irony considering Brandon's hope that *The Crow*'s success might finally move him beyond that legendary shadow. But the movie survives, and it remains a masterpiece of mood, melodrama, and goth aesthetic.

Lee plays Eric Draven, a Detroit-based musician who is murdered by members of a savage street gang who also rape and beat his fiancée, Shelly Webster (Shinas), leaving her comatose and on a slow, torturous fade toward death. The crime, committed the night before Halloween—what Detroiters refer to as "Devil's Night"—goes unsolved, despite efforts by an officer named Daryl Albrecht (Hudson) and Shelly and Eric's teenage friend Sarah (Davis) to piece together clues. A year later, summoned by the mysterious figure of a crow, an undead Eric pulls himself out of his grave, healed of his wounds. He returns to his apartment and experiences a sudden flashback of his and Shelly's murders. Recognizing the gang members—Tin Tin (Mason), Funboy (Massee), Skank

In the eighties, even as Hollywood continued to co-opt martial arts, the martial artists were mostly white: Van Damme, Seagal, Lundgren, Norris, Speakman. So when Brandon Lee was cast in *The Crow* I thought, "Finally, an Asian American action hero. And he's Bruce Lee's son, to boot!" And then he was killed on set by a malfunctioning prop gun. There's both poetry in that and fuel for pessimism. But when I rewatch *The Crow*—seeing Brandon in his black-and-white clown makeup deliver droll one-liners one moment and slink across the screen with balletic grace the next—it makes me glad he got to show the world a little bit of what made him special before he left us. Who knows what would have come next, had he lived. But what we got is what we got.

—BAO PHI ON *THE CROW*

(David), and their leader, T-Bird (Kelly)—Eric covers his face in harlequin makeup and sets out to obtain posthumous vengeance.

As he works his way through his murderers, news of the deaths reaches the crime boss who employs them, Top Dollar (Wincott). Top Dollar turns to his witchy lover/half sister, Myca (Ling), for advice, and she surmises that something more than human and less than alive is at play. She tells him the key to Eric's immortality is likely the crow; if the crow is killed, Eric will lose his powers. They abduct Sarah to set a trap: As Eric arrives, they shoot the crow with a rifle, rendering Eric mortal. But even a mortal Eric is enough to overcome the nefarious siblings, and Eric finally kills Top Dollar by flooding his mind with all thirty hours of Shelly's suffering at once, causing him to fall off the roof, catatonic, and die. With the last of their murderers gone, Eric returns to the grave and is reunited with Shelly in the great beyond. But *The Crow* would return, again and again—with four sequels and a forthcoming reboot speaking to the power of Lee's greatest and last performance.

Brandon Lee

Shopping for Fangs

1997, R, 90 MINUTES, MARGIN FILMS, USA

DIRECTORS: Quentin Lee, Justin Lin

STARRING: Radmar Agana Jao, Jeanne Chinn, Clint Jung, Lela Lee, John Cho, Peggy Ahn, Scott Eberlein, Daniel Twyman, Jennifer Hengstenberg, Dana Pan

WRITERS: Dan Alvarado, Quentin Lee, Justin Lin

The metanarrative of *Shopping for Fangs* is about identity and imitation, aspiration and longing, and ultimately, coming out of the closet—whether by embracing a hitherto hidden sexual orientation or by releasing the burden of toxic masculinity to accept manhood on your own terms, depending on which thread one follows in this dual-director film. Quentin Lee essayed the scenes focused on one plot—the odd waltz between a disaffected housewife named Katherine and her lesbian admirer Trinh—while Justin Lin, who would go on to direct *Better Luck Tomorrow* (2002) and save the *Fast and Furious* franchise, helmed the ones about Phil, a mild-mannered middle-aged payroll clerk who believes he's turning into a werewolf. Much like the film's clearest inspiration, Wong Kar-Wai's 1994 masterpiece *Chungking Express*, the two plots are lightly connected and only barely converge, though they speak to themes and ideas that ultimately prove to be similar.

Katherine (Chinn) has been experiencing amnesiac blackouts, creating periods of time that she can't explain. During one of these fugues, she misplaces her cell phone, which is found by self-avowed lesbian Trinh, a waitress at the Go-Go Café. (Trinh sports a platinum-blond wig and sunglasses throughout the film, in an homage to the great Brigitte Lin's character in *Chungking Express*, but for another reason as well, which becomes clear later.) Obsessed with Katherine, Trinh sends her suggestive texts and flirtatious pictures, causing turmoil in Katherine's rocky marriage to Jim (Jung).

Meanwhile, Phil (Jao) has been experiencing odd hair growth and changes in his physique and personality (he's more confident, eats raw meat, and is apparently immune to harm, getting hit by a car to no consequence). His brother-in-law, who's been conducting research on lycanthropy, suggests he's a skinchanger. But soon Phil's activities go beyond merely sexual adventurism and beef tartare: He starts finding

*S*hopping for Fangs was part of the so-called Class of 1997 that introduced new visions for Asian American feature filmmaking, alongside Chris Chan Lee's *Yellow*, Rea Tajiri's *Strawberry Fields*, and Michael Aki and Eric Nakamura's *Sunsets*. Of the quartet, *Fangs* was arguably the most ambitious, with its post-Tarantino set of overlapping stories about amnesiac alter egos, potential lycanthropes, and a young, melancholic John Cho spending quality time in San Gabriel Valley Asian diners. Its various plot lines are clearly meant to be an exploration of the malleability of Asian American identity without wearing those intentions on its sleeve. While both Lee and Lin would go on to make more polished films in their careers, few match the creative exuberance infused into their inaugural collaboration.

—OLIVER WANG ON *SHOPPING FOR FANGS*

corpses in his wake and wonders if he's the cause.

Ultimately, the truth about Katherine and Trinh is revealed, and Katherine asks her domineering husband for a divorce. Phil, meanwhile, confesses his possible murders to a church friend named Grace (Ahn), only to scare her away with his aggressive gestures. He tries chaining himself up to lock down the beast within and somehow experiences a revelation.

In the end, Katherine picks up a hitchhiking, clean-shaven Phil, and the two head off to somewhere, anywhere. The film is uneven, to say the least, and its ending feels a bit like the filmmakers ran out of ideas or budget, but the seeds of greater things within it are obvious, and future leading man John Cho delivers a charming performance, while Jeanne Chinn's turn is a tour de force.

Ringu

1998, NOT RATED, 96 MINUTES, ARROW VIDEO, JAPAN

DIRECTOR: Hideo Nakata

STARRING: Nanako Matsushima, Hiroyuki Sanada, Rikiya Ōtaka, Miki Nakatani, Yuko Takeuchi, Hitomi Sato, Daisuke Ban, Rie Inō, Masako, Yōichi Numata, Yutaka Matsushige, Katsumi Muramatsu

WRITER: Hiroshi Takahashi

BASED ON THE NOVEL *RING* BY KOJI SUZUKI

In the late nineties, Japanese horror movies took an eerily contemporary turn, adopting themes on media consumption and the viral spread of the uncanny through technology—television, videotapes, cell phones, and of course, the internet. These movies brought supernatural phenomena into our modern era while tapping into fears that we have moved from using devices to being used by them. No film did so more effectively than *Ringu*.

A death curse is scary but quaint; a death curse transmitted by watching a weird video clip feels like every day on the internet. *Ringu* begins with a pair of teenage girls, Tomoko (Takeuchi) and Masami (Sato), talking about a dark rumor going around their high school—the existence of a cursed videotape that, when watched, triggers a phone call that sets a countdown for your remaining days of life: "Seven days." Tomoko says she's seen the tape and then claims to have been joking. Alone later, Tomoko is startled when the TV turns on by itself. After trying to turn off the TV several times and failing, she is surprised by a mysterious presence and killed.

Her aunt Reiko (Matsushima), a journalist, is investigating the urban legend of the cursed videotape and hears at Tomoko's funeral that three other friends who saw the tape with her died at the same time. Reiko visits the rental cabin where Tomoko saw the video, finds it, and plays it for herself, seeing eerie, disconnected scenes in flickering black and white, ending with a shot of something emerging from a well. After the tape plays, Reiko receives a phone call: "Seven days." Aware she is now a carrier of the curse, she watches the tape with her ex-husband, Ryuji (Sanada), when they discover a strange audio message in a dialect native to the island of Oshima. Before leaving for the island, Reiko catches their six-year-old son, Yoichi (Ōtaka), watching the tape, explaining that his (dead) cousin Tomoko told him to.

Reiko and Ryuji learn of the creepy history of Shizuko Yamamura, a local psychic who committed suicide after being called a fraud, and her daughter Sadako, who inherited a more potent strain of Shizuko's abilities, even killing a journalist who mocked her mother. The truth of Sadako's curse: It can't be broken, only passed along. The only way to survive it is to show someone else the tape.

Ringu inspired an entire franchise of sequels and spinoffs in Japan, and a hit remake, *The Ring* (2002)

in the US, which itself had two successful sequels. *Ringu*'s influence didn't end with its direct extensions: It opened the way for a viral pandemic of similar Japanese horror films of varying quality, from *Pulse* (2001) to *Ju-On: The Grudge* (2002) to *One Missed Call* (2003), all of which were also remade in the US, with *varying* degrees of success.

Spirited Away

2001, PG, 125 MINUTES, BUENA VISTA PICTURES, JAPAN

DIRECTOR/WRITER: Hayao Miyazaki

STARRING: Rumi Hiiragi, Miyu Irino, Mari Natsuki, Takashi Naito, Yasuko Sawaguchi, Tsunehiko Kamijō, Takehiko Ono, Bunta Sugawara

By the time *Spirited Away* arrived on the international cinematic scene, its director, Hayao Miyazaki, had already been recognized by the cognoscenti as a genius of animation—a rare storyteller capable of weaving visual spectacles that delighted children and adults alike, bringing an unusually realistic depth and weight to tales otherwise fantastical; movies like *Nausicaä of the Valley of the Wind* (1984), *My Neighbor Totoro* (1988), and *Kiki's Delivery Service* (1989) were charming but also contended with darker aspects of the world, like degradation of the environment, fear of mortality, the burden of duty. *Princess Mononoke* (1997) unlocked another gear in Miyazaki's burgeoning imagination. His tale of a human girl and a wolf-spirit defending the virgin forest, both from the broken-gods-turned-demon that humans have accidentally created and from the humans themselves, is a remarkable achievement, weaving Shinto philosophy and the grim, gory sensibility of chanbara films into a critique of industrialization and humanity's push for progress at all costs. As great as *Mononoke* is, however, few people dispute that *Spirited Away* is even more of a masterpiece.

Spirited Away is the tale of a ten-year-old girl named Chihiro (Hiiragi) and her boorish parents, who spontaneously decide to explore an abandoned amusement park on the way to their new home. Seeing a giant spread of fresh and delicious food laid out in the park's restaurant, the parents dig in, while Chihiro politely demurs. She explores the rest of the park, encountering a mysterious boy named Haku (Irino), who tells her that she and her parents must leave the park and cross the river before the sun goes down. When Chihiro returns to her parents, she finds that they have been transformed into pigs—literal pigs—after engorging themselves, making it impossible for them to return to the human world. The park, part of the land of yokai, or supernatural beings, has trapped Chihiro, and she must follow its rules, which of all things includes getting a job.

Toshio Suzuki and Hayao Miyazaki in 2013

Haku introduces Chihiro to the yokai and a witch named Yubaba (Natsuki). Yubaba offers her a job, but as a price for the position, she takes away one of the kanji characters in Chihiro's name, which transforms it into "Sen." Yubaba's power over people lies in her taking away their names, causing them to forget their identities; Haku, too, is stuck in the park because he can't recall his full name.

Beginning her job as a bath attendant, Sen is generally abused by the other workers as the only human employee; because her peers refuse to train her, Sen allows a mute and dangerous spirit called No-Face (a.k.a. Kaonashi) into the bathhouse. As the shapeless masked figure wreaks havoc among the bathers, Sen cleans up a stink spirit, the former guardian spirit of a polluted river, and accepts a medicinal gift from him. Later, Sen gives an injured Haku a bite of the medicine provided by the stink spirit and forces him to cough up a coveted golden seal as well as a black slug. On the way out, she runs

into No-Face, who has engorged himself to an enormous size. She feeds him the other part of the stink spirit's magic medicine, and No-Face begins vomiting up everything he's eaten, including several of the bathhouse's attendants.

Having saved the bathhouse, Sen demands Yubaba release her and her parents and transform her parents back into humans. Yubaba says yes, if Sen agrees to a test—she must identify her parents from among her herd of pigs. Sen looks at the pigs and correctly says that none of them are her mom and dad. Defeated, Yubaba breaks her contract and returns Chihiro's name. Chihiro finds her parents and exits the park with them to find their car, which is years older and covered with the detritus of the passage of time.

Everything about *Spirited Away* is marvelous (even Disney's English dub of the film is pretty good!)—it is gorgeous, original, moving, and truly dark, with the vaguely horrific flavor that age-old fairy tales usually have but in a new and updated package. It made roughly $700 million around the world, $305 million of that in Japan, and for many years was the highest-grossing film in Japanese history. It won the Oscar for Best Animated Feature, becoming the first hand-drawn, non-English-language movie to win it, and is often cited as one of the greatest films of all time, animated or not. The accolades are well earned. Shockingly, Disney was reluctant to promote the film despite owning US distribution rights, since Miyazaki had retained merchandise and other rights for himself and Studio Ghibli. It went almost unseen in its first release, with the only advertising occurring in a single banner ad on a Disney site dedicated to marketing other movies. After the film won the Academy Award (something that then-Pixar chief John Lassiter demanded Disney help make possible), both Disney and American audiences finally tuned in. *Spirited Away* ended up grossing about $10 million in after-the-fact box office, and a generation of viewers, enthralled by the richly realized otherworld Miyazaki created here, was motivated to dive more deeply into the canon of anime.

Better Luck Tomorrow

2002, R, 101 MINUTES, MTV FILMS, USA

DIRECTOR: Justin Lin

STARRING: Parry Shen, Jason Tobin, Sung Kang, Roger Fan, John Cho, Karin Anna Cheung

WRITERS: Justin Lin, Ernesto Foronda, Fabian Marquez

Any history of the rise of Asian American cinema is going to include a few critically important works: *Chan Is Missing* (1982), for sure. *Crazy Rich Asians* (2018), naturally. And this film, the pivot point between the Asian American indie explosion of the 1980s and 1990s and the slow migration into the mainstream of the 2010s and 2020s (as seen in the career of its director, Justin Lin, who ended up in charge of the blockbuster *Fast and Furious* franchise).

Sung Kang, Jason Tobin, and Parry Shen

A stark, funny, deeply disturbing thriller, *Better Luck Tomorrow* was shot on credit cards and finished through the kindness of strangers, specifically a stranger better known as MC Hammer; when Lin ran out of money during production, he asked Hammer, whom he'd run into randomly at a video equipment expo, for help, and the rapper came through with completion funds. Hammer wasn't the only hero of *Better Luck Tomorrow*'s journey, though: After the film premiered at Sundance, an audience member asked why the film portrayed Asian Americans in such a bad light, and none other than legendary movie critic Roger Ebert stood up in its defense, stating that the (white) speaker would not dare to tell white people how to depict their community and shouldn't be lecturing Asians on how to do so either. Ebert's presence at the screening and public endorsement of the movie generated huge publicity and contributed to its pickup by MTV Films, in one of the first high-profile theatrical acquisitions of an Asian American indie film.

Better Luck Tomorrow's protagonist, Ben Manibag (Shen), is seemingly an archetypal Asian American overachiever, grinding his way toward the Ivy League and mooning over popular girl Stephanie (Cheung). But underneath his model minority veneer, there's a bad boy struggling to get out, as can be seen by his regular episodes of petty crimes with his oddball friend Virgil (Tobin) and Virgil's cousin Han (Kang). The crimes soon increase: Daric Loo (Fan), big man on campus and class valedictorian, pulls Ben and his pals into a cheating scam, convincing Ben to sell cheat sheets off stolen tests to desperate and lazy classmates. The cheat sheet business proves lucrative and a gateway to breaking bad—theft of school property, drug sales, and for Ben, drug use that verges on addiction. After waking up with a cocaine nosebleed, Ben tells the gang he's out, to refocus on academics and his growing relationship with Stephanie, whose wealthy private-school boyfriend, Steve (Cho), offers to give her to him, implying a favor to be repaid later. Steve calls in his chips by offering Ben and his boys a perfect crime: robbing his own parents' house.

Daric convinces Ben and the others to do it, suggesting it might be the ideal opportunity to give Steve some payback. On New Year's Eve, the four friends meet Steve, allegedly to do the job, but brutally assault him instead. Steve fights back, and Ben smashes Steve in the head with a baseball bat. Assuming Steve is dead, the panicked quartet tries to bury him but realize he's still alive when his body starts to quiver. Daric finally suffocates him to death with a gasoline-soaked rag, and they bury his corpse and go to a New Year's Eve party, where Ben arrives in time for a midnight kiss with Stephanie. Virgil, meanwhile, is so conscience-stricken over Steve's murder that he tries and fails to commit suicide by shooting himself in the head. After a lengthy hospitalization, Virgil is hanging out with Ben when they hear a muffled phone ringing. It's Steve's phone, which they forgot was in his pocket. They dig it up and see the call is from Stephanie. As the movie ends, Stephanie picks Ben up in her new car and asks him if he's seen Steve recently. He says no and kisses her, and they ride off. It's interesting to note that despite the concerns Sundance audiences had about the movie putting a stain on perceptions of Asian Americans, *Better Luck Tomorrow* is actually very loosely inspired by real events: the killing of Stuart Tay in Orange County, California, whose particulars, dubbed the "Honor Roll Murder," have striking similarities to the plot of *BLT*.

Oldboy

**2003, R, 120 MINUTES,
CJ ENTERTAINMENT NEON, SOUTH KOREA**

DIRECTOR/WRITER: Park Chan-wook

STARRING: Choi Min-sik, Yoo Ji-tae, Kang Hye-jung, Ji Dae-han, Kim Byeong-ok, Yoon Jin-seo, Oh Dal-su

**BASED ON THE MANGA SERIES *OLD BOY*
BY NOBUAKI MINEGISHI AND
GARON TSUCHIYA**

Park Chan-wook put himself on the cinematic map at the turn of the century with *Joint Security Area*, a twisty but conventional legal thriller that unpacks the circumstances behind a shooting incident in the Demilitarized Zone between North and South Korea. *Joint Security Area* was a gigantic success, becoming the highest-grossing movie in Korean history and earning Park accolades and awards from critics in Korea and abroad. More importantly for Park, perhaps, it earned him the trust to make films with far wilder and extreme material—beginning with 2002's

Sympathy for Mr. Vengeance, a grueling story of interlocking acts of bloody revenge, and continuing with this film, which has since been celebrated as one of the greatest Asian movies ever made.

Originating as an eight-volume manga series by Garon Tsuchiya and Nobuaki Minegishi, *Oldboy* is about an ordinary Korean businessman named Oh Dae-su (Choi) who is arrested for public intoxication on his daughter's fourth birthday, and subsequently drugged, kidnapped, and incarcerated in a locked and soundproof hotel room. With no human contact or interaction with the outside world, food is served to him through a small slot, the same Chinese food meal of fried dumplings every day, and the TV only provides him with news reports, including one that tells him his wife has been murdered and he is the main suspect. Fifteen years go by, with Dae-su barely keeping his sanity, spending his days exercising and teaching himself to fight while attempting to dig an escape tunnel and thinking endlessly of revenge against whoever subjected him to this mysterious imprisonment. And then, without warning, Dae-su

is hypnotized, drugged again, jammed into a large suitcase, and dumped on the roof of a tall building, where he sees a man about to commit suicide. He stops the man before he plunges over the edge and forces him to hear his bizarre story; when the man shares his story in return, Dae-su storms off, and the man throws himself to his death. The only words Dae-su heard from him is the sentence "Even though I'm no better than a beast, don't I deserve to live?" It is a line that will recur.

Dae-su tests his fighting skills, trained through fifteen years of shadowboxing in the hotel room, against a gang of thugs and proves himself quite capable of combat. A strange beggar hands him a wad of money and a cell phone—more signs something mysterious is still afoot. With money in hand, Dae-su wanders into a sushi restaurant and orders something "alive"—it turns out to be a wriggling octopus, which he gulps down whole. (Not a special effect! Choi swallowed that sucker.) Dae-su's mysterious captor then phones him, taunting him to come discover the reason behind his suffering. Dae-su collapses

I came upon *Oldboy* at a time in my moviegoing experience when I didn't think it was possible to be surprised anymore. I felt like I knew where this picture was going, but it eluded me at every turn, up to and including who and what was being avenged. In the end, it's like a movie Steven Spielberg might make if Spielberg had the muscle to produce something genuinely perverse and "feel-bad." It even works as a metaphor for the depersonalized aridity of modern existence, where the only way you can feel something is by eating a full-grown live octopus or taking on a hallway full of men with a claw hammer.

—WALTER CHAW ON *OLDBOY*

Oldboy is a movie I return to again and again. The entire film is brilliant, of course, but the first time I saw the fight sequence in the hallway, I didn't blink. Nothing is sped up. No wires. It isn't slick, it's effortful agony. There was what—one small effect in post (the knife in Dae-su's back)? Weapons are sticks and fists and that hammer. That hammer! One continuous shot, seventeen takes. You feel every ounce of bloody, brutal exhaustion. For anyone who has had to fight their way through hell—whether that means school/life-sucking job/parent of a newborn—you can tap right in. And then when he looks up at the end of the hall and the elevator dings open . . . I freaked the fuck out. BRILLIANT.

—JOY OSMANSKI ON *OLDBOY*

unconscious and is taken home by the restaurant's pretty young chef, Mi-do (Kang). Desperate for human intimacy, Dae-su makes a clumsy attempt to assault Mi-do, who fends him off and says she's not ready to have sex yet. Dae-su continues his search using the one clue he has: the fried dumplings he ate every day for fifteen years, which he knows came from a restaurant called Blue Dragon.

He and Mi-do visit a series of different Blue Dragons, sampling dumplings until he finds the ones he knows too well and follows a deliveryman to the private prison where he was held. Dae-su tracks down the prison warden, Mr. Park (Oh), and tortures him by pulling out his teeth until he explains all he knows: Dae-su was locked up for "talking too much." Dae-su then fights his way back out of the prison with nothing more than a claw hammer, in one of the most incredible fight scenes in cinematic history—a long, wide-angle side shot of Dae-su smashing and stumbling through two dozen punks armed with sticks, clubs, and knives.

At Mi-do's place, Dae-su finds her exchanging online messages with a person named Evergreen. He realizes Evergreen is his captor and accuses Mi-do of being a plant; she denies his allegations, but Dae-su finds the address of this torturer—a building across the street from Mi-do's place, occupied by a wealthy heir named Woo-jin (Yoo), who challenges Dae-su to discover the reason for his actions in the next five days. If he succeeds, Woo-jin will kill himself. If he doesn't, Woo-jin will kill Mi-do.

The ultimatum sends Dae-su into overdrive. He and Mi-do finally have sex, giving him more reason to solve the riddle. The clues start to come together—Dae-su finally remembers why Woo-jin is vaguely familiar: He was a high school classmate, a fellow "old boy," whose sister had committed suicide. Dae-su accidentally saw Woo-jin and his sister have sex, and blurted the fact of their incestuous relationship to a classmate, who then spread it to the rest of the school. The suicide of Woo-jin's sister, his lover, which he blames on Dae-su, is why the entire elaborate revenge plot was formed. And without revealing the final twist, the vengeance isn't over yet.

Oldboy set a new standard for genre cinema, taking a gory revenge thriller and turning it into a gut-punching reflection on the nature of humanity, social context, and the passage of time. It is exceedingly difficult to watch, and impossible to forget.

The Last Airbender

2010, PG, 103 MINUTES, PARAMOUNT PICTURES, USA

DIRECTOR/WRITER: M. Night Shyamalan

STARRING: Noah Ringer, Dev Patel, Nicola Peltz, Jackson Rathbone, Shaun Toub, Aasif Mandvi, Cliff Curtis

BASED ON THE ANIMATED SERIES
AVATAR: THE LAST AIRBENDER

When Paramount announced a live-action cinematic adaptation of Nickelodeon's incredibly popular animated series *Avatar: The Last Airbender* (2005–2008), the TV series' massive fandom held its collective breath. When it was revealed that it would be directed by M. Night Shyamalan—the polarizing and prolific Indian American director behind hits like *The Sixth Sense* (1999), *Unbreakable* (2000), and *Signs* (2002), and flops like *Lady in the Water* (2006) and *After Earth* (2013)—the fandom released that breath and began to scream.

Avatar was a character-driven epic journey playing out in gradual detail across a vast and diverse world; Shyamalan, meanwhile, was known for making movies built around shocking reveals and last-minute hidden twists, with little attention to character development or the deeper nuances of

Noah Ringer

worldbuilding. And getting those nuances was essential: The world of *Avatar* was a bold and intricate synthesis of an array of Asian and Indigenous cultures, its martial arts, magical systems, and foundational philosophy deeply informed by thorough research. Each of the four culturally divergent nations can magically control or "bend" a single element: Air, Water, Earth, or Fire. The Avatar is the being empowered by the Spirit World to bring unity to the four nations through his ability to master the bending of all four. The last Avatar, unfortunately, mysteriously disappeared a century ago as a young child, leaving the world without leadership or balance.

As the movie begins, the Fire Nation has aggressively moved to fill this vacuum, pitting them in constant war with the nations of Air, Water, and Earth. Amid this turmoil, Sokka (Rathbone) and his younger sister, Katara (Peltz), members of the Southern Water

I was living in Los Angeles and writing a dissertation on how Asian Americans have organized to fight for better representation in the media when all the activism surrounding *The Last Airbender* began. The activism surrounding it definitely had a huge impact, highlighting the practice of whitewashing stories and taking roles away from underrepresented performers. Since then, we have seen a huge interest in casting controversies and the invisibility of Asian Americans in Hollywood, and I know it connects back to those activists and others before them, who've been calling attention to these problems for a very long time.

—LORI LOPEZ ON *THE LAST AIRBENDER*

Tribe, find a twelve-year-old boy frozen in an iceberg, who is revealed to be Aang (Ringer), the missing Avatar. Sensing the energy release from Aang's awakening, Zuko (Patel), renegade prince of the Fire Nation, seeks to capture him. Sokka, Katara, and Aang flee on the back of Aang's pet flying bison to his home, the Southern Air Temple, which has become a place of desolation—after Aang's entombment, the Fire Nation destroyed the temple and slaughtered the Air Nomad people, leaving Aang as the titular last surviving Airbender.

The remainder of this joyless, chaotic mess of a movie is dedicated to Aang's attempts to learn other forms of bending while dodging the efforts of Zuko and the Fire Nation to eliminate him for good.

In its 103 minutes, *The Last Airbender* attempts to cram in a story line that took twenty half-hour episodes to tell on television. And, to the consternation of *Avatar* fans, its heroic characters and members of the "good" nations are played by white actors, with only the villainous Fire Nation portrayed by dark-skinned performers. It's rare a movie is so off the mark that it not only ends up being the first and last of a planned trilogy but actually adds a word to the culture referencing its biggest and most offensive mistake. *The Last Airbender* is one such movie: The fan movement that sprang up in protest of it referred to the film's casting decisions as "racebending," a term that stuck.

Revenge of the Green Dragons

2014, R, 94 MINUTES, A24, USA

DIRECTORS: Andrew Lau, Andrew Loo

STARRING: Justin Chon, Kevin Wu, Harry Shum Jr., Eugenia Yuan, Leonard Wu, Jin Au-Yeung, Jon Kit Lee, Shuya Chang, Celia Au, Ron Yuan, Billy Magnussen, Geoff Pierson, Ray Liotta, Geoff Lee

WRITERS: Michael Di Jiacomo, Andrew Loo

BASED ON THE *NEW YORKER* ARTICLE BY FREDERIC DANNEN

Produced by the legendary Martin Scorsese, codirected by brilliant Hong Kong director Andrew Lau (*Infernal Affairs*), and starring an exciting cast of up-and-coming Asian American talent, this movie had the potential to be the rare Chinatown gangster

I, along with many other fans of Asian American cinema, have longed for the day when an Asian American gangland epic would arrive that might capture the gravitas and epic themes of family and loyalty as *The Godfather*, or the acerbic dark humour and gritty naturalism of *Goodfellas*. So I greatly anticipated *Revenge of the Green Dragons*. The late, great Ray Liotta was in it! It was executive produced by Martin Scorsese! Excellent actors like Justin Chon, Eugenia Yuan, Ron Yuan, and Harry Shum Jr. comprised the main starring cast! "Finally," I thought to myself, "a movie about Asian American gangs that could approach the status and stature of the genre." But after the final frame rolled, my lofty expectations had been shattered. I should have known better. I remember seeing friends coming out of the screening and exchanging with them grimaces saying, "That was bad . . . very bad." And as of today, the "great Asian American gangster film" is still yet to be made.
—TIMOTHY TAU ON *REVENGE OF THE GREEN DRAGONS*

Justin Chon

movie worth watching: a gritty stereotype-free tale of the dark side of immigration and the American Dream deferred. Some of that promise lands; much of it sadly doesn't.

Very loosely based on a 1992 *New Yorker* feature by Frederic Dannen, the movie tells the story of Sonny (Chon) and Steven (Kevin Wu), foster brothers who get pulled into the orbit (and the maelstrom) of the Green Dragons, a violent street gang operating in Flushing, Queens. The Dragons shake down Chinese businesses for money, provide muscle for the human smuggling operation of Snakehead Mama (Yuan), and as the movie goes along, escalate to trafficking in heroin, hiding it by baking it into traditional moon cakes.

Sonny, the more pragmatic of the two, gravitates to the gang because it offers a sense of identity America itself refuses to offer its nonwhite

working-class immigrants. Hothead Steven gravitates to the freedom the gang offers to act spontaneously (and violently), in contrast to the lifetime of quiet drudgery and kowtowing to white customers promised by his mom's restaurant.

Their mentors are Paul Wong (Shum Jr.), the Dragons' smooth-talking, sharp-dressed leader from the shadows, and Ah Chung (Leonard Wu), the gang's brutal enforcer, and both brothers quickly find themselves in over their heads, with Paul preventing an all-out gang war by offering a deal to the Tiger boss: cutting him in on a heroin operation.

As Steven increasingly loses both his control and his soul, Sonny finds love—but is eventually forced to choose between his heart and his loyalty to his blood and found brothers. The outcome of his choice is tragic—and seems inevitable from the movie's beginning.

Umma

2022, PG-13, 83 MINUTES, SONY PICTURES ENTERTAINMENT, USA

DIRECTOR/WRITER: Iris K. Shim

STARRING: Sandra Oh, Fivel Stewart, MeeWha Alana Lee, Tom Yi, Odeya Rush, Dermot Mulroney

There's plenty of understated creepiness in the setup of *Umma*, Iris K. Shim's directorial debut, produced by horror great Sam Raimi. It's about the toxic ways we end up embodying our parents' flaws—becoming their worst selves in our worst moments, even as we swore never to do so. And it's about how immigrant trauma and isolation can twist and distort our identities and relationships, even with those we love most.

Amanda (Oh), a Korean American woman in her late forties, was brought to the US at a young age by her mother (Lee), recently deceased. As an adult, Amanda lives with her homeschooled teenage daughter, Chrissy (Stewart), on a deep-rural farm, raising chickens and bees by hand and eschewing modern technology—she claims an allergy to electricity. The allergy is more of a psychological reaction than a physical one: It turns out Amanda's mom, whom she calls "Umma," Korean shorthand for mother, used to punish her with a home-brewed electroshock device. But while Amanda rightly sees her mother as a monster, she has issues of her own. She refuses to allow her daughter to even consider going to college, telling her it's not safe. She won't even let her go into town unless it's on her weekly bike-supply runs. But the status quo—mother and daughter living quietly alone and apart from the rest of the world—can't last forever, as much as Amanda would love it to, and when a relative drops by with a bag containing nothing less than Umma's ashes in an ornate urn, the peace of their existence is shattered permanently.

Amanda is understandably less than thrilled at being left with the remains of the mother who tortured her for so long. She attempts to ignore the urn, but Umma will not let her forget. Weird things happen on the farm, from visions of restless and angry spirits to the sudden appearance of a demon fox—obvious signs the supernatural is afoot. When a terrified Amanda attempts to bury the urn, Umma uses the opportunity to possess her body, forcing her to wear Umma's cherished ceremonial mask and hanbok and to engage in jesa, a ritual of memorial for the dead. Chrissy returns to the house to discover the college application she was secretly completing destroyed, and a catatonic Amanda performing the jesa. Umma forces Amanda to attack her own child until Chrissy knocks the mask away and shocks Amanda out of her possessed state.

Horror from almost harming Chrissy leads Amanda to decide it's time to confront her mother on Umma's own ground. She returns to the place she buried the urn, only to be sucked into a plane of purgatory. There she encounters Umma's spirit and forgives her, while acknowledging the suffering that Umma experienced in her own journey to America. This reconciliation gives Umma the release needed to move on to the afterlife. The film ends with Amanda and Chrissy, both wearing hanboks, performing jesa in front of a formal gravestone installed at the farm. While *Umma* did not reach the heights of box office success, it demonstrated how stories that have become Asian American clichés—for example, tales of intergenerational angst—can be reinvented and retold in novel fashion, opening new perspectives and reaching new audiences.

> As a first-generation Korean American daughter, it made perfect sense to me that Iris Shim's feature film, *Umma*, would be a horror movie. *Umma*, the Korean word for mother, evokes visceral emotions to those who know firsthand the power, passion, and persistence of a Korean mom. Even at age fifty-two, I still buckle under the sharp words of my own umma, who raised four daughters with loving criticism and frighteningly high expectations that were never fulfilled.
>
> **—LEE ANN KIM ON *UMMA***

"Chaos [with] deliberate intent."

A Talk with **Ken Jeong** and **John Cho**

Though one is best known for comedy and the other for drama, there are few actors whose filmographies show more willingness to dive into the dark side of humanity than Ken Jeong (*Crazy Rich Asians*, *The Hangover*) and John Cho (*Searching*, *Star Trek*). By spelunking in the caverns of our collective unconscious, they've expanded the boundaries of what it means to be Asian American. In this candid and sometimes tongue-in-cheek Q&A, the two friends discuss the challenges of finding the humanity in fools and monsters, and the need to hold up a "true mirror" to ourselves, even if we may not like what we end up seeing.

I feel like you're two of our most fearless and risk-taking actors, so it made sense to me to ask you about the topic of taking on uncomfortable topics in Asian American cinema. I want to begin by asking about *Better Luck Tomorrow*, which is famous for having been challenged by an audience member who said, "How dare you represent Asian people that way!"

KEN JEONG: This is a safe space, so I want to just admit that what really offended me about *Better Luck Tomorrow* is that I was not actually in it. Maybe it's because I hadn't moved out to LA yet and had never been in a movie. But it still makes me super angry that I wasn't cast in one of my favorite movies of all time, and they had to bring in someone handsome and talented like John Cho instead. Seriously though—I love the movie so much because it proves to me how there can be diversity within diversity. It challenged everyone's expectations of what Asian Americans were allowed to be on-screen. That's why, twenty years later, it still endures.

JOHN CHO: I've really started to think about this issue in psychological terms. When a baby is born, it knows it has hands and feet, but it doesn't know that they're connected to its body. They're just these weird objects that move around. But once the baby sees itself in a mirror, it can make that connection, that these are all parts of "me." It takes an external device, the mirror, to form that sense of "me." Well, we, as Asian Americans, have for generations been bereft of that means of recognizing ourselves. Because for a community, that mirror is the screen.

It's theater, it's books, it's art, it's culture. If we have a true mirror, we can integrate ourselves in a true way. Otherwise we just look at that thing at the end of our arm or leg and think, *What is that thing? That's weird. It's not a part of me.*

KEN: It's not fair for him to answer second, because he ends up coming off as ten times smarter than me.

Okay, then, John, you answer this one first: So, would you say that to be whole, we need to embrace and integrate all of our different parts, heroic and villainous, embarrassing and inspiring?

JOHN: Yes. Ken and I were on a project together recently, where we play part of an Asian family and we're dealing with a complicated issue with a white family. And I wanted this [Asian] family to be as textured, layered, and real as the white family, even if it meant being dysfunctional. Because you need that balance. And we have a resistance to openly talking about the problems in our families. When I'm talking about my parents' generation in public, my instinct is not to slight them. But in private, I'll bitch and moan about them all day. There's that public-private divide—that we should keep our family problems in the family. Yet there's nothing that white America enjoys more than seeing negative depictions of themselves. There are movies filled with nothing but terrible [white] people that are huge hits. The fact is, if you think that you only have the one shot at representation, you're going to protect that depiction at all costs, even to the point of possibly fibbing. But of course, the real fib is that one representation can contain us all.

KEN: I don't want to go second anymore. How am I supposed to follow that? But I agree with whatever John was saying. Whatever we put up on-screen, I think it's important to start from a kernel of truth. I study my characters and try to figure out why they're like that—is it an inferiority complex? Is it codependency? Is it a sense of loss? So even if what you see on-screen is chaos, there's deliberate intent behind it. When I was up for *The Hangover*, my wife, Tran, had been diagnosed with stage three breast cancer. And she was getting better, but I still wasn't going to do the role—I wanted to be there for her. She told me to go do it. And I accepted the part, because if there was one thing I felt like I could do to help her fight, it was to make her laugh. But the anger and fear I had for her still came through—there's a scene in the movie where I just do a ten-minute improvised rant, it isn't even funny: It's rage; it's primal screaming. It's just "fuck cancer," all the way through.

JOHN: So what you're saying is that you're anti-cancer. Very controversial.

In some ways, you guys came into the industry at the end of an era when a lot of actors still felt like there wasn't a lot of choice. Do things feel different now?

JOHN: This business is never going to be easy. But young people coming into the profession always ask for career advice, and lately I've been saying, "There are a million obstacles, but act like there are no impediments. Be creative in a way that you don't think is possible yet. Be who you want to be, and let the world adjust to you, rather than modifying your creativity for the market." I think that's the last level of freedom for us. What kinds of parts would you take if there were no such thing as the history of Asian American cinema, the way we're treated in the world and all these political issues that we deal with every day?

KEN: See, this is what true representation looks like—John says something smart, so I can say something stupid.

Ken, you have a medical degree.

KEN: And I'll always have that over John! But I guess what I'd say is a twist on that "no small roles, only small actors" saying. You can find the humanity in any role. It takes work, and it takes pushing back, and sometimes it doesn't land. But you need to try. In *The Hangover*, a lot of people didn't get that I was speaking Vietnamese—they thought I was just throwing out gibberish. And that ended up shaping the character, because it wasn't originally written for me. Todd Phillips just said, "Don't be afraid to throw away the script and just go for it." So, as a weird love letter to Tran, I had her translate specific lines into Vietnamese as inside jokes for her. And here's the amazing thing, right? Because we did that, this whole backstory started to develop for Chow, in which it makes sense that he speaks Vietnamese. Maybe he's a refugee and he ended up falling into a life of crime to survive. Maybe he lost loved ones and that's why he feels he has nothing left to lose. When we shot the second movie in Thailand, a big destination for refugees after the war, Todd said to me, "Hey, just want you to know, we're only here because of what you brought to your performance."

JOHN: That's what I mean by plurality. Because in the simple act of bringing that kind of specificity to a character, it changes. It becomes human in a way that it wouldn't be otherwise. As Asian Americans we're still coming from the glare of the lobby into the darkness of the theater. So we need extra time for our eyes to adjust. And other people need time to buttress their sense of empathy for Asians on-screen.

KEN: Ha, you said "buttress."

JOHN: Really? That's how you want to end this?

7

The Family Way

THE JOY LUCK CLUB · THE WEDDING BANQUET ·
DOUBLE HAPPINESS · CHUTNEY POPCORN · THE DEBUT ·
MONSOON WEDDING · LILO & STITCH · PING PONG
PLAYA · IN THE FAMILY · SPA NIGHT · COLUMBUS · BAO ·
SEARCHING · MS. PURPLE · THE FAREWELL · TURNING
RED · EVERYTHING EVERYWHERE ALL AT ONCE

"Immigrant parents know how to adapt."
A Talk with **Nisha Ganatra** and **Kal Penn**

ILLUSTRATION (OPPOSITE) BY TOMA NGUYEN

The quantum unit of Asian community isn't the individual—it's the family. And not just the nuclear one but the full extended network of secondary and tertiary affiliates, unrelated uncles and aunties and "cousins" you've never met and wouldn't recognize on the street. As such, it's understandable that explorations of the complicated dynamics of family make up a disproportionate percentage of the Asian and Asian American cinematic canon.

Films about the tense negotiation of generational divides and familial expectation, like *The Joy Luck Club*, *Double Happiness*, *Chutney Popcorn*, *The Debut*, and *Spa Night*. Movies about the stress and tragedy of losing family members, or preparing for their loss, like *In the Family*, *Searching*, *Columbus*, *The Farewell*, and *Ms. Purple*, and the stress and joy of gaining new members, like *The Wedding Banquet*, *Monsoon Wedding*, and yes, the animated *Lilo & Stitch*. Growing up, or failing to do so, is a frequently explored subject, as in *Ping Pong Playa*, *Bao*, and *Turning Red*. And occasionally there are films that address all these topics, everywhere, all at once—like *Everything Everywhere All at Once*.

These films can serve as therapy, as a springboard to a confession, to ask uncomfortable questions or share inconvenient truths. They're in turn awkward, necessary, comforting, and chaotic . . . much like our families themselves.

The Joy Luck Club

**1993, R, 139 MINUTES,
BUENA VISTA PICTURES, USA**

DIRECTOR: Wayne Wang

STARRING: Tsai Chin, Kieu Chinh, Lisa Lu, France Nuyen, Rosalind Chao, Lauren Tom, Tamlyn Tomita, Ming-Na Wen, Michael Paul Chan, Andrew McCarthy, Christopher Rich, Russell Wong, Vivian Wu, Wu Tianming, Elizabeth Sung, Philip Moon

WRITERS: Ron Bass, Amy Tan

BASED ON THE NOVEL BY AMY TAN

Based on Amy Tan's novel of the same name published in 1989, *The Joy Luck Club* book spent a staggering forty weeks on the bestseller lists. Perhaps the most revealing thing about the movie is how hard it was to make, and how much more successful it could have been. Director Wayne Wang met with Tan to discuss his interest in adapting the book for film but expressed concern about how to adapt a novel that consists of sixteen different interwoven short stories into a cinematic narrative.

With development support from Carolco Pictures, they ultimately brought in veteran screenwriter Ron Bass to cowrite the screenplay with Tan; he proposed using voice-over narration and creating a new uniting event for the ensemble—June Woo's going-away party—to weave the book's many threads. But they ran into creative conflicts with Carolco, who was concerned about the box office potential of a film featuring eight Asian American women with no platform for a "proven star" (essentially, a non-Asian top-line talent). Bass and Tan completed the first draft of the script on their own in 1991, bringing it to Walt Disney chairman Jeffrey Katzenberg the following year. Though he too was unsure of its commercial potential, he believed it deserved to be made anyway, and the film secured its cast: four of Asian America's most eminent elder actresses (Tsai Chin, France Nuyen, Lisa Lu, and Kieu Chinh) and four emerging young talents (Tamlyn Tomita, Rosalind Chao, Lauren Tom, and Ming-Na Wen). *The Joy Luck Club* went into production in 1992 and was released the following year.

The members of the titular club—Suyuan (Chinh), Lindo (Chin), An-Mei (Lu), and Ying-Ying (Nuyen)—are a group of older immigrant women who meet regularly to play mahjong and share their nostalgic memories and modern-day interactions with their four daughters—June (Wen), Waverly (Tomita), Rose (Chao), and Lena (Tom), respectively.

The Joy Luck Club was the first time I ever saw myself on-screen. Before it I'd never seen Asian American women lead a major Hollywood film. June, Waverly, Rose, and Lena were all me: Chinese American daughters who bore the traumas of their mothers and their grandmothers. I cried watching Waverly tearfully telling her mother, "You don't know the power you have over me; one word from you, one look . . . because nothing I do can ever, ever please you." That scene perfectly captured my relationship with my own immigrant mother. Now as I raise my own family, I view the film through the lens of the Chinese immigrant mothers placing their hopes in their American daughters.
                                    —NANCY WANG YUEN ON *THE JOY LUCK CLUB*

(From left) Kieu Chinh, Ming-Na Wen, Tamlyn Tomita, Tsai Chin, France Nuyen, Lauren Tom, Lisa Lu, and Rosalind Chao

The movie opens at a surprise farewell party, celebrating June's upcoming trip to China to reunite with her half sisters, the left-behind daughters of her mother, Suyuan, who passed away a few months earlier and whose spot in the club June has filled.

Among those attending are the other club members and their daughters, all of whom have their own rich histories and ties, positive and negative, to one another. Lindo, a stern and forbidding figure, remembers her arranged marriage with a much younger boy at the age of fifteen, and how she exited that loveless marriage through a sly ruse. We then learn of her difficult relationship with her own daughter, Waverly, who gave up chess despite being a childhood prodigy; as an adult, Waverly is engaged to Rich (Rich), a well-meaning Caucasian man who inadvertently offends Lindo with his misuse of chopsticks and his clumsy statements about her cooking. The incident

strains Waverly and Lindo's already tense relationship, but eventually Lindo gives their union her blessing, and Rich shows his good intentions by practicing his use of chopsticks.

Switching to Ying-Ying, we learn of her youthful marriage to Lin Xiao (Wong), a handsome rogue who turns out to be an abusive philanderer (although the scene in which Ying-Ying first sees Lin Xiao, as he eats watermelon with his bare hands, is an iconic swoon moment for Russell Wong). Ying-Ying's degrading mental health leads her to accidentally drown her baby son—something that will haunt her for the rest of her life. It also helps her see that her daughter Lena is following a similar path, controlled by her domineering husband, Harold (Chan). Ying-Ying tells Lena to find someone new, and so she brings Ken (Moon) to the farewell party, an attentive and accepting man.

Meanwhile, An-Mei remembers the story of her mother (Vivian Wu), a widow who was raped and impregnated by a wealthy older man, Wu Tsing (Wu Tianming). She is forced into becoming his fourth wife by his conniving second wife (Sung), who takes her infant son upon birth and tells their husband that he is her own. After telling An-Mei the truth about her situation, An-Mei's mother kills herself in a way intended to frighten Wu Tsing with a potential curse. To appease her ghost, Wu Tsing resolves to honor An-Mei's mother as first wife and to raise An-Mei and her brother. An-Mei later advises her daughter Rose to take a stronger stance in her fraying marriage to Ted (McCarthy), an aristocratic heir whose mother disapproves of an Asian wife. Rose subsequently tells Ted to leave their house and she'll raise her daughter alone, as her mother did. The shock of her assertiveness causes Ted to stop taking her for granted, and the two reconcile.

Finally, we learn the story of Suyuan and June, which begins with the former fleeing Japan's invasion of China with her twin baby daughters. Near death from illness, Suyuan is forced to abandon her babies by the side of the road; she is rescued but never learns what happened to her children. Remarrying in America and birthing another daughter, June, Suyuan pushes her to excel, but June fails to meet her expectations, doing poorly in piano, getting mediocre grades, and eventually working as a freelancer for Waverly, with whom she's always had a rivalry. When Waverly dismisses June's ideas at a dinner party, Suyuan responds that "style" is something that can't be taught and must be innate. June later confronts her, assuming that the "style" comment was an implication she was always going to fall short of Waverly, but Suyuan meant Waverly is the one without "style"—that June's kindness and earnestness were something that Waverly, the one who always seizes the "best quality" for herself, was born without. June is the one with the "best heart." The movie ends with June meeting her long-lost half sisters and embracing them.

For Asian Americans, *The Joy Luck Club* was a historic breakthrough—the first Hollywood studio film with an entirely Asian American headline cast since the 1961 musical *Flower Drum Song*, and the first film that brought many Asian moviegoers to the theaters for multiple viewings, with daughters often bringing their mothers and grandmothers. The movie was earning $33 million on a $10 million budget. Some felt Disney didn't market it as well as they could have; in fact, in one marketing meeting with the studio, Wayne Wang—known for his even temper—erupted in anger after seeing that the initial poster concepts for the film featured either abstract designs or the younger female cast, facing away from the camera or shot from behind.

May Chin and Winston Chao

The Wedding Banquet

1993, R, 106 MINUTES,
SAMUEL GOLDWYN COMPANY, USA

DIRECTOR: Ang Lee

STARRING: Ah-Leh Gua, Sihung Lung, May
Chin, Winston Chao, Mitchell Lichtenstein

WRITERS: Ang Lee, Neil Peng,
James Schamus

The Wedding Banquet, Ang Lee's breakout as
a director, is a tour de force of intersectionality,
addressing issues of immigration, sexual orientation,
interracial relationships, and parental expectations
in a single tightly woven (and very entertaining)
package. It was one of the earlier Asian American
narrative features focused on LGBTQ issues, and
perhaps the earliest to specifically address "covering" and how cultural code-switching impacts
representations of sexuality. The film focuses on gay
couple Wai-Tung (Chao) and Simon (Lichtenstein),
living a pleasant double-income no-kids existence
in Manhattan, until Wai-Tung's Taiwan-based parents, Mr. and Mrs. Gao (Lung and Gua, respectively),
confront him about his unmarried status, asking
when he'll "settle down" and give them a grandchild.
Wai-Tung has never been able to tell them he's gay,
an unavoidable consequence of Wai-Tung's traditional upbringing. To fend off the Gaos' demands,

Wai-Tung explains he will only accept a woman who meets his strict specs—a dual PhD who speaks five languages, sings opera, and is at least 5′9″ tall. Well, never underestimate a parent's wish, as the Gaos' matchmaker *actually* finds him a woman who meets these conditions.

Simon intervenes and tells Wai-Tung to marry one of his rental tenants instead—Wei Wei (Chin), a recent immigrant from China needs a green card, thus killing two birds with one stone. Upon hearing that Wai-Tung has found his future wife, the Gaos announce they will travel from Taiwan to meet her. (In one of the funniest visual sequences, Wai-Tung and Simon prepare for the Gaos' arrival by "straightening up" the house, replacing gay iconography with Chinese brush paintings and traditional ornaments.) When the Gaos arrive, Wai-Tung tells them that he and Wei Wei intend to get married at city hall, but the sparse ceremony, combined with the revelation that Wei Wei is a penniless artist, breaks Mrs. Gao's heart.

To make up for their disappointment, the Gaos announce that their only son's marriage requires an elaborate wedding reception dinner; Wai-Tung and Wei Wei (and Simon, who has been introduced as Wai-Tung's friend and landlord) reluctantly go along with the plan. But during the packed and bustling banquet, the many guests force the "couple" to drink toast after toast of high-test liquor, then escort them to their wedding hotel room and force them into bed naked. Thoroughly intoxicated, Wei Wei and Wai-Tung have sex—leading to Wei Wei unexpectedly getting pregnant, to the triad's dismay and the Gaos' delight. But Mr. Gao, a stroke survivor, has another stroke, leading to an angry confrontation among the triangle and a confession by Wai-Tung of his real situation to his mother. Horrified, she begs Wai-Tung not to tell his father. But Mr. Gao is aware of the situation more than Mrs. Gao knows, and he admits as much to Simon, embracing him as part of the family while asking him to allow the sham marriage to continue for the sake of their future grandchild. But the existence of said grandchild is in doubt; Wei Wei has an appointment for an abortion but decides to keep the baby and raise him along with both of his fathers. As the film ends, the Gaos prepare to return to Taiwan, with Mrs. Gao now bonded with her "daughter-in-law" and Mr. Gao secretly accepting his "son-in-law." Though it was initially perceived to be a "niche film" with no "bankable stars," it defied expectations, as Lee would continue to do throughout his career, earning over $23 million on a budget of around $1 million—making it by far the most profitable film of 1993.

Sandra Oh and Callum Keith Rennie

Double Happiness

1994, PG-13, 87 MINUTES, FINE LINE FEATURES, CANADA

DIRECTOR/WRITER: Mina Shum

STARRING: Sandra Oh, Stephen Chang, Alannah Ong, Frances You, Johnny Mah, Callum Keith Rennie, Claudette Carracedo, Greg Chan, Mimi Mok

This lighthearted but clever Asian Canadian feature was a big-screen debut for both director Mina Shum and star Sandra Oh, whose performance won her Best Actress at the Genie Awards, Canada's

equivalent of the Academy Awards. The title, *Double Happiness*, plays a dual role—it's a reference both to the traditional Chinese symbol of great fortune and to the ambitions of Jade Li (Oh) to somehow lead a life that fulfills her and satisfies her parents . . . achieving "double happiness."

Jade, a twenty-two-year-old daughter of Chinese immigrants who still lives at home with her parents and sister, wants to be an actress. Her parents want her to give up the preposterous ambition and meet and marry a nice Chinese boy instead. Jade hopes to satisfy both her parents and her soul, although threading that needle looks increasingly challenging as the movie continues, especially when the arrival of her father's childhood pal Uncle Bing (Chang) tests the family's equilibrium. Because it's so important to Mr. and Mrs. Li (Chang and Ong) to save face in front of the old family friend, they go to great lengths to hide Jade's showbiz dreams while stepping up their efforts to find a suitable marriage prospect. Their preferred match: Andrew Chau (Mah), a handsome and charming young lawyer. Although Jade doesn't feel a particular chemistry with him, she gives him a chance to make her parents happy (and yes, he's handsome, charming, a lawyer, and so forth), but it turns out Andrew is hiding his own secret: He's gay.

Meanwhile, Jade is slowly falling for Mark (Rennie), a grad student with whom she had a one-night stand and who's been clumsily trying to get her attention since. Of course, he's a poor student studying for a useless degree (English!) and, yes, is not Chinese, making him far from an acceptable boyfriend candidate. Ultimately, Jade recognizes it's not always possible to make everyone happy, and part of growing up is making difficult decisions, including the very first one: leaving home to live on your own.

Though this film won its share of acclaim in Canada, it had limited exposure in the United States. Nevertheless, it's well worth watching simply for Oh's terrific and nuanced performance as Jade. The skills and charisma Oh demonstrated here quickly propelled her into other acting opportunities, such as a regular role on the HBO sports agent comedy *Arliss* (1996–2002), the movie *Sideways* (2004), and then a long, critically acclaimed run as Dr. Christina Yang on ABC's *Grey's Anatomy* (2005–2014). But until she was cast as the titular Eve in the smash hit BBC crime thriller *Killing Eve* (2018–2022), Oh had rarely been given the kind of prime center-stage showcase she deserves. Since then, Hollywood seems to have woken up to Oh's talents, and few actresses of her generation are in greater demand.

Chutney Popcorn

1999, PG-13, 92 MINUTES, SHOWTIME NETWORKS, USA

DIRECTOR: Nisha Ganatra

STARRING: Nisha Ganatra, Jill Hennessy, Sakina Jaffrey, Madhur Jaffrey, Nick Chinlund, Ajay Naidu, Cara Buono

WRITERS: Susan Carnival, Nisha Ganatra

A few movies lay claim to being the first "Desi American feature film"—that is, the first theatrically released movie with a South Asian American director and a South Asian American cast, focusing explicitly on matters taking place in the United States. There's *American Chai*, which won the Slamdance Film Festival's Audience Award in 2001 but wasn't officially released until 2002, which means that *American Desi*, released in March 2001, officially came out first—and both were beaten to theaters by *ABCD: American-Born Confused Desi*, which was released in 2000. Then there's this film, *Chutney Popcorn*, which landed in 1999 and as a result, squeaked past the others for the title . . . so long as you're not counting Mira Nair's *Mississippi Masala* from all the way back in 1991, and you probably should. Still, there's no question that *Popcorn* served as a milestone, as an Indian American film that both embraced the comfortable memes of diaspora movies—generational divide, interracial marriage, young people who aspire to art while their parents are more worried about security—while also pushing topical envelopes.

Reena (played by director Ganatra) is a young, gay Indian American woman in a committed relationship with girl-friend Lisa (Hennessy). Though she earns a living as a henna artist, her dream is to become a professional photographer, and she has real talent. What she doesn't have is her act together, with long-suffering Lisa serving as a constant anchor of calm preventing Reena from spinning into dis-organized chaos. Mom Meenu (Madhur Jaffrey) wishes Reena would settle down with the right guy and start a family (ignoring the fact that Reena is already with the right girl). Meanwhile, Reena's perfect older sister, Sarita (Sakina Jaffrey) is infertile, which causes problems for her and her husband, Mitch (Chinlund), until Reena impulsively offers to serve as Sarita's surrogate. The decision sends shock waves through

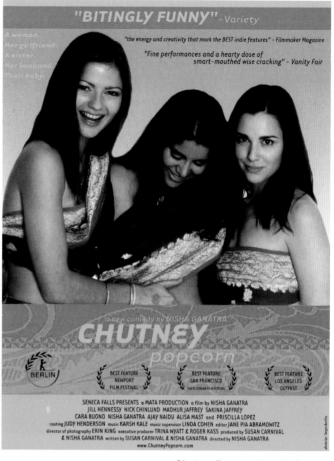

Chutney Popcorn theatrical poster

the family and upends Reena's relationship. But ultimately, the bonds of family—both blood and found—are strong enough to endure, and the arrival of the new baby boy heralds a fresh start for the clan.

I love this movie so much! Featuring a motorcycle-riding Indian American woman in love with another woman, *Chutney Popcorn* gave voice to another facet of the queer Asian American experience. And even though I'm not Indian American, I recognized within it so many aspects of what it means to be Asian American—including the scene where the protagonist Reena's sister Sarita has an argument with her white husband over Hinduism. As someone interested in religion, I saw her lived experience of faith bumping up against his academic approach to it: Another white guy trying to whitesplain Asian religions! It was just so classic. And familiar.

–LAURA MARIKO CHEIFETZ ON *CHUTNEY POPCORN*

(From left) Eddie Garcia, Dante Basco, Tirso Cruz III, and Gina Alajar

The Debut

2000, R, 88 MINUTES, CELESTIAL PICTURES, USA

DIRECTOR: Gene Cajayon

STARRING: Dante Basco, Tirso Cruz III, Eddie Garcia, Gina Alajar, Darion Basco, Dion Basco, Derek Basco, Bernadette Balagtas, Joy Bisco

WRITERS: Gene Cajayon, John Manal Castro

There are few coming-of-age films that center on Asian Americans, which is why the ones that do easily stand out. Those that center on experiences beyond those of East Asians—Chinese, Japanese, and Koreans—are so few as to virtually be unique, which gives *The Debut* disproportionate importance and influence in Asian American cinema: In addition to exploring adolescence from a new perspective, it's one of the earliest Filipino American feature films, just behind Rod Pulido's *The Flip Side* (2001), which actually screened at Sundance (the first Filipino American film to have that honor) but saw virtually no distribution afterward.

The Debut played a few dozen cities, earning $1.75 million at the box office, via the efforts of director Gene Cajayon, his stars, and an army of street-level promoters, who got the word out and audiences into the theaters. Cajayon's indie journey began a decade earlier, when he made a shorter version of the film as his film school thesis; it took him eight years to raise the money to start production in 1997, with a major grant from the National Asian American

Telecommunications Association (now called Center for Asian American Media) getting him just enough to roll cameras.

He cast Dante Basco (who'd garnered a substantial audience for portraying Rufio in the 1991 Steven Spielberg film *Hook*) as his lead, and Dante's three brothers Darion, Dion, and Derek in other roles for good measure. The Bascos would end up a core part of the effort to get word out about the film, using their extended networks in the Filipino American community to boost Cajayon's database of potential Fil-Am supporters—a list that grew to over twenty thousand. Cajayon used the list to recruit street teams in every city the film would travel to, getting supporters to visit churches, community organizations, and campuses, and hang posters in mom-and-pop stores to add people to the list. From their efforts, in cities like San Francisco and Los Angeles, *The Debut* ended up selling out screenings, matching or beating major Hollywood blockbusters like *Harry Potter*.

The movie's story couldn't have been better tuned to its primary target audience. Ben Mercado (Dante Basco) is a high school senior who has his heart set on attending the illustration program at CalArts. His parents have other ideas: They want him to accept a UCLA scholarship, setting him on a path to pre-med studies (since every family could use another doctor). Ben secretly sells his comic book collection to pay for his CalArts tuition, hiding the truth from his strict father, Roland (Cruz), a postal worker who has put aside his own dreams to ensure the family's well-being. Roland dislikes Ben's non-Filipino friends and suspects that Ben is embarrassed by his heritage and community—a "coconut," brown on the outside but white on the inside.

All of this comes to a head as Ben's sister Rose (Balagtas) prepares for her eighteenth birthday party—her "debut." But Ben plans to only make a quick appearance before joining his friends to attend a "rager" the same night. The plan falls apart when he meets and instantly falls for Rose's best friend Annabelle (Bisco). Unfortunately, Anna comes with baggage in the form of her thuggish ex Augusto (Darion Basco), who humiliates Ben in a game of pickup hoops in front of her, causing an angry Ben to let his friends drag him away to the other party. Another mistake: At the all-white high school bash, a drunk girl implies Ben eats dogs and then calls him a racial slur. He returns to his sister's birthday party, where Augusto corners Ben in a hallway and taunts him until he throws a punch, leading to a disruptive brawl. The incident leads Ben's grandfather Carlos (Garcia) to brutally criticize Roland for allowing gangsters into the gathering. Ben realizes the way Roland treats him is a legacy of how he has been treated by Lolo Carlos—a multigenerational cascade of disapproval and disappointment. As the film closes, Ben has a renewed respect for his heritage and has earned renewed respect from his father, after the latter finally sees his artistic talent for the first time—in a portrait he's been drawing of the three generations of Mercado men.

Unfortunately, the hard-earned success of *The Debut* didn't pave the way to Hollywood for Cajayon;

> **I**f there's one movie that students in my Asian American film history class love, it's *The Debut*. They adore the nineties Pinay vibe (breakdancing! turntablism! pagers!), the cute and smexy love triangle between Dante Basco, Darian Basco, and Joy Bisco, the lovingly photographed Filipino food spreads, and all the other little details that make this film FilAm AF. The agile comic timing and screen ability of all four Basco brothers makes me wonder why their careers didn't take off after this movie's success, but as usual, the answer is probably racism. I've watched this movie dozens of times in my classes, and I enjoy it every time.
>
> **—VALERIE SOE ON *THE DEBUT***

to date, it's the only feature film he's directed. But his star, Dante Basco, would direct something of a spiritual sequel to the film, making his directorial debut with the similarly Basco-sibling-powered comedy *The Fabulous Filipino Brothers* (2021).

Monsoon Wedding

2001, R, 114 MINUTES, FOCUS FEATURES, INDIA/USA

DIRECTOR: Mira Nair

STARRING: Naseeruddin Shah, Lillete Dubey, Shefali Shah, Vasundhara Das, Vijay Raaz, Tillotama Shome, Randeep Hooda, Rajat Kapoor, Jas Arora

WRITER: Sabrina Dhawan

Monsoon Wedding, director Mira Nair's foray into the Bollywood genre, uses a grand Indian wedding's vivid colors and wide-ranging diasporic abundance to bring to life a narrative that is in turn comic, romantic, dramatic, and of course, musical—because what would a Bollywood film be without music and dance? Its story focuses on the planning and celebration of the nuptials of Aditi (Das), the only daughter of Lalit Verma (Naseeruddin Shah) and his wife, Pimmi (Dubey), to Hemant (Dabas), the amiable computer-programmer son of a family friend based in Houston, Texas. Naturally, the ceremony must be epic to preserve face and properly send Aditi off to America. But epic means extensive and expensive—the entire Verma clan must be gathered to Delhi from across India and around the world, and the wedding production itself must have white stallions and synchronized dances and colored lights and strings of marigolds and thousands of yards of colored silk . . . you know, typical wedding expenses.

Meanwhile, a stressed Lalit is getting dubious advice from his wedding coordinator, P. K. Dubey (Raaz), and a legion of relatives, including his wealthy brother-in-law Tej (Kapoor). But Tej is hiding his own secrets; his benevolent offers to pay for Lalit's niece's college education are greeted not with gratitude but with horror from the young woman herself, Ria (Shefali Shah). The reason why comes out when Ria sees Tej coaxing Aliya, the ten-year-old daughter of a family friend, to take a drive with him alone, and a

I f there's one person who above all others inspired me to move to New York and become a storyteller, it was Mira Nair. I watched *Monsoon Wedding* a few years after moving, at the Brooklyn Academy of Music cinema near home, and I still recall the far-left angle from which I stared at the screen and the squiggly, animated string that launched the opening credits and told you nothing would ever be the same. Here was a fantastic tamasha, or spectacle, but one that was surprisingly urbane and moving. Her characters converged on Delhi from the US, the Gulf, and Australia. They weren't weighed down by boring "Am I of East or West?" tropes. They were sexy, callous, and caring, and they were also capable of terrible acts like child sexual abuse. This was revelatory. Because fun wasn't all that united our people, scattered as we were across the globe—secrets did too. Watching it twenty years later, I found the film even more powerful than when I first saw it.

—ARUN VENUGOPAL ON *MONSOON WEDDING*

(Standing) Kulbhushan Kharbanda, Kamini Khanna, Lillete Dubey, Naseeruddin Shah, Natasha Rastogi, Rahul Vohra, (in chairs) Ira Pandey, Rajat Kapoor, Vasundhara Das, Vimla Bhushan; (seated) Randeep Hooda, Shefali Shetty, Kemaya Kidwai, Neha Dubey, and Ishaan Nair

distraught Ria blocks the car with her body and pulls Aliya away, publicly accusing him of sexually molesting her as a young girl. The news shocks Lalit, who initially tells Ria that he believes her but can't send Tej away due to how much he literally and figuratively owes him.

Later, Lalit changes his mind and orders Tej and his own sister to depart, right before the wedding is to begin. But nothing comes easy, as the wedding itself almost runs aground due to bride Aditi's last fling with a married former lover, which she tearfully admits to her groom-to-be. To Hemant's credit, he tells her that marriage is not without risk, and she is worth

the risk, and the wedding seems back on course. Meanwhile, Aditi's cousin Ayesha (Dubey) is flirting with college student Rahul (Hooda), and of course it's monsoon season, so the skies are threatening to send a deluge crashing down on the festivities. Everything gets resolved by the film's finale, of course, with the rain holding off until after the bride and groom have been safely wed.

Monsoon Wedding received the Golden Lion (the Venice Film Festival's highest honor), earned over $30 million at the global box office against a budget of $1.2 million, and has even been adapted into a stage musical, directed by Nair herself.

Lilo & Stitch

**2002, PG, 85 MINUTES,
BUENA VISTA PICTURES, USA**

DIRECTORS/WRITERS: Chris Sanders,
Dean DeBlois

STARRING: Chris Sanders, Daveigh Chase,
Tia Carrere, Ving Rhames, David Ogden Stiers,
Kevin McDonald, Jason Scott Lee,
Zoe Caldwell, Miranda Paige Walls

This eccentric Disney animated feature focuses on an alien genetic experiment that escapes its creator and gets adopted by a young girl and her guardian older sister on Hawaii's island of Kauai. *Lilo & Stitch* explores an unexpectedly deep set of themes: refugeeism, permanent foreigner status, the meaning of humanity and the nature of friendship, and the ways that the state attempts to regulate family.

Experiment 626 (Sanders) is a furry blue creature that vaguely resembles an insane koala; decanted in the lab of Dr. Jumba Jookiba (Stiers), 626 bolts when the Galactic Federation decides to crack down on Jumba's dangerous research. Meanwhile, Lilo Pelekai (Chase) is a young girl whose parents died in a car crash, leaving her to be raised by her older sister, Nani (Carrere). But Nani's competence as a guardian is constantly being observed by an intimidating all-business social worker, Cobra Bubbles (Rhames), and often put to question—for example, after Lilo beats up her nemesis Mertle (Walls), because Mertle called her "crazy." After the fight, Nani realizes that Lilo is lonely and needs a companion. She takes her to a shelter so she can adopt a dog, who turns out to be Experiment 626, quickly renamed Stitch by the enchanted Lilo.

But the Galactic Federation has tracked 626 to his new home and sent Jumba and an Earth-relations representative, Pleakley (McDonald), to recapture him. Their first attempt ends up nearly destroying the restaurant where Nani works, causing her to get fired; the loss of her job may mean Lilo will have to be placed in a foster home. Continued chaos from Jumba, Pleakley, and Stitch end up ruining every subsequent job opportunity Nani pursues, putting her guardian status on the edge. To let off some steam, Nani, Lilo, and Stitch go for a day at the beach with Nani's friend (and would-be boyfriend) David Kawena (Lee), but another Jumba attempt to snag Stitch leads to Lilo almost drowning. Cobra tells Nani that this is the final straw, and if Nani doesn't get a job the next day, he will be collecting Lilo for foster care.

Stitch, blaming himself for the situation, flees the Pelekai family and finds Jumba on the verge of disaster himself: His assignment to capture Stitch has been transferred to a much larger by-the-numbers Federation officer named Gantu (Richardson). With Nani away for a job interview, Gantu and Stitch destroy the house, confirming to Cobra that Lilo is not safe with Nani. As they argue, Lilo and Stitch are captured by Gantu and taken to his ship, where Stitch manages to escape but is unable to free Lilo. Upon returning to Earth, Stitch convinces Jumba and Pleakley to help him free Lilo, explaining to them the meaning of the word "'ohana," which he'd learned from Nani and Lilo: "'Ohana means family. Family means no one gets left behind or forgotten."

Jumba, Pleakley, Stitch, and Nani chase after Gantu in Jumba's spaceship and succeed in rescuing Lilo, but the Grand Councilwoman of the Galactic Federation (Caldwell) is on Earth to greet them as they arrive. She forces Gantu into retirement for his failure, tells Jumba to get ready to go to jail, and orders Stitch to return with her. Stitch simply asks for the chance to say goodbye to his 'ohana, which triggers a realization in Lilo. She promptly grabs and shows her stamped shelter receipt where they adopted Stitch, telling the Councilwoman that she paid for him, and as a result, taking him away would be like stealing. The Councilwoman is impressed by Lilo's resourcefulness and Stitch's genuine love for her and his new place. She decrees that Stitch will be formally and permanently exiled to Earth, in the guardianship of Lilo, Nani, and Cobra Bubbles, who turns out to have been a CIA agent in a former life and a friend of the Councilwoman's after the first human-alien encounter in Roswell, New Mexico. At the film's end, Stitch's 'ohana gather to rebuild their house, an oddball extended family that now includes Jumba and Pleakley.

Lilo & Stitch is special for many reasons. For one, it centers on Hawaii's multicultural and majority Asian and Pacific Islander society—the main characters are all of multiracial Native Hawaiian and Asian descent, and minor characters like Mr. Wong and Mrs. Hasegawa populate the town. For another, it's a Disney film that focuses not on romance but on Lilo and Nani's relationship as sisters, a sibling narrative that *Frozen* (2013) is often credited as pioneering. It also became Disney's first international animated franchise, with Stitch moving on to other friends after Lilo grows up and goes to college in two TV series that continue his story: first with Yuna, a resident of Japan's southern Ryukyu Islands in the anime series *Stitch!* (2008–2015), and then *Stitch and Ai* (2017), made for China's CCTV, which shows Stitch befriending a Chinese girl named Wang Ailing.

> **A**s a person born and raised in Hawaii of Hawaiian ancestry, what really resonated with local people the most was that two actors born and raised in Hawaii played main characters with authentic pidgin accents and didn't overdo it—Tia Carrere and Jason Scott Lee were simply being their "local" selves. It was soothing to hear an unforced cadence of island pidgin English without trying to be a pidgin English accent. And Tia singing "Aloha 'Oe" still makes people teary-eyed.
>
> **—BROOK LEE ON *LILO & STITCH***

Ping Pong Playa

2007, PG-13, 96 MINUTES, IFC FILMS, USA

DIRECTOR: Jessica Yu

STARRING: Jimmy Tsai, Andrew Vo, Khary Payton, Jim Lau, Roger Fan, Elizabeth Sung, Javin Reid, Kevin Chung, Peter Paige, Smith Cho, Scott Lowell, Stephnie Weir

WRITERS: Jimmy Tsai, Jessica Yu

Jimmy Tsai

The only narrative feature made by documentarian Jessica Yu, *Ping Pong Playa* is quite a departure from her usual subject matter: She won an Academy Award in 1996 for her short documentary *Breathing Lessons*, about Mark O'Brien, a poet in an iron lung; her other acclaimed works include *Men of Reenaction* (1996), about Civil War reenactment fanatics, and *Last Call at the Oasis* (2011), about the looming American water crisis.

This film, by contrast, is about a young slacker named Christopher "C-Dub" Wang (Tsai), a trash-talking wannabe hoopster in his twenties who swears he'd be in the NBA if it weren't for his height. As it is, he lives an aimless post-college life, living at home, helping his parents' ping-pong-focused sporting goods store, and resentfully absorbing his elder brother

Michael's (Fan) condescending advice. Both Michael and Christopher have grown up playing table tennis, taught by their parents, who were former top players in their youth. Training young kids in the game is a big part of the family business, so when Mrs. Wang and Michael are both injured in a minor traffic accident, C-Dub has no choice but to take over as a teacher and the Wang family representative at the local table tennis tournament, the annual Golden Cock Competition. Initially reluctant, he leans into the challenge, taking a young student named Felix (Vo) under his wing, attempting to woo Felix's big sister Jennifer (Cho) and successfully defend his family honor and Chinese ping-pong in general from the irritating Gerald (Paige), a white player who seeks

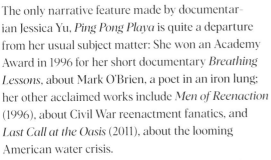

This was the last movie I saw before becoming a father. I took my baby mama to see it in the theaters. I don't know if seeing an Asian American film that pushed the boundaries on how an Asian man could be represented on-screen induces labor, but the next morning her water broke, and less than twenty-four hours after watching the final credits, my daughter Klee was born. I think it was a fitting way to quite literally mark the birth of a new generation of Asian America.

—MICHAEL KANG ON *PING PONG PLAYA*

to launch a rival table tennis academy focused on European training methods.

As a sports comedy, it shouldn't be a surprise that C-Dub wins, earning respect from his family, his students, and even Jennifer in the process. This movie was lead actor Jimmy Tsai's only feature film performance; he'd originally created the character of fast-talking hustler C-Dub in a series of comedic web sketches framed as ads for an athletic clothing company, Venom Sportswear, which Yu saw and found hilarious. Yu and Tsai cowrote the script, and Tsai served as a producer on the film.

In the Family

**2011, NOT RATED, 169 MINUTES,
E.D. DISTRIBUTION, USA**

DIRECTOR/WRITER: Patrick Wang

STARRING: Sebastian Banes, Patrick Wang, Trevor St. John, Kelly McAndrew

---

This quiet, deeply moving drama was Patrick Wang's feature directorial debut, and it caused something of a sensation upon its release; while Wang didn't come out of nowhere (having directed and acted in a few short films and having directed a handful of theater productions at New York's Stella Adler Studio and Neighborhood Playhouse), the film was initially overlooked, being rejected by most of the major festivals. Though it was finally screened at the San Diego Asian Film Festival, the Hawaii International Film Festival, and the Whistler Film Festival, Wang decided to take a major risk by booking the Quad Cinema in New York City to give it a theatrical run, renting the screen out of his own pocket. Suddenly, critics hailed it as the unexpected arrival of a major indie filmmaking talent, and Wang received an Independent Spirit Award nomination for Best First Feature.

The film focuses on Joey Williams (played by Wang himself), a gay man whose partner, Cody (St. John), is killed in a car accident. Together Joey and Cody had been raising Chip (Banes), Cody's six-year-old son from a prior marriage, but Cody's sudden death puts Chip's custody in question, as Cody left behind an outdated will remanding Chip to his sister Eileen (McAndrew) in the event of his untimely passing. They live in Tennessee, a state with few protections for gay partners, which doesn't make Joey's case for custody any stronger. Eileen's initial unwillingness to share custody or give him any visitation rights pushes him to pursue a quixotic legal battle for the boy he sees as his son. The courtroom fight turns ugly when the lawyer Eileen has hired goes for the jugular, questioning Joey's name (an orphan originally named Chin Mae Lee, he was given the name Joey by his foster parents, the Williamses), his relationship with Cody ("When did you seduce him?"), and even his intentions with Chip ("Are you a pedophile, Joey?"). Joey's measured honesty and his sincere love of Chip come through in his responses, making Eileen regret both the interrogation and allowing their dispute to go

In the Family finds its way into the most tender part of your heart and never lets go. It inspires intense loyalty to writer/director Patrick Wang, because even though your brain knows this is fiction, your heart believes he's Joey, the character he plays. To love this film is to believe in a world where the humble Joeys of the world can navigate stubborn prejudices and loud injustices with quiet strength and sheer mission-driven goodness.

—ADA TSENG ON *IN THE FAMILY*

Sebastian Banes and Patrick Wang

to court. Ultimately, the unusual family finds a way to move forward together, filling in some of the Cody-shaped gap in their mutual lives and looking ahead to what's best for the son Cody left behind.

Wang has gone on to make two more films, the novel adaptation of *The Grief of Others* (2015) and the broadly acclaimed two-part comic musing on the nature of art and art as commerce *A Bread Factory* (2018).

Spa Night

2016, NOT RATED, 93 MINUTES, STRAND RELEASING, USA

DIRECTOR/WRITER: Andrew Ahn

STARRING: Joe Seo, Haerry Kim, Youn Ho Cho, Tae Song, Ho Young Chung, Linda Han, Eric Jeong, Yong Kim

This assured and deeply moving feature debut from Andrew Ahn isn't the movie many people may assume, given how most films about sexual self-discovery operate. More simply, it's not a "coming out" movie—David (Seo) doesn't arrive at a point where he really knows or understands his sexual orientation in the film, though he clearly is not "fully straight." For some viewers who frame this as a queer film first and foremost, that may seem like a cop-out; but for those who are watching it as Asian Americans, gay or straight, it may simply seem familiar: The process of coming to terms with identity is more complicated when one stands at multiple marginal intersections, and as the film shows, it's often not until the relative freedom of college that young Asians finally feel the agency to make choices—who they are, who they love, what career they wish to pursue.

David is the eighteen-year-old only son of Jin (Cho) and Soyoung (Haerry Kim). His parents are loving and supportive of him, though he seems to constantly fall short of their expectations, particularly academically; his grades and test scores reflect his apathy toward his studies, and his growing sense that perhaps college isn't for him. The family lives in LA Koreatown and operates a restaurant, until it

Joe Seo

is abruptly shut down when Jin falls behind on rent payments. Loss of the business forces Soyoung to take a job as a waitress at church friend Mrs. Baek's (Han) successful establishment; David looks for work to help provide for the family. Meanwhile, a distraught Jin drowns his sorrows in alcohol, unable to lift himself out of his sense of failure.

Jin and Soyoung urge David to focus less on the present and more on his future, pushing him to visit Mrs. Baek's son Eddie (Song) at USC. David agrees and joins Eddie for an evening that begins with a flirty coed gathering and ends at an all-male Koreatown spa, where David begins to have new feelings he's not quite able to process. Driven to explore them further, he takes a job at the spa and soon realizes it is a hot spot for gay men seeking anonymous hookups. He is both mesmerized and made uncomfortable by this revelation, and when he finally indulges his sexual longing with another patron—only to be caught by his boss (Chung)—he is driven to both ritually apologize to him and brutally cleanse and scrub himself, though it is unclear whether he is removing a sense of shame or peeling away the facade of the life he feels obligated to. The final scene shows David running, fleeing from a climactic fight between his parents, but also running toward something—a future that is uncertain, choosing to embrace what comes next.

Spa Night is a narrative about the complexity of embracing gay identity in a traditionally conservative culture, and the battle one has with it and with oneself. The queer Asian narrative has seldom been portrayed in cinema with such thoughtfulness and authenticity; Ahn defied what is expected and created a story that impacted me and my own queer identity in a way that nothing else has.

—DINO-RAY RAMOS ON *SPA NIGHT*

Haley Lu Richardson and John Cho

Columbus

2017, NOT RATED, 100 MINUTES, OSCILLOSCOPE, USA

DIRECTOR/WRITER: Kogonada

STARRING: John Cho, Haley Lu Richardson, Michelle Forbes, Rory Culkin, Parker Posey

The cinematic debut of pseudonymous video essayist Kogonada, who first garnered notice with artful

visual critiques and deconstructions of great filmmakers for *Sight and Sound* and the Criterion Collection, *Columbus* centers on two people facing very similar circumstances: Jin (Cho) is a book translator whose estranged father, an architecture historian, is on his deathbed. Casey (Richardson) is a high school graduate and aspiring architecture student who has held off on going to college to care for her mother, a recovering (but not recovered) drug addict. They're bound together in space and subject by buildings: Encountering one another when Jin bums a cigarette from Casey, they strike up a conversation and then an odd friendship, as Casey attempts to incite in Jin the same kind of appreciation for the built environment that she has gained from living in the titular town of Columbus—not Ohio but Indiana, a small Midwestern burg with the distinction as one of the nation's great centers of Modernist architecture, due to the lifelong investment and patronage of one of the town's wealthiest scions.

Jin shares with Casey his resentment of his father, who loved architecture more than his son, in Jin's mind. Casey, in turn, tells Jin about her dreams and her fears, that leaving her mother would be signing her death warrant. It is the very Modernist architecture that Casey obsesses over that ultimately changes her mind—wide glass windows giving her a view of her mother not at work at her cleaning job as she had claimed, which almost certainly means she has relapsed. This proves to be the final nudge to unhook Casey from Columbus, from stasis, from spending her youth mothering a mother who refuses to grow and change.

Jin asks his father's protégé Eleanor (Posey) to provide Casey with the introductions she needs to pursue her academic ambitions. Eleanor, who has just rejected Jin's profession of love for her—he has nursed a crush on her for decades—agrees, perhaps by way of apology. Casey leaves, and Jin stays to watch over his father, the two "crossing the line" and exchanging places—the child who has no connection to his parent embracing his filial role, and the child who has been too deeply tethered to hers finally cutting the cord. The film, made for just $700,000, was celebrated by many critics as among the best of the year, due to its strong core of Kogonada's studied aesthetics and the pair of brilliant performances by Cho and Richardson.

Bao

2018, G, 8 MINUTES,
WALT DISNEY STUDIOS, USA

DIRECTOR/WRITER: Domee Shi

STARRING: Sindy Lau, Daniel Kai Lin, Sharmaine Yeoh

The first and only short featured in this collection, *Bao* was created as the thirty-fifth in Pixar's series of brief animated films designed to encourage young animators to experiment and stretch their storytelling skills. And *Bao*'s impact was disproportionate to its running length: Not only did it win Asian Canadian Domee Shi an Academy Award but it also gave her

Domee Shi's animated short *Bao* won her an Oscar and helped propel her into the front ranks of animation directors—but the millions of people whose hearts it touched may wish Shi had expanded her debut effort before moving on to *Turning Red*. Well, never say never: Here (opposite) **Cryssy Cheung** imagines what a live-action feature adaptation of *Bao* might look like (and the answer is . . . a horror comedy).

LOVE CAN CONSUME YOU.

BAO

THE MOVIE

The mother and her baby bao

the freedom to work through key ideas that became running themes in her feature film debut, *Turning Red* (2022)—whose success led to a promotion to Pixar vice president of creative, making her one of four people at the studio shaping its future output.

In *Bao*, a mother cooks a meal of steamed meat buns—"baozi"—for herself and her husband, only to have one of the baos sprout a face, arms, and legs and come alive just as she's about to eat it. Though she's initially shocked, she is quickly won over by its cute antics and decides to name it Bao and raise it as her offspring. But as Bao grows older and begins to wander through the world alongside his mother,

he encounters danger—a dog almost runs away with him; a soccer ball nearly squishes his head—causing Mother to become extremely protective of her beloved bun-boy. Still, everyone grows up, even a delicious blob of starch and protein, and Bao soon chats with friends on the phone, drives fast cars, and suddenly brings home a blond bombshell, his new fiancée.

As he packs his bags and readies to leave with her, Mother panics and blocks the door; he tries to get around her, only to have Mother grab him and tearfully . . . swallow him whole. Having cannibalized her darling child, Mother goes to her bed, catatonic in depression, until she hears her husband come home,

As a Taiwanese American, I know all about immigrant parents who are unable to express themselves verbally and instead, show their feelings through food. A bao is a dumpling, but it's also short for bao bei—a darling. At first, I watched this film through the eyes of a child, finding comfort in the image of a selfless mother whose life revolved around feeding her family. But rewatching this film after dropping off my son at college, I realize how revolutionary this eight-minute film really is. It's not the story of an ideal mother but an imperfect middle-aged woman learning to let go.

—GRACE HWANG LYNCH ON *BAO*

along with someone else—her adult human child, an exact simulacrum of the steamed bun she imagined. It turns out that the whole fantasy was just an internal reflection of Mother's empty-nest concern, anxiety, and overprotectiveness for her son. The short ends with a shot of the family together, including human Bao and his blond bombshell wife, making steamed buns—with daughter-in-law showing she's quite good at bun making herself, producing three for Mother's inspection. Could she have . . . a set of triple buns in the oven? We'll have to wait for the sequel—or the feature film adaptation!—to know for sure.

Searching

**2018, PG-13, 102 MINUTES,
SCREEN GEMS, USA**

DIRECTOR: Aneesh Chaganty

STARRING: John Cho, Debra Messing, Michelle La, Sara Sohn, Joseph Lee, Steven Michael Eich, Ric Sarabia, Sean O'Bryan, Colin Woodell

WRITERS: Aneesh Chaganty, Sev Ohanian

In this feature debut, Aneesh Chaganty demonstrated a new and definitively postmodern way to weave the intricate narrative of an investigative thriller, telling the story of a father searching for his missing daughter entirely via computer screens, smartphones, streaming media devices, and webcams. The storytelling method was so unfamiliar to the lead, John Cho, that initially, he refused to take part in the film—telling Chaganty that he wasn't interested in being in a "YouTube movie." But Chaganty persisted in pursuing Cho, explaining that the movie's conceit was intended to demonstrate the reality of how our lives are shaped by and reflected in the data we leave behind, while putting the protagonist at the very center of the narrative: Cho and other actors would be constantly in view, from the perspective of the cameras that are embedded in all our technology. Fortunately, Cho agreed to play the role, and proved more than up to the challenge of working under the constraints of "screenlife" performance (in most cases, Cho was acting toward a blank screen, his eyes following line-of-sight dots, or with actors on video teleconference platforms).

The film begins with a montage of the lives of the Kim family—David (Cho), Pam (Sohn), and Margot (as a teenager, La)—over the years, seen from the vantage point of their Windows PC. Through video clips, saved photos, and YouTube streams, we see Margot grow from a small child to an adolescent; we observe the deep love between David and Pam, and the special closeness that exists between Pam and her daughter, Margot; and we watch, our hearts breaking, as Pam is diagnosed with lymphoma and eventually passes away from her illness.

In the present, David and Margot's relationship is strained, as David chides Margot for not taking out the trash, and she tells him she'll do it after she comes back from her group study session. Margot never comes home, and when David wakes up, he sees he's missed two calls from her. He angrily messages her again about the trash, which has begun to smell. But hours later, with Margot still out of contact, David begins to worry. She doesn't answer her phone. He calls her piano teacher, only to find that Margot had canceled her lessons six months ago, meaning that she'd been taking the money David gave her for each lesson and using it for an unknown purpose.

An increasingly concerned David calls the police, reaching Detective Rosemary Vick (Messing), who, as a single mother herself, seems empathetic to David's concerns. She tells him to follow Margot's data trail and reach out to her classmates for any information. David realizes as he compiles a spreadsheet of responses to his inquiries that Margot isn't who he thought she was—rather than being a sunny, cheerful girl with a lot of friends, she is distant, isolated, and generally seen as an outsider.

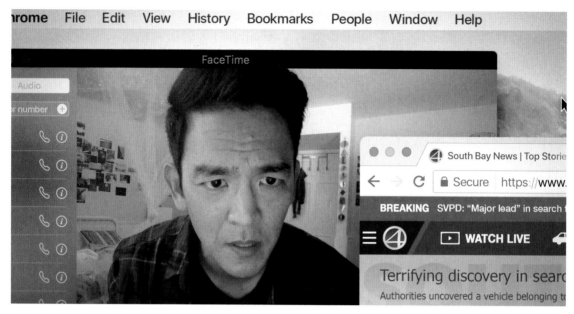

John Cho

As the film goes on, Vick contacts David to show him more evidence that Margot was hiding a secret life. David himself uncovers unexpected truths about Margot's relationships with her mother, her uncle, and ultimately, David himself, all by spelunking through her digital history. There are red herrings aplenty and a conclusion that ends with a spectacular twist. But patient and observant viewers will have had the opportunity to fairly solve the mystery early in the film, though knowing the answers doesn't prevent you from enjoying the ride.

Searching, made for under $1 million, was an enormous hit, earning over $75 million at the global box office. It also demonstrated how a movie that doesn't directly focus on issues of race or ethnicity can still be subtly shaped by casting Asian American leads, with key aspects of the story, from the nature of the father-daughter relationship to Margot's love-hate attitude toward piano to even the film's saturation with social media all playing differently, and more authentically, because of the Asian family at the movie's center. Director Chaganty even admits to being inspired to make the movie in part by his time working as a marketing video producer for Google, which released a viral ad for Google Chrome called "Dear Sophie" that featured an Asian father, Daniel Lee, creating a digital hope chest for his young daughter.

> I love how this movie is a modern-day updating of the epistolary novel—a story told through letters and journal entries, like *Dracula* and *Frankenstein*. And I love how the family at the center of this just happened to be Asian American, that it wasn't the focus of the film. A tightly made, innovative movie that ended with a real surprise, it broke new ground in how it showed how much of our lives are lived on and captured through digital media. The artifacts of our digital lives are such an interesting lens through which to tell a mystery story.
>
> —JENNIFER 8. LEE ON *SEARCHING*

Jake Choi and Tiffany Chu

Ms. Purple

**2019, NOT RATED, 87 MINUTES,
OSCILLOSCOPE, USA**

DIRECTOR: Justin Chon

STARRING: Tiffany Chu, Teddy Lee, Octavio Pizano, Jake Choi, James Kang, Mark Krenik, Crystal Lee, Alma Martinez, Ronnie Kim

WRITERS: Justin Chon, Chris Dinh

Set within and shaped by the hidden world of Los Angeles's Koreatown, the largest center of Korean population outside of Korea itself, *Ms. Purple* is a deeply felt examination of the relationship between siblings, a family dimension often sidelined in Asian American cinema in favor of parent-child (or even grandparent-child) dynamics. It is a brother and sister pair who stand, and try to remain standing, at the center of this film—Kasie (Chu) and Carey (Lee), albeit siblings who've been separated for years.

Abandoned by their mother at a young age—she left the family to pursue a wealthier marriage prospect—they were raised by their brokenhearted, occasionally brutal father Young-Il (Kang), whose violence toward Carey drove him to flee the house at age fifteen. But when a dying Young-Il's live-in nurse (Martinez) quits and advises Kasie to put him in hospice care, Kasie reaches out for Carey's help; he's

> **K**oreatown, Los Angeles is like if Seoul, Korea and Oaxaca, Mexico had an urban-planning baby 2.7 square miles in size. As a third-generation Chinese American who's lived here for over twelve years and who was elected to represent Subdistrict 5 of the Wilshire Center Koreatown Neighborhood Council for the last four, I often feel like I live abroad, in a place where I can pass as a local more than any white person can. My neighborhood is an open-air attic of secrets, traumas, and stories hiding in plain sight behind wrought-iron gates, abandoned couches, and MS-13 graffiti. Even what spare greenery we have—nonnative palm trees swaying alone or in pairs at sunrise—are emblems of displacement that have rooted themselves and now look the part of local fauna. Justin Chon's wounded-family drama was shot in the blocks around me—in norebangs, a computer gaming hall, the parking lot of the Rodeo Galleria, and more. Seeing my neighborhood as a backdrop for this story about two siblings who are trying to decide how to care for their ailing father felt voyeuristic, heartbreaking, and satisfying all at once. Now Koreatown isn't just some neighborhood where you party, eat, vomit—usually just outside my building—before heading back to the Westside. It's also the backdrop for the modern American family drama.
>
> **—KRISTINA WONG ON *MS. PURPLE***

doing a lot of nothing (playing video games in internet cafés, mostly) and agrees to serve as a fill-in caregiver on her behalf. Kasie can't do it herself because of the nature of her job as a karaoke room hostess. She spends her nights serving men drinks and fending off advances when they go too far, and spends her mornings shaking off the drunken haze that's a constant hazard of her profession.

There's initially a wary bitterness to the reunion of the siblings. Kasie has been bearing the burden of their father's care for so long alone. Eventually, they fall back into old patterns of comfort as they accept that they're the only family they have left. Their scenes together drive the movie, more than Kasie's interactions with her arrogant, monied boyfriend (Kim) or her low-key potential love interest, Octavio (Pizano). Carey's willingness to provide care for the father who drove him away shows residual compassion, but nevertheless, he finds himself so stir-crazy in one scene that he rolls his father's sickbed out onto the streets of Koreatown, eventually landing at his favorite bar, to the surprise of other patrons.

Ms. Purple is a quintessential indie gem, focusing on a small world within a small world, within a very large one that seems almost infinitely distant for the story's trapped characters. Kasie is given a chance to show fire in a climactic scene where she pushes back, violently, against the abusive karaoke patrons, backed up by the establishment's other hostesses, a found family that offers more support than the one in which she was born.

The Farewell

2019, PG, 100 MINUTES, A24, USA

DIRECTOR/WRITER: Lulu Wang

STARRING: Awkwafina, Tzi Ma, Diana Lin, Zhao Shu-zhen, Lu Hong, Jiang Yongbo, Chen Han, Aoi Mizuhara, Zhang Jing, Li Xiang, Yang Xuejian, Jim Liu

Lulu Wang's sophomore feature film is a deeply personal and semi-autobiographical family drama whose

(From left) Jiang Yongbo, Aoi Mizuhara, Chen Han, Tzi Ma, Awkwafina, Li Xiang, Lu Hong, and Diana Lin

central conceit plants squarely in the rift between cultures. It proved to be a challenge to green-light, since investors and studios found it hard to believe a family would hide a terminal medical diagnosis from a loved one. Yet for Chinese and other Asian cultures, withholding news can be a sign of respect (because giving someone news of their impending doom is tantamount to wishing it on them) and a means of ensuring they face the world and their remaining days with peace and positivity. Wang ultimately told her story as a segment on the hugely popular public radio show *This American Life*, which proved to be key in getting the film's funds.

Wang's self-insert in *The Farewell* is Billi (Awkwafina), a Chinese American writer whose dreams have been dented by a rejection from a major

Films about the Asian immigrant experience tend to feature the friction between two genera-tions: those who move to the States as adults, and their American-born children. It wasn't until Awkwafina's Billi in *The Farewell* that I saw my own experience fully represented on-screen. Like director Lulu Wang, I moved to the US with my parents when I was a child, part of the oft over-looked "1.5 generation." I still hold memories of my (happy) childhood in China, and I still struggle with my parents making the decision to take me away from the only home and family I knew. To see a character who looked like me voice these complex, sensitive thoughts out loud felt like a breath of fresh air and a gut punch at the same time; and it reminded me again that what I always thought were deeply personal feelings are more universal than I realized.

—LINDA GE ON *THE FAREWELL*

fellowship. That's just the first body blow she sustains in the early moments of the movie: Her parents share news that her beloved Nai Nai (Zhao) has terminal cancer and has just months left to live. The entire family intends to hide the diagnosis from Nai Nai, instead using a ruse that Billi's cousin Hao Hao (Han) is getting married as an opportunity for one last extended family reunion. And they don't even want Billi to attend, fearing she'll give away the secret. Billi is aghast that they would deny her the chance to see her beloved grandmother one last time, and surreptitiously flies to Changchun, China, on her own, promising her parents that she won't reveal the diagnosis. Her vow is constantly tested, however, as she grows increasingly angry about the family's elaborate attempts to hide the truth from Nai Nai. Billi finally confronts them, and her uncle Haibin (Jiang) explains to her that by keeping up the fiction, they're taking the emotional burden of the diagnosis on themselves, rather than putting it on Nai Nai's sole shoulders—reflecting how the East emphasizes the group, while the West prioritizes the individual.

Billi later learns that Nai Nai herself never told her late husband that he was terminally ill either. The burden is a hard one to carry even for Haibin, who bursts into tears during the wedding banquet; so does Hao Hao, confusing guests. (The whole thing has been staged, with Hao Hao and his Japanese girlfriend of a few months agreeing to the plot for Nai Nai's sake.) Billi keeps up the lie until she leaves, sharing a tearful goodbye, perhaps a final one, with her grandmother as she prepares to leave for home. It ends with a stark and heart-wrenching ending: Billi's back in New York, walking down a busy street, and then suddenly stops and shouts out loud with all of her soul—a scream that leaps from her body and seems to impact halfway around the world as we cut to startled birds flying out of a tree in Changchun. Grandma is gone, we must assume. Or is she? A final intertitle appears before the credits, sharing a shocking fact: Six years after the end of the film, both the fictional Nai Nai and her real-life inspiration are still alive—and still unaware they were ever sick.

Turning Red

2022, PG, 100 MINUTES, WALT DISNEY STUDIOS, USA

DIRECTOR: Domee Shi

STARRING: Rosalie Chiang, Sandra Oh, Ava Morse, Hyein Park, Maitreyi Ramakrishnan, Orion Lee, Wai Ching Ho, Tristan Allerick Chen, James Hong, Addie Chandler

WRITERS: Domee Shi, Julia Cho, Sarah Streicher

The post–*Crazy Rich Asians* era has seen a notable boom in both quantity and quality of Asian American (and Canadian!) works on the big screen. In tandem with more and better, we've also seen the arrival of stranger, more idiosyncratic, distinctively personal movies, broadening out and deepening the spectrum of what it means to tell Asian American stories. This Pixar animated feature—the first from Domee Shi, creator of the Oscar-winning short *Bao*—springs from her direct childhood experience and her feverishly wild imagination: It's a love letter to the ethnic swirl of Toronto, to boy-band hysteria, to growing up in a traditional immigrant household, and to puberty and all its mysteries, tragedies, and delights—delivered via the warm, furry embrace of a giant magical red panda.

Meilin Lee (Chiang) is a defiantly uncool Chinese Canadian girl—she has a sticker on her flute case that says "THIS GIRL LOVES MATH"—who's living her best life in early 2000s Toronto with her besties Priya (Ramakrishnan), Abby (Park), and Miriam (Morse). In addition to swooning over the definitely swoon-worthy multiethnic crooners of 4*Town, she finds herself suddenly in her feels over the bland but cute

(From left) Abby (Hyein Park), Priya (Maitreyi Ramakrishnan), Mei Lee (Rosalie Chiang), and Miriam (Ava Morse)

convenience store clerk Devon (Chandler). She doodles romantic pictures of him spontaneously in the margins of her homework and wakes up in the middle of weird, but hot, fantasies about him.

Mei soon learns she's part of a lineage of Chinese women who have inherited the protection of the Red Panda spirit, lending strength and ferocity when needed to defend their families. It also transforms them when they get overwhelmed by emotion, which starts to happen to hormone-driven Mei more frequently. The realization that any loss of self-control can lead Mei to transform into a giant furry beast is initially terrifying to her, though her parents—especially her mother, Ming (Oh), who has overcome her own inner red panda—take it in stride. Mei, too, quickly sees the upside in her alternate identity: It gives her the ability to intimidate and then appease her biggest bully, Tyler (Chen), and even more

The creators of *Turning Red* aren't just brilliant storytellers, they also made an enormous and genuine investment to ensure the story was told with authenticity. The incredible attention given to details elevated the film and helped to achieve both cultural specificity and universal impact. *Turning Red* proved that stories celebrating our community can still shatter records and resonate with audiences of all backgrounds.

—JEREMY TRAN ON *TURNING RED*

importantly, it provides her with a unique way of earning money to buy her squad 4*Town concert tickets, by turning herself into a pay-per-fur sideshow for her fellow students.

Of course, she can't risk going panda at the concert, so she agrees to undergo a special ritual that Ming and her other female relatives have all undergone, which seals their Red Panda spirits in a special talisman. But right before the ritual begins, Mei's father, Jin (Lee), shows her the video she took of herself in panda form, dancing with her friends, and tells her she shouldn't be ashamed of her panda. He also shares that Ming had the biggest, most ornery panda ever, one the ritual could barely even control. Mei ultimately decides to keep her panda and flees the ritual to the Skydome to join her friends. Ming is so enraged about Mei leaving that her talisman bursts, releasing her panda form . . . an out-of-control monster the size of a skyscraper. Ming and Mei battle at the Skydome until the other women in their family arrive and try to restrain Mei in their panda forms. When Mei accidentally knocks Ming unconscious, the women quickly perform the ritual to seal Ming's panda, as well as their own, with the help of 4*Town's spontaneous singing. Mei decides once more to stick with her panda self, and Ming ultimately accepts Mei's decision. Fortunately, Mei's panda form proves just as popular with patrons of the small family-operated temple as it was with her classmates, ensuring a constant flow of donations, which are needed to pay off the destruction from the panda rampage.

Turning Red is nonstop fun, and a breakthrough film for Disney Pixar—a feature set in the present day, in the real world, featuring a cast of characters that is nearly all Asian, across a distinctive and diverse spectrum: Mei's friend group, which includes a Chinese American, a Korean American, and an Indian American; her bully, Tyler; even three of the five 4*Town boys—Tae Young (Grayson Villanueva) and both Aaron T. (Topher Ngo) and Aaron Z. (Josh Levi)—appear to be of Asian or multiracial Asian heritage. Few movies have done a better job of demonstrating how empowering it can be to see a world where being Asian isn't odd or exotic, but just . . . normal.

Everything Everywhere All at Once

2022, R, 139 MINUTES, A24, USA

DIRECTORS/WRITERS: Daniel Kwan, Daniel Scheinert

STARRING: Michelle Yeoh, Stephanie Hsu, Ke Huy Quan, Jenny Slate, Harry Shum Jr., James Hong, Jamie Lee Curtis, Tallie Medel

The sophomore feature effort of the Daniels (the directorial duo of Daniel Kwan and Daniel Scheinert) is almost as impossible to describe as it is to resist. It draws from the same surreal black humor as their debut, 2016's *Swiss Army Man*, about a suicidal man's unusual friendship with a slightly reanimated corpse, but it's more of a spiritual successor to the Daniels' breakout music video—their visual interpretation of DJ Snake and Lil Jon's "Turn Down for What." In the video, Kwan plays a protagonist whose reaction to the song is so turnt (as Lil Jon himself might say) that he humps his way down through the floors of his apartment building, shocking the occupants of lower levels. *Everything Everywhere* isn't built around the same kind of transgressive sexual absurdity (though there's an eye-popping kung fu sequence in which an antagonist's fighting style is fueled by the use of a, uh, posterior self-pleasuring device), but it does share its basic throughline of a protagonist breaking through barriers, intersecting with strange new worlds.

Evelyn Wang (Yeoh) is an immigrant Chinese American woman trying to simultaneously manage a failing laundromat and hold together a fragmented

Michelle Yeoh

This movie made me think a lot about my parents' regrets. As kids, my sister and I would listen to their stories about the lives they lived before we were born: the cities they moved to and could have stayed in, the jobs they could have had, the trips they wished they took. In our two-story house in a quiet suburb, it felt like the versions of themselves they dreamt about were a faraway fantasy. The ways they reflected on "what could have been" were echoes of generational trauma felt from their parents, whose immigration stories were also filled with "what ifs." I catch myself sometimes thinking along those same lines: about the cities I should've stayed in, the jobs I should have taken, the missed opportunities I won't ever get back. But I don't want to live in regrets hidden behind stories—and I don't want generations after me to do that either. We all make choices in life about where to go, who to spend our time with, what to do to fill the hours in the day. Through Evelyn's eyes, I came to understand the significance of choosing to be deeply and wholly present in this universe—for the people I love and the people who love me, even when it isn't always easy.

—TRACI LEE ON *EVERYTHING EVERYWHERE ALL AT ONCE*

family. Her endlessly cheery husband, Waymond (Quan), isn't much help; neither is her sullen daughter, Joy (Hsu), who is ground down by Evelyn's constant microaggressions and refusal to publicly accept Joy's girlfriend, Becky (Medel). Meanwhile, the laundromat is being audited by savage IRS agent Deirdre Beaubeirdre (Curtis), who's so good at her soul-crushing job that she has multiple awards on her desk (shaped like said posterior self-pleasuring devices). All of this is going on as Evelyn is planning a last-ditch attempt to save the laundromat by throwing a grand Lunar New Year party for its semi-regular customers. But as Deirdre interrogates her, Evelyn is sucked backward into a storage closet and confronted by Waymond—or rather, a version of Waymond from the "Alpha" timeline, who has temporarily co-opted her own Waymond's body.

Alpha Waymond tells her she is uniquely capable of saving the cosmos: of all the Evelyns in the multiverse, because her multitude of failures have turned her into a giant mass of pulsating, unfulfilled potential. This means she's capable of "verse jumping" to an unparalleled number of different "possibilities," leveraging the abilities and know-how of thousands of Evelyns in thousands of other universes. This is essential because it will take the combined skills of all those Evelyns to stop the dimension-hopping monster known as Jobu Tupaki from destroying *every* timeline that exists.

Evelyn, naturally, does not believe this Waymond, until he demonstrates skills her own Waymond couldn't have, like the ability to use a fanny pack as a devastating improvised set of nunchucks. But Evelyn isn't the only person capable of verse jumping so easily; Jobu Tupaki can do so with frictionless ease. Complicating matters, Jobu Tupaki is none other than the Alpha variant of Evelyn's own daughter, Joy. What follows, put as succinctly as possible, is a messily brilliant and brilliantly messy slapstick action science-fiction martial arts fantasy that is, at its core, one of the most heartfelt and authentic Asian American family dramas ever created. There are incredible fighting sequences, choreographed by the Martial Club, a group of self-taught martial artists whose kung fu cinema–inspired videos have made them YouTube-famous. There are any number of worlds to explore, each one a variant of the one Evelyn calls home, due to decisions she made and didn't make: the wuxia timeline, where Evelyn is expertly trained in kung fu. The period-romance timeline, where Evelyn and Waymond never got married but reconnect years later in a set of wistful scenes that pay loving homage to Hong Kong auteur Wong Kar-Wai. There's even a "hot dog fingers" timeline (where everyone has mustard-shooting fingers that are made of hot dogs) and a timeline where the only sentient things on Earth are animated rocks that communicate via subtitles.

Ultimately, Evelyn learns how to trigger her powers effectively—each requiring a random "improbable" act to unlock, like giving yourself paper cuts, eating a tube of lip balm, or hugging a foe and telling them you love them. Along the way, she learns a lot about herself, her husband, and most of all, her daughter. By the end, mother and daughter have found a path to reconciliation, while also satisfying the oppressive demands of the IRS. The movie is both unrecognizably weird on its surface and deeply moving and authentic in its body and bones, and its box office success demonstrates how well it managed to satisfy so many audiences: It made over $100 million on a budget south of $25 million, powered by the Daniels' relentless originality and career-defining performances by newcomer Hsu, long-lost veteran Quan, and especially the marvelous Michelle Yeoh. To cap it all off, EEAAO won a staggering seven Oscars, including Best Picture, Best Directing, Best Original Screenplay, Best Film Editing, Best Supporting Actor (Quan), Best Supporting Actress (Curtis), and Best Actress for Michelle Yeoh, making her the first Asian woman to win the honor, and just the second woman of color to win Best Actress . . . ever.

"Immigrant parents know how to adapt."

A Talk with **Nisha Ganatra** and **Kal Penn**

It's often said that the family is the basic unit of Asian community—the indivisible atom of our cultures. Is that why families are at the center of so many of our cinematic works, or is it simply that storytelling is such an effective form of therapy for creators seeking to unpack, reflect on, and resolve their inherited traumas and childhood domestic dramas? In this Q&A, filmmaker Nisha Ganatra (*Late Night, Chutney Popcorn*) and actor Kal Penn (*The Namesake, Harold and Kumar Go to White Castle*) share their thoughts about the complications, contradictions, and limitations of Asian American family stories, the ways that they bridge generations and cultures, and how—like families themselves—they ultimately push creators to leave the nest and foray beyond.

What is it about family stories that make them so alluring for Asian American filmmakers?

NISHA GANATRA: My first film, *Chutney Popcorn*, which I've been told some people call the "first Indian American narrative feature," was about a lesbian woman who offers to be a surrogate for her sister who can't have a baby, and the chaos and comedy that ensues from that. It's both an Indian American family comedy and a gay romantic comedy, which makes it part of a small but wonderful subgenre—I'm thinking of some amazing movies like *Saving Face* and *The Wedding Banquet*. My theory is, maybe there's permission to tell these family stories through the lens of being LGBTQ, because, look, we've already disappointed our immigrant parents by being filmmakers, so why not just skip ahead in the disappointment graph and publicly talk about being gay too? Let's just double down; what do we have to lose?

KAL PENN: I think family stories just give off a feeling of universality. From a business perspective, it might also be a result of decisions that happen at the studio level. I'd be really curious to know if we've seen more Asian American family stories because they fit into a business quadrant in a way that others don't. We have so much talent within this community, and it's not like we're a one-note group of people with just one particular type of story. But one of the things we always push up against is this notion of Asian Americans being perpetual foreigners, right? So maybe immigrant family stories are the more palatable or profitable narratives right now.

Is there a particular challenge in telling stories about something as intimate as family?

NISHA: Well, yes, because you're mining from your personal experience, and you never know when you'll accidentally hit a nerve. When I was writing *Chutney Popcorn*, I interrogated my aunt about what pregnancy felt like and how it changed her world, because I had no idea what it was like. I was constantly interviewing them about it, and fortunately, they didn't raise an eyebrow. I didn't tell them about the gay stuff. As a result, my dad first found out I was gay when he attended the film's premiere at the Los Angeles Independent Film Festival. I never had the chance to warn him, and I was sitting there in my seat thinking, "Wait . . . is this how I'm coming out to my father?" To his credit, he was totally cool with it. His biggest criticism was that there was no dad in the film. "My story's not in there at all," he complained. So, my next film, *Cosmopolitan*, was inspired by him and his story, and his response after he saw it was, "I guess the lesson is to be careful what you wish for."

KAL: I need to begin with a bit of a tangent. I know you talked to [John] Cho—I'm not sure if he told you how I ended up being in *The Namesake*, but it happened like this: He and I are both avid readers, and I think this was when we were making the second *Harold and Kumar*. Out of the blue he asked me,

"What do you think of Jhumpa Lahiri?" And I said to him, "Jhumpa who?" and he flipped out. "You don't know who Jhumpa Lahiri is?" He used the same tone with me as when he found out I'd never tried scotch. And yes, people need to know that John Cho is the man who taught me how to drink scotch. But he also gifted me a copy of *Interpreter of Maladies* and said, "Jhumpa Lahiri won the Pulitzer for this." Well, I obviously loved it. Then when *The Namesake* came out, after we read it, we called each other and said, "Okay, well obviously we're going to try to get the rights to this, right?"

We reached out as fast as we could, only to find out that Mira Nair had already optioned the film. And that actually made us breathe a huge sigh of relief: "Thank God it's her; we could not have done justice to this book." After that, it was all about trying to get cast in the film. I campaigned aggressively for it. And one of the reasons I ultimately landed the audition was that Mira's twelve-year-old son was a huge *Harold and Kumar* fan.

But to your point about intimacy: Jhumpa's book was an incredibly intimate story. You learn that Gogol, the protagonist, lost his virginity at Yale, in this one specific dorm room that you can actually go find on campus. She even tells us his ATM passcode. I mean, it's all there, right? So as somebody who loves backstory, that intimacy was wonderful to me. Fourteen-year-old me connected with *The Catcher in the Rye* because of its detail and intimacy, even though I'm obviously not a rich, white New England boarding school kid.

And Jhumpa's writing made me feel that way—except this was *our* story. I just thought, "Wow, this is . . . this is incredible." And I shared my feelings about that with a couple folks in my parents' generation: "Hey auntie, did you read this book *The Namesake*?" And they said something to the effect of, "Yeah, I didn't understand what the big deal was. It's just our story. I lived it; why do I need to read a

novel about it?" I was like, "Oh my gosh, such a classic cynical auntie response."

So that's one challenge to telling these stories—to the people who actually lived them, all of that exploration of sacrifice, connection, disconnection, reconnection may feel like it's nothing new. For them, that intimacy is just familiarity. But for us, the generations coming up, we experience them with a different set of eyes.

What do Asian American family stories teach us?

NISHA: I think they teach us that every Asian American family is different! For me, in *Chutney Popcorn*, I wanted to focus on the idea that despite all the things this family put one another through, they were going to find a way to stay together—that all of the craziness was just part of the love that they have for one another. And that the baby at the end is going to be okay, because this family is gonna get their shit together for the next generation. I had a very painful relationship in some ways with my mom, because she always let me know that she had all these expectations of me and I wasn't meeting them, but I never once doubted that she loved me and that I was the most important thing in her life. And that's something I always took for granted and never really celebrated, until I made that film.

KAL: These movies bring complexity to how people see us. It's common for Asians to be born with a name and then to adopt a new one for whatever reason as they grow older. Like, my name is Kalpen Modi, and professionally I ended up using just Kal Penn. But in *The Namesake*, Gogol is born with a Russian author's name, and he changes it to Nikhil to embrace his Indian cultural roots—it's the opposite journey that many of us take.

That specificity makes him more human; it allows more people to really see him. It's part of why people who are fourth-generation Americans from non-AAPI communities come up to me and say how much they love *The Namesake*, how it made them call their parents as soon as they got out of the theater. Fans of that movie are touched by the family element of that story irrespective of their own background. It makes me a little emotional even saying it.

There are so many dimensions of complexity to families, and Asian ones in particular—immigrant status, culture and language differences, generation gaps. I think that's why family ends up as such a good foundation on which to build all kinds of stories.

KAL: Oh, definitely. The first time I remember seeing Indian Americans on-screen that were not cartoon characters voiced by white actors or people in brownface was in [Mira Nair's] *Mississippi Masala*, with Sarita Choudhury and Denzel Washington. I saw it with my parents and my cousin—I was probably twelve years old at the time—and it was the first time I'd ever seen characters who looked like us on-screen, who were flawed and complex and a little racist, and who made love. They were all of the things we never see ourselves as on camera.

NISHA: The complexity of our family situations is a major source of drama, but also comedy. There's a scene in *Chutney Popcorn* where the mom, played by the incredible Madhur Jaffrey, is trying to conduct a Hindu ritual to bless the baby before birth. And so you have me—I ended up playing the lead in my first film because the only other Indian American lesbian actress I knew couldn't do it last minute!—in the traditional "mother-to-be" role for the ritual. My girlfriend [was] played by Jill Hennessy as the "husband," and my sister—Madhur's real-life daughter, Sakina Jaffrey—was in the "brother" role. And then when [the mom] gets to Nick Chinlund, who plays the white biological father of the baby, she's just like, "Well, you just stand over there." This ritual doesn't accommodate the unique shape of this

family situation, yet they make it work. And you know what's funny? Four years ago, I had a baby girl, and at the baby shower my mom basically reenacted that scene from the movie!

Immigrant parents are constantly being challenged to adapt what they've brought here to the American culture in which we were raised. Which is why there's nothing more resourceful than an immigrant parent.

KAL: My parents are from the post-1965 wave of immigration, which means, you know, my dad's an engineer and the only reason he was allowed to come to America is because there was a shortage of American-born engineers. Of course, he's going to encourage his kid to do something like that. It's literally what got him here. But I wanted to apply to NYU's acting program, and I remember my parents telling me, "Nope, you're not going to do that." But I did anyway and got to the audition stage, which meant taking an hour-long trip into Manhattan, because we lived in New Jersey at the time. Well, it snowed the night before my audition, and I woke up to my dad saying, "Get up, get up, you're going to be late." I said, "Dad, the trains are going to be shut down," and he said, "I know! That's why I'm driving you."

NISHA: Immigrant parents know how to adapt. My mom would take us to the Sikh temple when we were growing up because the Hindu temple was too far away. She was like, "Oh, it's fine; God is God." I love the fact that back then, there were so few of us that we would all come together and mingle just because we were the only South Asians around. And movies were a big part of it: Bollywood would unite us across historical divisions of class, caste, language, ethnicity, and faith. Its biggest stars include actors who are Hindu, Muslim, and Sikh, and they'd all show up on-screen together as equals, and we'd cheer for them together. So that's what's in our souls, you know?

8

What the Heart Wants

THE CHEAT · SAYONARA · BRIDGE TO THE SUN · COME SEE THE PARADISE · JU DOU · CHUNGKING EXPRESS · DILWALE DULHANIA LE JAYENGE · IN THE MOOD FOR LOVE · MY SASSY GIRL · SAVING FACE · EVERYTHING BEFORE US · THE EDGE OF SEVENTEEN · TO ALL THE BOYS I'VE LOVED BEFORE · ALWAYS BE MY MAYBE · THE HALF OF IT · FIRE ISLAND

"Romance is not practical."
A Talk with **Simu Liu** and **Alice Wu**

ILLUSTRATION (OPPOSITE) BY TOMA NGUYEN

In 2018, Asian America cracked open the gates of Hollywood with a battering ram of love, as rom-com *Crazy Rich Asians* smashed box office expectations and seemingly upended decades of top studio resistance to telling Asian stories and casting Asian performers. But it's worth noting that Asian America's cinematic odyssey began with romance as well.

Though silent-era star Sessue Hayakawa's early career saw him consigned to playing villains, traitors, and ne'er-do-wells, his simmering good looks and aura of sexual threat—as evidenced in his breakout film, *The Cheat*—made him extremely popular among (mostly white) female audiences in roles as a "forbidden lover." He was, at one point, one of the highest-paid stars of the time, earning the present-day equivalent of $150,000 a week at the peak of his career.

In the 1930s, the industry's self-imposed Hays Code prevented on-screen depictions judged to be immoral, including miscegenation. As a result, Hayakawa could not be shown on-screen as having a romance, even a forbidden one, with a non-Asian woman. That, and the rise of sound in motion pictures, ended his staggering run of success: The "talkies" caused audiences to learn that Hayakawa had a Japanese accent, which quickly led his fan base to lose interest.

By the 1960s, Hollywood began to phase out the production code, eventually replacing it with the motion picture rating system. Films like *Sayonara* and *Bridge to the Sun* depicted once-taboo interracial relationships, making them so mainstream that it would be decades before a Hollywood studio would make a movie focused on romance between a pair of Asian leads.

In the meantime, Asian Americans turned to films abroad to sate our passion for passion: We swooned over movies like *Ju Dou, Chungking Express, Dilwale Dulhania Le Jayenge, In the Mood for Love*, and *My Sassy Girl*, and so did a growing non-Asian audience. Indie movies like *Saving Face* and *Everything Before Us* gradually reintroduced romance to the Asian American canon, until the breakthrough success of *To All the Boys I've Loved Before* and other films made it safe once again for Asians to love one another on-screen—three generations of movie lovers who grew up and came of age from the forties to the nineties likely never saw a Hollywood film in which two Asian characters kissed.

The Cheat

**1915, NOT RATED, 59 MINUTES,
PARAMOUNT PICTURES, USA**

DIRECTOR: Cecil B. DeMille

STARRING: Sessue Hayakawa, Fannie Ward,
Jack Dean

WRITERS: Hector Turnbull,
Jeanie Macpherson

This film served as Japanese American silent star Sessue Hayakawa's big breakout—the role that turned him into a secret object of desire for millions of women across a nation that still largely saw Asians as an invasive species. He was framed as the villain in this somewhat lurid melodrama about a spoiled society woman named Edith Hardy (Ward) who spends money with abandon despite warnings from her husband, Richard (Dean). But even without money, Edith must keep up appearances, and so as treasurer of the local Red Cross, she attends a fundraising ball hosted by the fabulously wealthy Japanese ivory merchant Hishuru Tori (Hayakawa).

She catches Tori's eye, and he brings her to his artifact room to show her many valuable items he's gathered in his world travels. Anything he wants, he gets—and what he gets, he keeps. To demonstrate this to her, he takes a hot branding iron and sears his mark into one of his treasures, which both draws her to him and terrifies her. After the gala, a friend tells her of a scheme that can double her money in a day. Tired of living on the cheap, she takes the $10,000 in funds raised from the Red Cross gala and gives it to her friend. But the tip proves to have been a scam, and her friend says the money is gone. With the Red Cross seeking to pick up the proceeds the next day, Edith begs Tori for a loan to cover for her theft. He agrees, if he can sleep with her. She agrees, with great trepidation.

Shortly after she has transferred the money to the Red Cross, Richard tells her that his stock investments have proven wildly successful, and they are now very wealthy. Edith asks him for $10,000, saying she needs it to pay off a debt from gambling at bridge, and he gives it to her without question. But when she seeks to repay Tori, he rejects the money, telling her that their bargain was set and can't be unwound: He will have her, then and there. She struggles in his

I always associate this film with *The Clansman*, a.k.a. *The Birth of a Nation*, as foundational textbook lessons by masterful Hollywood directors both in how to make motion pictures and how to appeal to the most visceral racist emotions of white America. Like the Black politicians hideously portrayed by D. W. Griffith as dangerous rapists threatening the sanctity of white womanhood during Reconstruction, Sessue Hayakawa's Tori is framed as preying on a white woman he seeks to brand as his sexual conquest. But unlike Griffith's crude characters in stereotypical blackface, Hayakawa appears suave and handsome, making his performance subversively alluring. The message at the time, however, was clear: Don't be seduced by the romantic charm, cultural sophistication, or economic power of those "sneaky Japs." This builds over the next quarter century until the mass incarceration of Japanese Americans becomes a commonsense proposition for most white people steeped in Yellow Peril thinking.

—SCOTT KURASHIGE ON *THE CHEAT*

embrace, and finally, to prove that she is irrevocably his, he takes the branding iron and presses its hot tip against her shoulder. She screams and flails at him to get away, finally grabbing hold of a pistol and shooting him in the shoulder. Richard bursts into the room to find his wife disheveled and Tori wounded. When the police arrive, he tells them he was the one who shot Tori, who allows the ruse to continue as Richard is arrested. The case goes to trial, and Richard makes it clear he intends to take the fall for the shooting, and Tori is happy to see him imprisoned, as it will give him free rein to pursue Edith. Richard is found guilty, to Tori's satisfaction, until Edith bursts out that she was the one who shot him—pleading that it was in self-defense against his brutality. In her defense, she pulls her dress away from her shoulder and displays the brand that has been burned into her lily-white skin. Horrified, the onlookers in the court rush at Tori

to lynch him, but the judge prevents them from doing so. Richard is declared innocent, and a docile Edith leaves the courtroom with him.

The depiction of an "exotic oriental man" as a ravenous sexual beast, barely disguised in the trappings of an elegant gentleman, was par for the course for the time; women fainted in theaters when Hayakawa thrust himself upon star Fannie Ward, ostensibly out of fear, but almost certainly from lust as well.

ABOVE: Fannie Ward (left), Utake Abe, and Sessue Hayakawa
OPPOSITE: *The Cheat* turned Sessue Hayakawa into a sex symbol—but his role in the film was as its villain, a framing that he'd have to tolerate through most of the movies he made in his career. Here (opposite) **Jiyeun Kang** reimagines *The Cheat* as it was really experienced by its female viewers—as a dark, sultry romance of forbidden pleasures and temptations.

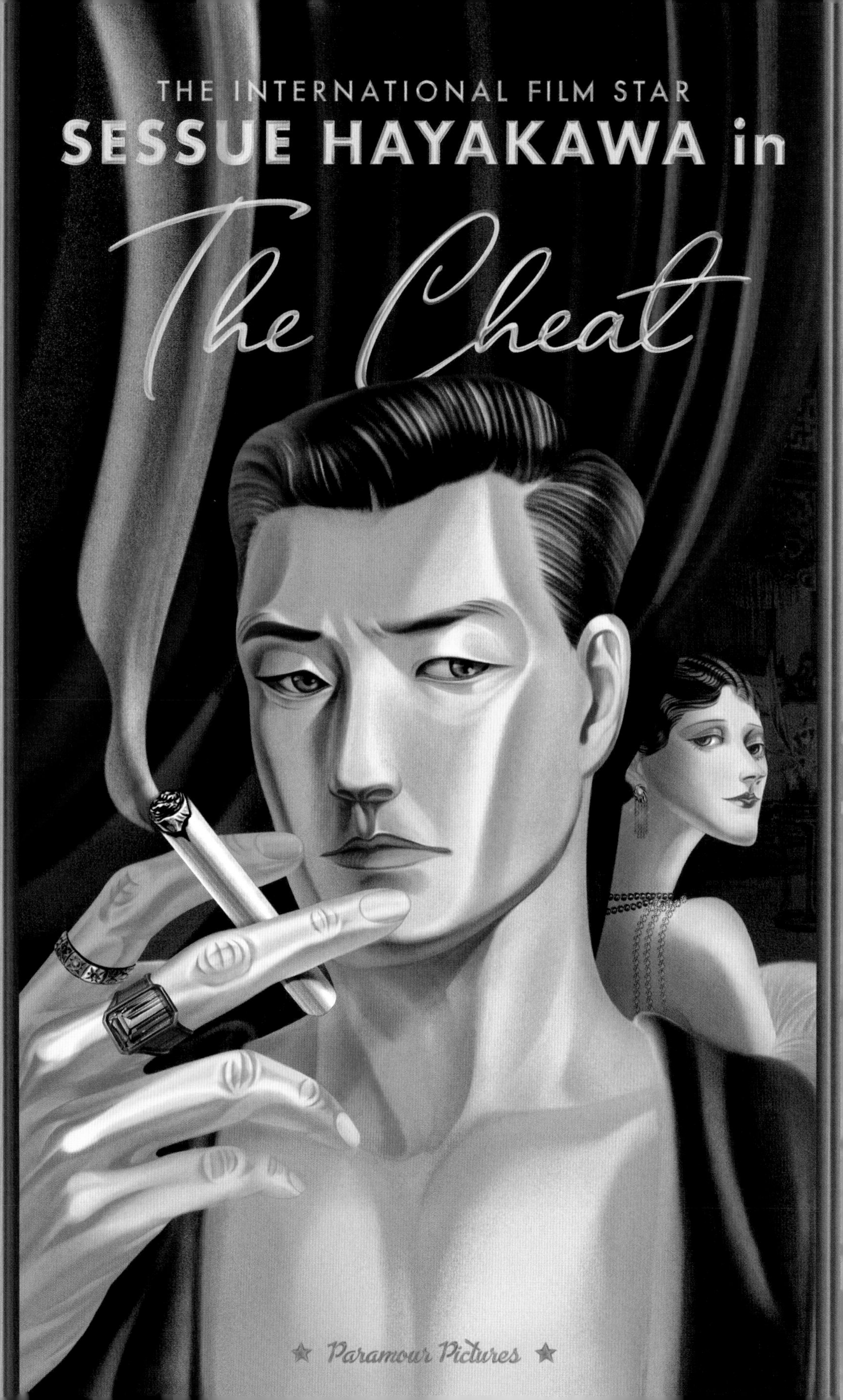
THE INTERNATIONAL FILM STAR
SESSUE HAYAKAWA in
The Cheat
Paramour Pictures

Miyoshi Umeki and Marlon Brando

Sayonara

**1957, NOT RATED, 147 MINUTES,
WARNER BROS., USA**

DIRECTOR: Joshua Logan

STARRING: Marlon Brando, Patricia Owens,
James Garner, Martha Scott, Miiko Taka,
Miyoshi Umeki, Red Buttons, Ricardo
Montalbán

WRITER: Paul Osborn

**BASED ON THE NOVEL BY
JAMES A. MICHENER**

It's hard to imagine that up until 1948, interracial marriage was still illegal in thirty-one states, including California, and of these, sixteen continued to enforce anti-miscegenation laws until 1967, when the Supreme Court case *Loving v. Virginia* struck down racial marriage restrictions across the full United States. *Sayonara*, based on a book by bestselling war novelist James Michener, was one of the first and highest-profile movies to focus on prejudices encountered by contemporary interracial couples. The film won four Academy Awards, including a Best Supporting Actress honor for Miyoshi Umeki, the first ever awarded to an Asian woman.

Marlon Brando plays hotshot Air Force pilot Major Lloyd Gruver, who earned his nickname "Ace" through his fighter duty in the Korean conflict. His commanding officer transfers him to noncombat duty at Japan's Itami Air Force Base. Ace becomes embroiled in the legal struggle of one of his airmen, Joe Kelly (Buttons), to obtain military approval for his desire to marry a Japanese woman, Katsumi (Umeki).

Ace is initially against Joe's romance, even referring to Katsumi using a slur. He soon apologizes, however, and agrees to be Joe's best man.

Ace's awakening has just begun: He soon falls in love with Hana-ogi (Taka), the star of a Japanese musical theater troupe. Eileen (Owens), Ace's now ex-fiancée, also finds a Japanese lover, in Kabuki performer Nakamura (played in yellowface by Mexican American actor Ricardo Montalbán). But before any of these new romances can truly blossom, tragedy strikes: Joe and a pregnant Katsumi, threatened with separation by a military that disapproves of their relationship, take their lives in a double suicide. The mixed couples find no approval among the Japanese populace either, who beset the military base with anti-American protest signs, degenerating into street fighting. But Joe's death only makes Ace even more resolved to marry Hana-ogi, who has been sent from Kobe to a theater in Tokyo, in part to separate her from Ace. He tracks her down to a new performance venue and begs her to accept him as her husband, despite the potential troubles. She agrees, and they exit the theater together to find themselves surrounded by reporters from both Japanese and American publications asking how they intend to explain their romance to the military brass. The movie ends with its own title, as Ace and Hana-ogi's final message is short and sweet to those who refuse to accept them: "Sayonara."

Bridge to the Sun

1961, NOT RATED, 113 MINUTES, MGM, US/FRANCE

DIRECTOR: Etienne Périer

STARRING: Carroll Baker, James Shigeta, James Yagi, Tetsurō Tamba, Sean Garrison, Ruth Masters, Nori Elisabeth Hermann, Emi Florence Hirsch, Hiroshi Tomono

WRITERS: Charles Kaufman

BASED ON THE AUTOBIOGRAPHY BY GWENDOLEN TERASAKI

Arriving a few years after the big-budget interracial romance *Sayonara*, this film, *Bridge to the Sun*, is well ahead of its time in how it explores the challenges faced by a real-life cross-cultural married couple, diplomatic aide Hidenari Terasaki and self-described "Southern belle" Gwen Harold. The pair wed in the mid-thirties and managed to preserve their marriage throughout the bloody war between their two

countries, despite the resilient prejudices of the people
around them in Japan and
the US.

"Terry" Terasaki
(Shigeta) meets Gwen
(Baker) at a Japanese
embassy reception, and
they're immediately drawn
to each other. Despite their
differences, they fall in
love and decide to marry.
Gwen's aunt wonders out
loud why she'd marry
him over a "nice, clean"
American young man, and
Terry's boss, the Japanese
ambassador, warns Gwen
that through his relationship with her, Terry is
endangering his career—a
word of advice tinged with
foreboding. They wed any-
way and move to Tokyo
after Terry is recalled to
his home country. Shortly
after Gwen gives birth
to their daughter, Mako
(Hirsch), Terry is posted to
Washington, DC, and brings
the family with him.

James Shigeta and Carroll Baker

Late 1941 arrives, and
the world is at war; while America is officially neutral,
more voices urge the US to enter the conflict. Given
Imperial Japan's allied status with Germany, that
would put the two nations at violent odds—something
Terry personally and politically wants to avoid. He
even commits a major breach of protocol, contacting
US president Franklin D. Roosevelt to urge him to
preserve peace, but it is too late; militarists have surrounded the emperor, and a decision from the throne
itself cannot stop the inevitable.

On December 7, 1941, Japan strikes first, bombing Pearl Harbor, Hawaii, and pushing the US into
the war. In the wake of the surprise attack, Terry
is deported to Japan; Gwen and Mako go with him
rather than be separated, and to flee the anti-
Japanese fervor erupting around them. But they
encounter similar anti-American hatred once they
arrive, especially given Terry's status as a pacifist
within the diplomatic corps. In one air raid, Gwen is
horrified to see Mako's school targeted, and she runs
to her to find her unharmed but sad and terrified:
Even before the bombing began, her classmates had
been bullying her as the "American kid." The family

relocates out of Tokyo to a friend's empty house on the city's outskirts. But war fervor is taking over everyone, even former supporters of peace like Terry's cousin Ishi (Tomono), who has joined the kamikaze corps. Terry again pushes Gwen to return to America, telling her that staying in Japan would not be safe, but she refuses to leave him. The war weighs heavily in Japan, and US invasion is imminent, as Gwen and Terry become targets of military police as a suspect couple with obvious American ties. (Meanwhile, Mako, a child of war, is growing up cold and inured to loss, refusing to mourn even as friends of hers are killed around her.) Shortly after invasion, the emperor delivers his famous radio address—his first speech given in public—and announces Japan's surrender.

With the war over, Terry once more pleads with Gwen to return to the US with Mako. This time feels different; Gwen knows that it is Japanese wartime custom for soldiers to send their families away before they die. She agrees to leave, and after they kiss for one last time, Terry waves goodbye to her and Mako as they depart, assuring her they'll be together again soon, though both know this to be untrue. As the ship sails off and Terry's figure disappears in the distance, Gwen breaks down in tears. Though not a critical or box office success, *Bridge to the Sun* remains a curious and compelling document—one of the few movies of its era to focus on an interracial couple as part of a tight-knit family rather than in the context of courtship, showing the social, cultural, and political challenges they face to stay together.

Come See the Paradise

1990, R, 138 MINUTES, TWENTIETH CENTURY FOX, USA

DIRECTOR/WRITER: Alan Parker

STARRING: Dennis Quaid, Tamlyn Tomita, Sab Shimono, Shizuko Hoshi, Stan Egi, Ronald Yamamoto, Akemi Nishino, Naomi Nakano, Brady Tsurutani, Elizabeth Gilliam, Shyree Mezick, Caroline Junko King, Pruitt Taylor Vince, Colm Meaney, Becky Ann Baker

This film, in retrospect, feels like a complement to *Bridge to the Sun* (1961), telling the story of an interracial couple on the other side of the US/Japan war divide. Though it has been criticized by some as a "white savior" story—telling the tale of a traumatic chapter in Japanese American history through the convenient lens of a white protagonist's drama—it was also the first Hollywood film to depict the incarceration of Japanese Americans in a sympathetic and emotionally nuanced light, while giving Tamlyn

Tomita (best known at the time for her role as Kumiko in 1986's *The Karate Kid Part II*) her first substantial dramatic role.

Tomita plays Lily Kawamura, who, at the beginning of the film, is seen walking with her young daughter Mini (Gilliam) and telling her about her father, Jack (Quaid). In the run-up to World War II, two decades earlier, Jack had been a motion picture projectionist involved in labor organizing in the profession. During a protest against non-union theaters in New York, a member of the union sets a venue ablaze, leading to a death that in part implicates Jack. He moves cross-country and takes a job in Los Angeles to escape the law—ironically as a non-union projectionist—at a movie theater owned by a Japanese American family, the Kawamuras.

Dennis Quaid, Caroline Junko King, and Tamlyn Tomita

While working there, Jack falls in love with his boss's daughter, Lily, and ends up eloping with her to Seattle, given the disapproval of the Kawamuras and the laws against miscegenation that still operated in California. The couple has a daughter named Mini—but when the US enters the war, the incarceration of Japanese Americans sweeps up both Lily and Mini, who are sent away to the Manzanar camp, leading to an extended family reunion under the darkest of circumstances.

Jack, meanwhile, has been drafted into the army, and it is months before he can make his way to the camp, meeting with his father-in-law, Hiroshi "Harry" Kawamura (Shimono), to tell him that he has gone AWOL from his unit and is prepared to spend the rest of the war with the Kawamuras behind barbed wire. Harry tells him to return to the army and finish his service, after giving his belated blessing to their marriage—but after Jack rejoins his unit, he is immediately arrested by FBI agents for arson and manslaughter, as they have finally tracked down his connection to that crime. The movie ends with Lily and an adolescent Mini at the station as the train arrives, bringing Jack, who has completed his prison time, back together with the daughter who barely remembers him and the wife he hasn't seen for decades in a heartwarming reunion.

At the time of this film's release, Dennis Quaid had come off a string of box office hits, and Alan Parker's prior film, *Mississippi Burning* (1988), was similarly a critically acclaimed social-issue movie; but while *Burning* was a commercial success and received seven Academy Award nominations, *Paradise* went largely unnoticed and underseen, in part because it was only shown in a handful of theaters in a few major cities. Would a smaller movie with a lower budget—*Paradise* cost $17.5 million, more than

Burning—and, perhaps, a more Japanese American–centered story have found its niche? We'll never know. There hasn't been a major studio release focused on the Japanese American incarceration since.

Ju Dou

1990, PG-13, 95 MINUTES, MIRAMAX, CHINA

DIRECTORS: Zhang Yimou, Fengliang Yang

STARRING: Gong Li, Li Baotian, Li Wei, Zhang Yi, Zheng Jian

WRITER: Heng Liu

This stunning work by Zhang Yimou was one of the milestones of the arrival of the "Fifth Generation" of mainland Chinese filmmakers—the first to graduate in 1982 from the nation's only film school, the Beijing Film Academy, after the chaos of the Cultural Revolution. Like his fellow Fifth Generation standout Chen Kaige, Zhang had been sent down to the countryside to engage in hard labor with almost no exposure to any kind of media; at BFA, he was given access to a wide range of formerly banned foreign films. The work of the Fifth Generation would be deeply shaped by both their Cultural Revolution experience and the brash visual and narrative experiments of French New Wave directors like Godard and Truffaut. *Ju Dou* shows earmarks of both sets of influences in its oblique criticism of authoritarian rule; its interweaving of dark, gritty reality with stunningly framed and colored imagery; and its subversive narrative, which deals overtly with sexuality, violence, and rebellion within the boundaries of a nontraditional family unit.

Gong Li plays the titular woman, a defiant, independent beauty who is given to a cruel and wealthy old man as a bride because her parents are too poor to provide her with a proper dowry. The man, Yang Jinshan (Li Wei), is the owner of a textile dyeing factory, which produces brightly colored cloth in bulk for sale to the apparel trade. Jinshan has already beaten two prior wives to death for not producing an heir for him—crimes whose atrocity is made even greater because Jinshan is the one who is impotent.

Jinshan's sole employee is his much younger nephew Yang Tianqing (Li Baotian), who instantly falls for Ju Dou but is too weak to do anything but secretly spy on her bathing. Ju Dou, aware that he's peeping, uses her bathing rituals to reveal the new bruises and contusions that Jinshan leaves on her body after each violent attempt at sex. The ill

Li Baotian and Gong Li

treatment moves Tianqing's empathy, even as her willing exposure of skin moves his lust. Soon, the two fall into an affair beneath Jinshan's eyes, which leads to Ju Dou getting pregnant. The two assert to Jinshan that the baby is his, which he accepts with surprising naivete. But after Jinshan suffers a stroke that leaves him paralyzed, Tianqing and Ju Dou engage in their affair openly before Jinshan, who is

When I was in grad school, I used to frequent a video store called Kim's Video Underground, and I still remember the time I rented this movie. Its title was labeled in yellow grease pencil on a flimsy DVD case, and there was a ripped photocopied cover on the front. It's a sexy, thrilling film, awash with the vibrant colors of yellow and red banners—a tightly woven 1920s-era story about a forbidden romance between a fabric dyer and his adoptive uncle's wife. The story is simple, perhaps too simple by today's standards, but I love the performances, the POV camerawork, its soundtrack, and its important look at oppression, rebellion, and legacy. Twenty years ago, I watched *Ju Dou* hunched over, wearing bulky headphones, because I was embarrassed what my roommates would think of the risqué images flickering on my monitor. Today, if anyone were to walk into my room while I was watching *Ju Dou*, I'd dim the lights, turn up the volume, and invite them to stay.

—DENNIS LIU ON *JU DOU*

now physically incapable of interfering with their love. But there is a more vulnerable individual within the house, Tianqing and Ju Dou's young son, Tianbai (Zhang), and Jinshan targets him for revenge, trying to set fire to the house to kill the child. Jinshan's plan is thwarted, but he obtains psychological vengeance when Tianbai addresses him as "Father." Jinshan's joy at being seen as Tianbai's father ends when the child accidentally tips his wheelchair into a dye vat, where the old man drowns.

Ju Dou and Tianqing are still together seven years later, still in love, and still operating the factory. But as a sullen teenager, Tianbai (Zheng) despises his parents, still believing that Jinshan is his father and feeling deep shame and horror at their open affair. Tianqing and Ju Dou have sex in the factory's cellar and fall into a daze due to a combination of fumes and low oxygen. Tianbai drags the pair out of the basement and drowns Tianqing in another dye vat. As Ju Dou realizes with horror what their son has done, she sets fire to the house and wanders the burning ruins alone, having lost everything in her life that matters to her. Along with Chen Kaige's *Farewell My Concubine*, *Ju Dou* is frequently considered to be a high-water mark for the directors of the Fifth Generation.

Chungking Express

1994, PG-13, 102 MINUTES, MIRAMAX, HONG KONG/CHINA

DIRECTOR/WRITER: Wong Kar-Wai

STARRING: Brigitte Lin Ching-Hsia, Takeshi Kaneshiro, Tony Leung Chiu-Wai, Faye Wong, Valerie Chow

Gorgeously shot and acted with agile, improvisational grace by the biggest stars in Cantonese cinema, *Chungking Express* is both a love letter to Hong Kong and a love letter to love; an elaborate neon journey around some of the island's most unique locations (including the densely packed enclave of Chungking Mansions, a single building housing thousands of low-income and mostly immigrant individuals and their ad hoc businesses, and the endless outdoor escalators that connect the wealthier private domains of the Mid Levels with the raucous streets of Central), and a pair of interwoven romantic pas de deux, each featuring a cop and a mysterious woman.

In the film's first story, a police officer named He Qiwu (Kaneshiro) is spending a month in mourning over his April 1 breakup with a girl named May by eating tins of pineapples, her favorite fruit, each of which has the expiration date of May 1—which also happens to be Qiwu's birthday. As he grieves his lost love and his lonely birthday at a seedy club, he runs into a striking, nameless woman in a blond wig, sunglasses, and trench coat (Lin). They strike up a conversation and eventually end up going to a hotel, where she falls asleep exhausted, leaving him to watch old movies on TV. After he departs to go jogging, she wakes up, heads to the Chungking Mansions, and shoots the drug lord who sabotaged her smuggling operation, then sends a "Happy Birthday" text to Qiwu, who is at a neighborhood snack bar where he's friends with the owner.

At the snack bar, he runs into a new employee named Faye (Wong)—the deuteragonist of the second story line. Faye is a dreamy young woman enamored with both the song "California Dreamin'" (by the Mamas and the Papas) and a different police officer, known only as Cop 663 (Leung); that cop, coincidentally, is also going through relationship troubles with his flight attendant girlfriend (Chow). The flight attendant drops by the snack bar to leave Cop 663's keys and a breakup letter, which Faye reads. She tells Cop 663 she has a letter for him from his girlfriend, but 663 refuses to read it, telling her to keep it for him. Faye subsequently uses 663's keys to break into his apartment, cleaning up and redecorating his apartment on the sly. Cop 663 notices that things are becoming cleaner and less miserable in his environment but doesn't consider why until he runs into Faye in the act. He realizes she's been interested in him all along and asks her on a date (suggesting that they meet at a restaurant called California). He gets stood up by Faye, and the owner of the snack bar tells 663 that Faye has flown to California, the state—although she has left him a boarding pass she's sketched on a napkin, which is valid on the one-year anniversary of their date.

A year later, Faye, who has taken a job as a flight attendant, returns to the old snack bar, which she discovers 663 has purchased and is renovating. He invites her to the grand opening of his new place and hands her the tattered boarding pass, which he has kept the whole time. She takes a napkin and begins to sketch him a new one, asking him where he wants to go. His response: "Wherever you'll take me."

While *Chungking Express* was a box office disappointment upon its release, it quickly became a hugely influential cult hit after the fact, with directors ranging from Quentin Tarantino (who released it in US theaters under his vanity label Rolling Thunder) to *Moonlight* Oscar winner Barry Jenkins calling it a major influence, and international film critics regularly calling it one of the greatest films of all time. Like so many of Wong's films, it captures both a fleeting moment in time and a transient emotional state in a way that seals them in cinematic amber, giving deeper meaning and unexpected spotlight to small gestures and happenstance, much like one does in the early days of a romance.

Dilwale Dulhania Le Jayenge

1995, NOT RATED, 181 MINUTES, AMAZON PRIME VIDEO, INDIA

DIRECTOR: Aditya Chopra

STARRING: Shah Rukh Khan, Kajol, Amrish Puri, Farida Jalal, Satish Shah, Achala Sachdev, Himani Shivpuri, Pooja Ruparel, Anupam Kher, Parmeet Sethi, Mandira Bedi, Anaita Shroff Adajani, Karan Johar, Arjun Sablok

WRITERS: Aditya Chopra, Javed Siddiqui

One of the most beloved movies in Bollywood canon, this film served as director Aditya Chopra's debut and a showcase for the talents of superstars Kajol and especially Shah Rukh Khan—the actor known as the "King of Bollywood." Prior to *DDLJ*, as the movie is frequently called, Khan had been primarily known for his powerful performances as villains and antiheroes; this film gave him the means to transition to romantic lead, and from there to iconic status as the industry's most popular actor.

The Maratha Mandir theater in Mumbai; Shah Rukh Khan on-screen

For NRIs—Non-Resident Indians living abroad—*DDLJ* served as a loving inclusion of their diasporic experience into a cinematic industry that was often the main means they stayed tethered to their distant home. Khan and Kajol play Raj and Simran, respectively, two young NRIs living in London. Simran's family is strict and traditional, while Raj's is more freewheeling and progressive; Simran's father (Puri) has already promised to betroth her to Kuljeet (Sethi), the son of a close childhood friend (Shah) in India. While Simran is brokenhearted at having to marry a stranger, she accepts her duty and asks only that she be allowed to go on a trip with her friends before her engagement. Her father reluctantly agrees, and she sets off on her journey across Europe.

It's on this trip that Raj and Simran meet and fall in love. Simran shares her secret with her mother (Jalal), unaware that her father is listening in; he explodes at her and vows that the family will leave for India immediately. Unaware of this, Raj dreamily tells his father (Kher) about the amazing woman he met, and is encouraged by him to go pursue her, even though Raj knows that Simran is already set to be wed. Raj shows up at her house the next day but is told by their next-door neighbor that the family is gone—they've sold the house and left for the motherland.

Back in India, Simran meets Kuljeet and finds him arrogant and unpleasant. She longs for Raj but is told by her mother that their love is impossible due to her father's intransigence. Raj shows up on their doorstep the very next day, having tracked her down with the help of their friends, and Simran asks him to run away with her. He refuses: He will only marry her if her father gives his blessing. Instead, Raj makes friends with Kuljeet, and as Kuljeet's best new pal, insinuates himself into the good graces of Simran's family. But Raj's true identity is soon discovered—first by Simran's mother, who tells them to quickly elope, and then by her father, who slaps Raj in the face for his lies and sends him on his way.

A heartbroken Raj heads for the train station, where he encounters a furious Kuljeet and a gang of his friends; they attack him and are only stopped when Simran's and Kuljeet's fathers arrive. Raj boards the train, but when Simran catches up, she demands to join him, saying she can't live without him. Her tears and sincere emotion move her father, who finally relents and lets her go, and she runs and catches the train just before it leaves the station.

DDLJ earned $60 million around the world, making it the highest-grossing Indian film of its time. It also holds a distinctive world record as the longest running film in Indian cinematic and possibly world history: As of 2021, over a quarter century after it was first released, it is still being screened to nostalgic audiences at one theater in Mumbai, the Maratha Mandir cinema.

In the Mood for Love

2000, PG, 98 MINUTES, USA FILMS, HONG KONG/CHINA/FRANCE

DIRECTOR/WRITER: Wong Kar-Wai

STARRING: Maggie Cheung, Tony Leung Chiu-Wai, Siu Ping Lam, Rebecca Pan, Kelly Lai Chen, Joe Cheung, Chan Man-Lei, Chin Tsi-Ang, Roy Cheung, Paulyn Sun

If director Wong Kar-Wai's *Chungking Express* (1994) is an ode to love, *In the Mood for Love* is an elegy to it, a reverie on broken promises, missed opportunities, and ultimately, the passing of the mood for love. Like *Chungking*, it's a film that feels sumptuously larger than the moments it captures, but unlike *Chungking*, which is airy, light, and full of ping-pong coincidences that send characters rebounding through one another's lives, *Mood* is slow, deeply measured, each scene unfolding like a delicate and ephemeral blossom, until the moving path of fortune ultimately pushes the central pair apart.

Set in 1962 within the community of Shanghainese expats in the then-British colony, the film follows Chow Mo-wan (Leung), a reporter, and Su Li-zhen (Cheung), an office worker at a trading company, from their first encounter as apartment-complex neighbors whose spouses are mostly absent. Mo-wan and Li-zhen initially keep apart from one another, but after discovering that their respective partners are having an affair, they lean on one another for comfort.

Mo-wan invites Li-zhen to help him write a serial wuxia story he's penning for his newspaper; she agrees, but their collaboration leads to unwanted attention from others in the complex. As a result, Mo-wan rents a hotel room where they can work in private. Their relationship develops into mutual attraction, and when Mo-wan is offered a job in Singapore, he invites Li-zhen to go along. She accepts but is delayed in getting to his hotel and misses him. A year later, Li-zhen travels to Singapore to visit him, even calling him at the newspaper where he works, but says nothing when he answers the phone. Mo-wan only realizes that she was present when he sees a cigarette butt with her color of lipstick in an ashtray in his apartment. Later, Mo-wan talks about how in ancient times, people would hide secrets by whispering them into the cavities of trees, then sealing the holes with mud.

Three years pass, and Li-zhen visits the old complex again and finds that her former landlady is moving to the US. She asks her if the apartment is available for rent, and the landlady says yes. Mo-wan returns to Hong Kong as well and visits the complex to find that his former landlords have moved away; the new owner of the apartment tells him that next door also has new tenants, a woman and her son. At the end of the film, Mo-wan leaves without seeing Li-zhen again, and we see him traveling to Angkor Wat in Cambodia, where he finds a hollow in a wall and whispers something into it, before sealing the cavity with mud.

In the Mood for Love has been justifiably and almost universally acclaimed as one of the greatest films of all time; a remarkable achievement, given the tortured path of its creation, almost entirely due to Wong's unique, almost conversational filmmaking process: no script, just an outline, and constant reshooting of scenes again and again with different notes and improvisations until he gets what he instinctively wants. Fortunately, Leung and Cheung were both veterans of his process from prior movies and were willing to withstand the months and months of repetition it required; unfortunately, Wong's frequent collaborator, director of photography Christopher Doyle, was unable and perhaps unwilling to stay through Wong's months of iteration for this film, leaving the film for Taiwanese cinematographer Mark Lee Ping Bin to complete. (Doyle returned for *In the Mood for Love*'s 2004 sequel, *2046*, but similarly left midway through production.) *In the Mood for Love* forms a loose "love trilogy" together with *2046* and 1990's *Days of Being Wild*, with *Wild* focusing on longing and loneliness, *Mood* on missed opportunities, and *2046* on the lingering hollow mark left by the one that got away.

W hen I began the research for my book *Last Boat Out of Shanghai: The Epic Story of the Chinese Who Fled Mao's Revolution*, Wong Kar-Wai's *In the Mood for Love* was one of the first films I turned to. This sensual, haunting film transported me into that unsettled, disquieting world of displaced people who had lost all, including their connection to time, place, and the familiar that once was—postwar Hong Kong, when the colonial city's population had doubled almost overnight to two million. Like the star-crossed characters gorgeously played by Tony Leung and Maggie Cheung, many were from Shanghai: sophisticated, worldly exiles crammed together into steamy, sweaty, dingy, congested subdivided rooms, all yearning for what no longer existed and could never be. Instead, there was just the quiet desperation of longing, love, and loss in the narrow, winding streets of old Hong Kong. A feeling I hoped to convey and that I've embraced as a cautionary tale.

—HELEN ZIA ON *IN THE MOOD FOR LOVE*

My Sassy Girl

2001, NOT RATED, 137 MINUTES, ASIAN CRUSH, SOUTH KOREA

DIRECTOR/WRITER: Kwak Jae-yong

STARRING: Jun Ji-hyun, Cha Tae-hyun, Kim In-moon, Song Ok-sook, Han Jin-hee, Im Ho, Yang Geum-seok

BASED ON THE NOVEL BY KIM HO-SIK

Coming just a few years into the explosive rise of Korean pop culture known as "Hallyu" or the "Korean wave," this hilarious and heartbreaking comic romance was a huge success in its native country, in part because of how it played against conventional gender tropes that dominate depictions of Korean romance. Rather than being sweet and gentle, the female love interest is aggressive and violent; she drinks, swears like a sailor, lies whenever she opens her mouth, and drags the hapless male protagonist through an endless series of humiliations.

Gyeon-woo (Cha) is a kindhearted but passive engineering student who has had little luck with relationships. He finally gives in and heads to the train to see his aunt, who apparently knows of the perfect girl for him. In the station he sees a drunk girl (Jun, whose character is never named) teetering at the edge of the platform and pulls her out of harm's way just as the train arrives. He helps her onto the train, finding himself simultaneously attracted and repulsed by her, especially after she vomits on another passenger before fainting onto his shoulder. Gyeon-woo, panicked, takes her off the train at the next station and plants her on a bench, but he is unable to go through with abandoning her and finally takes her to a nearby hotel so she can sleep it off.

When the girl's phone rings, Gyeon-woo answers it without thinking; asked a battery of questions about where the girl is, he stammers out ambiguous responses, triggering the police to track the phone location and burst into the room, spraying Gyeon-woo's face with mace and dragging him off to prison. The next day, released from jail, he gets a phone call from the girl, who asks to meet to get a rundown of the night before. Unfortunately, after the meetup it all happens again: At the restaurant, she gets thoroughly

I'm pretty sure I first watched this movie via Napster download in my college dorm. But the low resolution of the video didn't affect how much I loved it. This was the first Korean movie I, and apparently many people around me, ever watched: Every girl I knew was trying to act "sassy," and every guy was dreaming of finding his own edgy princess (if she looked like Jun Ji-hyun it wouldn't hurt either). Personally, I felt empowered seeing a modern love story with an Asian male lead who was relatable to me compared to the hyper-macho leads I saw in American movies. The awkwardness, emotional vulnerability, and humor of Cha Tae-hyun's character made me feel confident in myself, and in playing my own characters in that fashion when it came time to write male leads. To this day, I'm still humming the soundtrack, still threatening "joo-gu-lae!?" and still adding hints of *My Sassy Girl* in much of my work, knowing that anything I make will still never be THE *Sassy Girl* (as the American reboot has shown!).

—PHILIP WANG ON *MY SASSY GIRL*

drunk while explaining that the reason she behaves as she does is that her boyfriend has left her, and Gyeon-woo has no choice but to bring her back to the same hotel again. But now that the ice has broken between them, the girl pops up regularly, pulling pranks on him (like dragging him out of his college while announcing that she's pregnant with his child), beating him when she's in a frustrated mood, and teasing him when she's feeling playful.

But every time you think you've pinned down their relationship, *My Sassy Girl* pulls you in a new direction, like its female lead does to Gyeon-wan. There are long gaps when the two don't interact at all, and any number of accidental, absurdly coincidental reunions. The twist ending of the film seems both confounding and entirely reasonable given the bizarre physics of the romantic world in which these two live. But it's an enormous credit to the two stars who occupy so much of the movie's screen time that you're never bored, and always willing to suspend disbelief, just to see what will happen next.

The sheer power of Jun Ji-hyun and Cha Tae-hyun's stardom can be seen in the fact that, despite never being released in the US, *My Sassy Girl*'s popularity throughout Asia led to it being remade in Hollywood with an all-white cast, led by Elisha Cuthbert as "the girl." Without its Korean leads, the remake fell painfully short of the original, both critically and commercially, totally missing both the whimsy and the heartfelt sincerity that made the original such a delight.

Saving Face

2004, R, 91 MINUTES, SONY PICTURES ENTERTAINMENT, USA

DIRECTOR/WRITER: Alice Wu

STARRING: Michelle Krusiec, Lynn Chen, Joan Chen, Jin Wang, Guang Lan Koh, Jessica Hecht, Ato Essandoh, Wang Luoyong, David Shih, Brian Yang, Nathaniel Geng, Mao Zhao

It's not going too far out on a limb to say that, for decades, *Saving Face* was the closest thing to a perfect romantic comedy that Asian American cinema had to offer—a heartfelt, nuanced, clever, and funny take at looking for love in all the wrong places and finding it right in front of you. But *Saving Face* was also the most sharply drawn comedy of Chinatown intergenerational manners since 1989's *Eat a Bowl of Tea*, and the most satisfying queer Asian American relationship story since 1993's *The Wedding Banquet*, all of which can be summed up as: If you haven't seen it, go see it.

Dr. Wilhelmina Pang (Krusiec), known to her friends as Wil, is a successful surgeon and a mostly

I saw *Saving Face* right when it came out, before I graduated high school. I knew right away how special it was, and after almost twenty years, I continue to rewatch it. It so perfectly captures the stakes of striking out from your own tight-knit immigrant community by being different, and the intense joy of finding out who around you will continue to love you when you show them who you truly are. The title still tickles me, as there's no direct Chinese translation for "saving face," because typically in Chinese we only speak of not wanting to "lose face" or hoping to be "given face" by others. Basically, the title is even more Chinese American than most people realize, and it's just perfect for a bona fide Chinese American classic.

—FRANKIE HUANG ON *SAVING FACE*

closeted lesbian whose mother, Hwei-lang Gao (Joan Chen), is determined to set her up with a "nice Chinese boy." Instead, at the dinner where Hwei-lang hopes to introduce her to the son of a friend, Wil meets Vivian (Lynn Chen), the daughter of another of Hwei-lang's social group, a recent divorcée. The two instantly hit it off, and the sparks that fly aren't merely platonic. But when Wil runs into Vivian again at the hospital where she works, Wil learns that Vivian's estranged father is none other than Dr. Shing (Wang Luoyong), Wil's boss. As if that weren't enough of a shock, she comes home to find her grandfather in a rage, threatening to turn her mother out onto the street after Hwei-lang reveals that she's pregnant and refuses to reveal the name of the father. With nowhere else to go, Hwei-lang moves in with Wil.

The presence of her pregnant mother makes it even more complicated for Wil to pursue her relationship with Vivian, but they manage to make it work, with Wil attending one of Vivian's dance performances and learning afterward that the two were friends as young children—and that Vivian had kissed Wil after she defended her from bullies. The two revisit that moment in the present, kissing each other after returning to Vivian's apartment. But as they date, Wil remains unwilling to kiss Vivian in front of others, especially her mother. (Wil later learns that her mother knows she's a lesbian but has refused to accept it, hoping it's just a phase.)

Meanwhile, Wil has pushed Hwei-lang to go on dates of her own, and Hwei-lang considers accepting a marriage proposal from Stimson Cho (Geng), a stable man who has always been enamored of her and is willing to be a father to Hwei-lang's unborn child.

Vivian reveals to Wil that she's been invited to join a prestigious dance program in Paris and is considering accepting. Dr. Shing leans on Wil to encourage her to take the offer, and Wil pulls away from Vivian, not wanting to be an obstacle to her professional growth. Nonplussed that Wil isn't trying to make her stay, Vivian accepts the offer, just as Wil's grandmother suddenly passes away, which pushes Hwei-lang to say yes to Cho's proposal. But Wil knows that Cho isn't the one Hwei-lang loves, after she discovered a secret letter pleading for Hwei-lang to ignore their difference in age and let him marry her. Armed with the letter, Wil breaks up the wedding ceremony, pointing to elderly pharmacist Old Yu (Mao) and encouraging him to follow through on his offer. Old Yu denies having written the letter, and suddenly, Little Yu (Yang), Old Yu's twentysomething-year-old son, stands up and says that he's the one—the letter's author and the baby's father.

In the chaos that erupts afterward, Wil pulls her mother out of the event and onto a bus, finally talking with her about love and the choices that one makes and doesn't make in the glare of the public eye. Hwei-lang explains why she initially didn't accept Little Yu's offer, and why she's going to now—and tells Wil that she, too, needs to choose to make her love public. With that encouragement, Wil races to the airport to catch Vivian before she leaves. But Vivian refuses to stay unless Wil makes the same kind of public declaration that Little Yu did, by kissing her then and there, in front of everyone. Wil can't bring herself to do it, and Vivian gets on the plane and leaves. Three months later, Wil attends a dinner in Hwei-lang and Little Yu's honor and once again sees Vivian, who has come back to visit her mother. Realizing that she's been given an unexpected second chance, Wil asks Vivian to dance, and then kisses her in front of everyone. Some people are shocked; Hwei-lang and Vivian's mom give them their blessing. And as the credits roll, Hwei-lang prods Wil with the *next* item on her checklist—when will Vivian and Wil give her a grandchild?

Everything Before Us

2015, NOT RATED, 99 MINUTES, GODIGITAL, USA/CANADA

DIRECTORS: Philip Wang, Wesley Chan

STARRING: Aaron Yoo, Brittany Ishibashi, Brandon Soo Hoo, Victoria Park, Randall Park, Joanna Sotomura, Chris Riedell, Ki Hong Lee

WRITERS: Wesley Chan, Chris Dinh, Philip Wang

This quietly compelling near-future romance drama was the first feature film to be made by Philip Wang and Wesley Chan, cofounders of the seminal YouTube production company Wong Fu; Wang and Chan raised over $350,000 through crowdfunding from 6,500 donors to cover much of the production cost.

The film imagines a world in which everything in one's life is shaped—or even determined—by a metric called emotional integrity, a kind of intersocial credit score that is influenced positively by being in successful, long-term relationships and negatively by break-ups, infidelity, and dishonesty toward one's partner. EI is seen as a predictor of maturity, stability, team spirit, and trustworthiness; those with low EI scores can't get jobs or bank loans and may end up pushed to the fringes of society in favor of those with more robust relationship histories. EI scores are tracked by a government entity called the Department of Emotional Integrity (DEI), which issues initial EI baseline determinations with written tests and then "audits" the EI of every adult American on an ongoing basis, tracking relationship successes and failures—and apportioning

Victoria Park and Brandon Soohoo

blame for the latter based on face-to-face interviews with couples.

Ben (Yoo) is rejected for a prestigious design job because of his low EI score, the result of a breakup with his ex-girlfriend Sara (Ishibashi), in which he was assigned the majority of the blame. His friend Henry (Riedell) pushes him to go to the DEI to attempt to get his and Sara's scores rebalanced. During the audit, Sara and Ben disagree over the reasons for their breakup but eventually agree to sign off on a fifty-fifty split of the blame, allowing Ben to get the job he's been seeking. At his new company, Ben meets and begins dating a coworker, Anna (Sotomura), but ends up kissing his ex Sara while painting a mural on a blank wall at her new café. When Anna finds out about Ben's kiss, she threatens to break up with him, jeopardizing his EI score and job. DEI agents audit Sara's EI record, accusing her

When this film premiered, it felt like a glimpse into a collective far-off future. The idea of a "Department of Emotional Integrity" and every individual being assigned a social/relationship score seemed so implausibly distant. And then almost overnight, social technology accelerated, and it felt like all of a sudden Big Brother was watching over our online behaviors—stop pushing ramen ads to me!—and online apps where we could rate and judge one another had suddenly become woven into the culture. When the film came out, it was still escapism. But now it's reality. How did Wong Fu possibly predict this?

—DAN MATTHEWS ON *EVERYTHING BEFORE US*

of engaging in a fraudulent relationship with her high-EI friend Jeremy to boost her score; after the investigation, Sara's EI score is slashed, even as Ben's plummets due to his breakup with Anna. Sara loses her café, and Ben his design job.

Meanwhile, Seth (Soo Hoo) and Haley (Victoria Park) are attending different colleges while maintaining a long-distance relationship, which they've dutifully registered with the DEI. But Seth is jealous and suffocating, constantly visiting Haley and even transferring to her school without warning her. When she decides to attend a party thrown by a frat with a bad record of sexual misbehavior, Seth becomes angry, only to have Haley accuse him of stifling her independence and ruining her college experience. Haley, who has plans to study abroad in London, breaks up with him. Ben and Seth meet one another at the DEI, and Ben counsels Seth to prioritize the memory of what he and Haley had over the opportunity to exact revenge.

Inspired by Ben's advice, Seth ends up taking 100 percent of the blame for their breakup. Ben, who has been brought in as a witness to help the DEI make its case against Sara, instead tells the auditors that he loves her, and that the system they've created to enforce better relationships wrongly prevents them from developing in ways that allow true love to root and blossom. Against DEI policy, the lead auditor (Randall Park) shares Ben's testimony with Sara, which sets them on the path to reconciliation. Meanwhile, Seth and Haley part ways amicably, each starting new and separate lives.

Everything Before Us is an impressive effort by a set of young creators honed on the tropes of social media to expand their range and narrative maturity. A passion project funded by fan fervor and starring many of Wong Fu's talented friends, it paves a fresh track alongside the studio and conventional indie film routes—showing how stories can be built in collaboration with audiences from inception, by tightly knit groups of mutually supportive creators. In that sense, its message of the central importance of relationships in the not-so-distant future might well be prophetic.

The Edge of Seventeen

2016, R, 104 MINUTES, STX ENTERTAINMENT, USA

DIRECTOR/WRITER: Kelly Fremon Craig

STARRING: Hailee Steinfeld, Woody Harrelson, Kyra Sedgwick, Haley Lu Richardson, Blake Jenner, Hayden Szeto, Eric Keenleyside, Alexander Calvert, Nesta Cooper, Meredith Monroe

This teen romance was Hailee Steinfeld's breakout movie as an adult lead, after being nominated for a Best Supporting Actress Oscar at the age of thirteen for her performance in 2010's *True Grit*. It gave the multiracial actress (her maternal grandfather is half–African American and half-Filipino, and she has been vocal about her pride in those roots) ample room to show her emotional and comic range, earning her widespread critical acclaim, and Golden Globe and Critics' Choice nominations for best actress.

In *Edge of Seventeen*, Steinfeld plays a, wait for it, seventeen-year-old named Nadine Franklin who's growing up in Portland, Oregon, and struggling to find her social compass in the years after her beloved father's sudden passing. Her elder brother, Darian (Jenner), is no help: He's a sculpted jock who gets all the attention in high school, and their mother, Mona (Sedgwick), remarks to herself how lucky she is to have raised such a "perfect child" as Darian . . . in Nadine's presence. The only person she feels truly connected with is her best friend, Krista (Richardson), but even that bond is stretched and broken when Krista hooks up with none other than Darian. Nadine, feeling betrayed, turns to another

Hailee Steinfeld and Hayden Szeto

classmate, Erwin Kim (Szeto), for counsel. It's clear that Erwin has a crush on her, but Nadine's eyes are on another guy—handsome bad boy Nick (Calvert), who barely knows she exists.

When Nadine is dragged to a popular-people party by Krista and Darian, she finds herself pushed to the sidelines as Darian introduces his new girlfriend to all the cool kids; after a partygoer comments on what a dud Nadine is given that she's Darian's sibling, she leaves the party in a huff, calling Erwin to help her escape. They end up at an amusement park, where Erwin—thinking this is an opportunity

The best coming-of-age films make me cry. I shed tears of joy over youthful antics being depicted on-screen, and tears of sadness over adolescent angst. *The Edge of Seventeen*, though, had me sobbing until I couldn't tell the difference. The movie plays many of the genre's greatest hits: There's the spunky protagonist who thinks she has all the answers, and the cast of adults who are as wise as they are wry. Yet, the film feels fresh, thanks in large part to a script that understands how equally hilarious and miserable the liminal space between childhood and adulthood can be, and to a dazzling performance from Hailee Steinfeld. Her Nadine is so fully realized she might as well be, well, real; she's smart but shortsighted, defiant but vulnerable—a teenager, in other words. I wouldn't return to my own seventeenth year, but I'd gladly watch hers again, anytime.

—SHIRLEY LI ON *THE EDGE OF SEVENTEEN*

to move from friend to more—tries to kiss her on a Ferris wheel, only to be rebuffed. Fortunately, the miscommunication doesn't end their friendship, despite Nadine explaining to Erwin how she sees him in clumsily devastating fashion, comparing him to a "really nice old man, in a wheelchair, in a convalescent home." Erwin still stays friendly to her and even lets her crash his huge, luxurious house to use his swimming pool. During their evening together, Nadine discovers that he is a talented illustrator/animator and accepts his invite to check out his work at the school's showcase.

Meanwhile, Nadine's relationship with her mother is degenerating, culminating in an argument that ends with Nadine taking her mom's car. Still steaming, Nadine composes a sexually explicit text to Nick and realizes that sending it would be catastrophic—while also realizing she just sent it. Nick's response the next day is to invite her to hang out, but as soon as he picks her up, it's clear that his intentions are to make good on her sexting overtures. Angry and disappointed, she fights him off and ends up calling her favorite teacher, Mr. Bruner (Harrelson), who takes care of her until her brother arrives. On their way home, Nadine angrily accuses Darian of showing up only so he can play hero, and he responds that all the things that she thinks are perfect in his life are just a facade—he's as anxious and uncertain of the future as she is, and the one true thing that has kept him anchored is Krista. Their candid conversation brings them together as they haven't been since before their father died.

The next day, Nadine watches Erwin's animated film, about an alien boy in love with a human girl who looks oddly like Nadine. The film is hilarious and snarky but also sincere, and it makes Nadine realize just how much Erwin cares—and how much she's taken him for granted. After it ends, she hands him a bunch of flowers that she's picked and tells him how great he is—the best thing in her world, actually, like Krista is for Darian. The conclusion sweetly subverts the typical romantic tropes of teen rom-coms by having the dorky-but-earnest-guy-friend character win the protagonist's heart instead of the popular and handsome crush—a subversion made particularly interesting by the casting of Chinese Canadian Hayden Szeto in the dorky-but-earnest-guy-friend role.

To All the Boys I've Loved Before

2018, TV-14, 99 MINUTES, NETFLIX, USA

DIRECTOR: Susan Johnson

STARRING: Lana Condor, Noah Centineo, Janel Parrish, Anna Cathcart, Andrew Bachelor, Trezzo Mahoro, Madeleine Arthur, Emilija Baranac, Israel Broussard, John Corbett

WRITER: Sofia Alvarez

BASED ON THE NOVEL BY JENNY HAN

Along with box office sensation *Crazy Rich Asians* and the sleeper hit *Searching*, this film was a key part of the hype around "#AsianAugust"—a hashtag that went viral on social media as a defiant statement of pride in Asian America's arrival on the pop culture main stage. The other two films were released theatrically; *To All the Boys* landed on Netflix. Though it was based on a *New York Times* bestselling YA novel by Jenny Han, there were no outsized expectations for the film; it was released as part of Netflix's first real play at romance, what they called their "Summer of Love." Yet *To All the Boys* quickly distinguished itself as a standout success and was even singled out in the company's annual report as one of its "most viewed original films ever, with strong repeat viewing."

To All the Boys stars Lana Condor as shy high schooler Lara Jean Covey, who has developed the

Noah Centineo and Lana Condor

habit of writing love letters to her crushes and storing them in a box in her closet, never to be mailed. But Lara Jean's little sister, Kitty (Cathcart), has different plans in mind when she discovers the box. The following Monday, Lara Jean runs into Peter Kavinsky (Centineo), who shows her the letter, addressed to him, and asks what it's all about—causing her to spontaneously faint. She wakes up to find him leaning over her in concern and sees, out of the corner of her eye, yet another former crush approaching, letter in hand, so she pulls Peter into a kiss to avoid being confronted once again, before escaping the mortifying scene. She later explains the kiss to Peter, and her explanation sparks a thought from him: Maybe they could publicly pretend that they're dating. That would simultaneously help fend off any additional letter recipients while also making Peter's ex-girlfriend Gen (Baranac) jealous. Lara Jean agrees, and they launch the ruse.

But as is often the case, their acting proves too effective: They begin to catch real feelings for each other and end up kissing in a hot tub during the school ski trip. Somehow, video of the hot tub kiss ends up on social media—taken from a particularly salacious angle—causing the whole school to buzz about the nature of their relationship. With Lara Jean's life crashing down around her ears, Kitty admits that she was the one who sent her letters, sending Lara Jean into a fury that only their older sister, Margot (Parrish), home from college for a visit, can calm. Margot tells her that Kitty simply did what Lara Jean always wanted to do herself if she'd had the confidence. Together, they manage to get Instagram to take down the video, and when school starts again after Christmas break, Peter tells everyone that nothing happened in the hot tub. But to Lara Jean, he finally tells her that he's in love with her for real, and they share a final kiss before walking off into tomorrow together.

Following the booming success of *To All the Boys*, Netflix moved the book's two sequels, *P.S. I Still*

Love You and *Always and Forever, Lara Jean*, into rapid development—followed by a spinoff TV series, *XO, Kitty*, focused on the adventures of Lara Jean's little sister in Korea, making this the first legitimate Asian American multimedia franchise.

Always Be My Maybe

2019, PG-13, 101 MINUTES, NETFLIX, USA

DIRECTOR: Nahnatchka Khan

STARRING: Ali Wong, Randall Park, James Saito, Michelle Buteau, Vivian Bang, Daniel Dae Kim, Keanu Reeves

WRITERS: Ali Wong, Randall Park, Michael Golamco

It's indicative of how much the world has changed for Asian Americans in Hollywood that this film became a reality: an offhand remark made by star and co-writer Ali Wong in a *New Yorker* interview. When asked what her dream project would be, she mentioned that she and *Fresh Off the Boat* star Randall Park had always talked about making a romantic comedy—"our version of *When Harry Met Sally*." The

mental image of longtime friends and famously funny people Wong and Park as rom-com protagonists went viral on social media, prompting producers and studio execs to begin reaching out to the pair about the project, which at the time was not a project, or even a script. The sudden interest inspired Wong, Park, and their mutual friend Michael Golamco to begin writing one, and in record time, they had something to pitch to Netflix—where Wong's stand-up comedy specials had already established a substantial fan following among viewers and Netflix execs.

With *Fresh Off the Boat* creator Nahnatchka Khan attached as director and Netflix enthusiastically behind the project, the creators were free to fulfill their wildest rom-com fantasies—and the results were indeed wild. Wong and Park play Sasha Tran and Marcus Kim, next-door neighbors who grew up as the closest of childhood friends, until as high school students they had a fumbling first sexual encounter in Marcus's car in the wake of the untimely death of his mother. After they make love, due to a combination of guilt and awkward inexperience, Marcus treats Sasha poorly, and they end up having a fight that drives a wedge between them for the next sixteen years. In that interim, Sasha has become a celebrity chef, inspired by the cooking lessons that Marcus's mother had given her. She's engaged to Brandon Choi (Kim), a wealthy Elon Musk–type who treats Sasha more as a brand to manage than a lover or life partner. Marcus, meanwhile, has mostly stalled out in life, working with his widowed father (Saito) doing air-conditioning repairs, while fronting a mostly obscure alt-rap band called Hello Peril and dating a dreadlocked bohemian named Jenny (Bang).

Ali Wong and Randall Park

After Sasha dumps Brandon (he delays their wedding date to take a soul-searching trip to India with *Top Chef* host Padma Lakshmi), she almost immediately runs into Marcus when he and his father are hired to install her air-conditioning. After some initial friction, they decide to let bygones be bygones and resume their friendship, though Marcus admits to his father that he regrets having clumsily ruined their chance at more. His father urges him to tell her, but by the time he builds up the confidence to do so, she's already moved on to a new love interest: Keanu Reeves (playing a hilarious version of himself). She invites Marcus and Jenny to join them for a double date that begins with a pretentious dinner at a hot spot called Maximal, featuring absurd dishes. (A beef entrée comes with headphones playing a recording of the cow being killed while you eat it.) But the restaurant is just the disastrous appetizer for the date's catastrophic main course, which takes place when Keanu invites everyone back to his hotel room and demands they play a game of confessing secrets. Sasha's secret is that she still has feelings for Marcus, which leads Keanu to threaten to kill him, and Marcus to punch Keanu in the face in preemptive self-defense. Sasha

Ali Wong. Randall Park. Daniel Dae Kim. Keanu Reeves. Need I say more? Big-studio comedies with all–Asian American casts are few and far between, and *Always Be My Maybe* set a contemporary gold standard for streaming success. As a comedy creator and performer, I found the film's hilarious but real characters, simple story, and love quadrangle to be inspiring and unlike anything I'd ever seen on-screen before. In pitches, Hollywood executives are constantly asking folks who look like us to add an identity conflict or culture clash to our stories, and it was nice just to see two friends falling in love and all the ridiculous shenanigans that go along with that. Movies like *Always Be My Maybe* normalize Asian Americans in leading comedic roles and open doors for the next crop of filmmakers like myself.

—SUJATA DAY ON *ALWAYS BE MY MAYBE*

and Marcus leave in an Uber, while Jenny stays behind to keep "talking" to Keanu. When they arrive at Sasha's apartment, they make love for the first time as adults, closing the gap that has existed between them since their teenage years.

But the pair have a ways to go to get to their happy ending. It takes self-reflection and humility on the part of Marcus and candor and commitment on the part of Sasha for the pair to finally feel safe and complete—making it the rare rom-com to acknowledge that meet-cutes and hot sex aren't quite enough to paper over youthful trauma and years of distance.

Always Be My Maybe proved to be enormously popular, and in the process gave a career boost to both Randall Park—as he leveraged the goodwill from *Always* to launch his own production company with Golamco, Imminent Collision—and Keanu Reeves, whose supremely self-satirizing performance reminded people of how exceptionally good he is at comedy, while unleashing a new barrage of internet memes celebrating his unique awesomeness.

The Half of It

2020, PG-13, 104 MINUTES, NETFLIX, USA

DIRECTOR/WRITER: Alice Wu

STARRING: Leah Lewis, Daniel Diemer, Alexxis Lemire, Enrique Murciano, Wolfgang Novogratz, Catherine Curtin, Becky Ann Baker, Collin Chou

The Half of It, the second feature film from Alice Wu, director of the iconic 2004 rom-com *Saving Face*, came after a gap of almost two decades; it bears much of the same DNA as Wu's first film—it's about a young woman who can't quite publicly express her love for another woman, whose choices in life are constrained by the feelings of responsibility she owes to the single parent who raised her—but it addresses its underlying themes with a very different perspective. Most notably, *The Half of It* displays a pragmatic maturity about what's possible in a world that often denies, dismisses, or suppresses the kinds of love we can't choose—a wistful melancholia that serves as ground for budding hope. Though it takes the shape of an adaptation of the classic story of Cyrano de Bergerac—the brilliant, ugly man with a gigantic nose who serves as ghostwriter for the love letters of a handsome but vapid friend—by making "Cyrano" female, it invokes issues of sexual identity and the cold dynamics of parental/societal/religious approval to complicate and enrich the well-worn trope.

Ellie Chu (Lewis) and her single father, Edwin (Chou), are the only Asian family in the tiny, conservative fictional town of Squahamish, Washington. Mostly ignored by her classmates (unless they need to pay her to write them an A-grade paper), Ellie dreams of leaving the town for university—her dream school is the liberal arts mecca of Grinnell College—but can't imagine abandoning her father, still brokenhearted over the death of her mother years later, or putting the burden of college costs on his finances, which are uncertain enough that their power is constantly in danger of being shut off.

When Paul Munsky (Diemer), a good-natured but tongue-tied football player, offers Ellie a substantial sum to write not an English essay but a love letter, she initially says no. The letter is intended for Aster Flores (Lemire), the gorgeous and popular daughter of the minister at the town church, and Aster already has a boyfriend, wealthy, arrogant Trig Carson (Novogratz). But Paul's sincerity and Ellie's electricity bill convince her to serve as his courtship surrogate, and she begins a love campaign on his behalf, writing texts, messages, notes, and letters in his name to woo Aster. In the process, Ellie investigates her target and discovers Aster's hidden artistic soul, suppressed because she's been convinced by her father that the arts are inappropriate and impractical as an ambition.

Leah Lewis and Alexxis Lemire

The two girls bond deeply in their proxy communications (Ellie as Paul) and, eventually, in person (Ellie as Ellie). Aster invites Ellie to join her at a secret local hot spring; Aster dives in in the buff, while shy Ellie stumbles in wearing all her clothes. During their

get-together, Aster tells Ellie that Trig is planning on proposing to her, a move her father approves of but that she's less enthusiastic about, in part because of her growing attraction to Paul, or at least the "Paul" she knows through her messaging platforms; the

I've never thought of myself as a romantic person. The nineties rom-coms I watched growing up seemed to always imply that there was only one way to fall in love: Boy meets girl, girl gets swept off her feet, boy and girl go to prom (or some other big dance in a gymnasium), and it ends with a "happily ever after." That was a narrative I never saw myself fitting comfortably into. It seemed like every film about an awkward teen girl ended with her taking off her glasses because a boy she was in love with told her to, and suddenly her life was changed for the better. But I was always waiting, searching for someone who looked—and felt—like me. So, when *The Half of It* came along in 2020, it was a surprise in the best way. I saw myself in Ellie. I saw how non-romantic love can be grounding and can serve as a path toward authenticity. Watching the film, I found myself not only transported back to high school but dropped in a queer love story that didn't put romance on a pedestal as the be-all, end-all of happiness. I wish I had this film growing up. I'm grateful I have it now.

—TRACI LEE ON *THE HALF OF IT*

face-to-face dates they've had have been just short of disastrous. Their time together helps Ellie to conclude she's falling for Aster herself, creating a complicated love triangle made even more difficult when Paul, tossed in a whirlwind of confusing emotions, kisses Aster, attempts to kiss Ellie (to her horror), and then realizes the true orientation of Ellie's feelings, which he declares a sin. The three-legged stool fully collapses at Aster's father's church, where Paul and Ellie—the church's organist, despite not being a believer—interrupt Trig's proposal to Aster by sharing their own respective definitions of love. Ellie's declaration happens to include language that "Paul" had shared in a prior letter, leading Aster to realize the trickery in which the two have engaged. She slaps Paul and stomps out of the congregation.

In the wake of the explosion, Ellie has decided to attend Grinnell, at her father's urging, and seeks out Aster to apologize to her before she leaves. Aster tells Ellie that in a different time and place, she might have been in love with her and suggests that they could have been together. Also, she's applying to art school, emboldened by Paul's (a.k.a. Ellie's) supportive words. Ellie impulsively kisses her and tells her that she'll see her in a few years (i.e., a different time and place). She leaves for the train, where she says bye to Paul. As the train pulls away, Paul runs after it, keeping pace, in a callback to a movie the two of them saw together while Paul was trying to learn the meaning of romance.

The movie ends with a message that is quite different than the one in *Saving Face*: As Ellie says in her church speech, love isn't by nature patient or kind, but horrible, selfish, and bold; one shouldn't expect

perfection, an ideal "other half," but rather another flawed human, trying and failing to fit. True love is not pushing someone to change but loving someone despite their inability to change. The message may be just as well applied to movies as to relationships: If *Saving Face* was something close to a perfect Asian American rom-com, hitting the tropes and expectations of the genre in virtuoso fashion, then *The Half of It* is purposely imperfect—a non-rom-com that ends in satisfying, deliberately unsatisfying fashion.

Fire Island

2022, R, 105 MINUTES, HULU, USA

DIRECTOR: Andrew Ahn

STARRING: Joel Kim Booster, Bowen Yang, Conrad Ricamora, James Scully, Margaret Cho, Zane Phillips

WRITER: Joel Kim Booster

This deliriously unexpected and outrageously queer rom-com was originally commissioned by the short-lived short-format streaming platform Quibi, which famously raised $1.75 billion—$1 billion of which went to developing original content—before imploding and selling off its library of content assets

(From left) Bowen Yang, Tomas Matos, Matt Rogers, Torian Miller; (from bottom left) Joel Kim Booster, Margaret Cho

for less than $100 million. The thesis of Quibi was that younger audiences had no attention spans and wanted to watch videos of no more than ten minutes in length on their mobile devices; as a result, Quibi productions were chopped up into brief mini-episodes and formatted exclusively for phones. But it's hard to imagine *Fire Island*, originally commissioned for Quibi, working as effectively in ten-minute expository chunks.

The film, a loose adaptation of Jane Austen's classic *Pride and Prejudice* set in the gay hot spots of New York's Fire Island, works precisely because of its ability to luxuriate in creating its characters rather than clipping them into brief stereotypes. (It also helps that in its feature-film version, *Fire Island*'s director is Andrew Ahn, whose 2016 film *Spa Night* demonstrated his deft skill at depicting the intersections of queer and Asian American culture, though this is a decidedly different kind of movie.)

Fire Island begins with a crew of longtime friends arriving for their annual holiday at the gay vacation mecca, led by Noah (Kim Booster, who also wrote the screenplay) and his best friend, Howie (Yang). Noah is unapologetically there to get some, while introverted Howie is prepared for another week of people watching and maybe catching up on his reading. This year, though, Noah isn't having it—he's determined to get Howie laid, and he vows to be celibate himself until the deed is done. It's especially urgent because according to their "den mother" and host Erin (Cho), this might be the last holiday on the island for the friends: The personal injury settlement with which she's been paying for her Pines cottage has run out, and she must sell the place.

That night, the friends head to the island's biggest bar, and Noah spots someone who looks like an ideal match for Howie—a handsome doctor named Charlie (Scully). But Charlie's not alone; he too has a friend in tow, sullen, bookish lawyer Will (Ricamora). If Charlie's going to be freed up to get to know Howie, Noah has no choice but to entertain Will, even though the two have taken an instant dislike to one another. The next day, Noah invites Charlie (and Will) to dinner at their place. But while shopping for groceries, Noah runs into a hot guy named Dex (Phillips) who clearly rubs Will the wrong way. Out of spite and more than a little attraction, Noah invites Dex over for dinner too. At the meal, despite their antipathy, it's clear Noah and Will have more in common than either wants to admit (beyond both being Asian). Dex and Noah flirt, but Noah's first focus is connecting Charlie and Howie.

The next day, the group heads for the big weekly underwear party in Cherry Grove, where Noah runs into Dex and finally gives in to temptation and has sex with him in the dark room, but Will's sudden appearance leads to a chaotic fracas in which Dex gets smacked in the nose, and Noah sees Charlie kissing someone other than Howie. As Noah and Will walk back to the Pines, they fight, with Noah calling Will a stiff-necked, judgmental jerk and Will calling Noah vain and self-involved; neither is entirely wrong.

The group heads to an after-party, in which Noah tries to comfort Howie over Charlie's apparent betrayal but ends up provoking him. Howie accuses Noah of assuming they've had the same journey just because they're both gay and Asian, and they part ways in a huff. The next day, Noah wakes to read a letter from Will, explaining his history with Dex—who he says hurt someone important to him—and telling him not to trust him. Meanwhile, Charlie has come over to talk to Howie, and what Charlie says causes Howie to throw himself into Erin's pool. It seems that the man Charlie was making out with the night before is his ex, who has Lyme disease; the diagnosis has motivated Charlie to leave the island to take care of him. Noah and Will then run into each other at a drag bar, where Will shows Noah Dex's social media—which is full of thirst-trap pictures tagged with hashtags designed to lure Black and Asian activist types. Red flags abound. Noah and Will continue to get closer, with Noah even convincing Will to get onstage with the drag queens to give a comically awkward performance.

Eventually, Will is able to help give Dex his comeuppance, when the latter posts a video of himself having sex with another of their friends without consent, and Will invokes his legal prowess to intimidate Dex into removing the video. Will's gavel drop convinces Noah that it's worth giving a relationship with him a chance. And meanwhile, Howie's public announcement of his feelings gets Charlie to change his mind and pursue him before he leaves the island, even if it takes Noah and the crew hijacking a water taxi to make their meet-cute reunion happen.

Fire Island is far from a perfect movie, but it's fun, clever, and proud of what it is and the community it represents—and it underscores the degree to which Asian American stories are now able to embrace specificity while appealing to smaller, more intersectional audiences, rather than watering down narratives to accommodate the "masses."

"Romance is not practical."

A Talk with **Simu Liu** and **Alice Wu**

It took a while for stories of Asian love to make it to American screens, but once they crashed the party, movies like *Crazy Rich Asians* and *Always Be My Maybe* showed that Asians are quite capable of delivering the swoon. In this Q&A, actor Simu Liu (*Shang-Chi and the Legend of the Ten Rings*) and filmmaker Alice Wu (*Saving Face, The Half of It*) talk about the racial politics of romance, the aching need we sometimes have to touch and be touched, and the ways in which love is a many-splendored—and gendered—thing.

We'll get right into it. Why do you think it took so long for Asian American romances to appear on-screen?

SIMU LIU: Well, historically, cinema has been framed from a predominantly white male perspective. That means Asian male characters would rarely be three dimensional or aspirational, much less romantically appealing. And meanwhile, Asian women were often fetishized as docile, submissive sex objects. You can see how that combination might serve as an obstacle to depicting Asians through a romantic lens. I can't say that I even remember seeing two Asian people kissing in a Hollywood film until I reached adulthood.

ALICE WU: But most Asian American indie films haven't focused on romance either. And I think there are reasons for that: Ours is still a majority immigrant community, and if you're the new kid on the block, that first generation basically has to just figure out how to survive. Romance is not practical. In a lot of ways, it's the opposite of practical. So maybe it takes two or three generations to get to a point where you're ready to make romance a focus, something you can tell stories about. And I think American romantic cinema is a late bloomer—but as a result, our romantic movies contain all the beauty and the pain of being a late bloomer.

I can see that. A lot of us—not all!—were definitely slower to experience romance than our non-Asian friends.

ALICE: Well, I was a very quiet kid, and we moved every two or three years. And so I ended up being more of an observer than a doer. I'd see people who really knew how to work it and were popular and socially integrated, and I was always so impressed. I was like, "Wow, how did they do that?" Because I had zero idea. I ended up watching movies to try to understand them—like, "What is this world they belong to?" And now maybe I'm making movies to try to understand them?

SIMU: But movies and TV didn't reflect the world we actually lived in. I was big into, you know, teen dramas, all the shows featuring brooding white emo kids. And even though I didn't see myself depicted in them, some of their themes translated over to me. Oh, so the jocks are the cool kids? And the cool kids get girlfriends? I guess that means I have to be good at sports and go to parties and try to be on top of the social hierarchy. And because I'm Asian and I'm fighting the shadow of Long Duk Dong, it's even harder: I have to be *really* good at sports, go to a *lot* of parties, and be at the *very top* of the social hierarchy if I want to have romantic options at all. Everything I saw in the media portrayed me as undesirable, so my assumption was that in every room I walked into, that was something I had to overcome. I guess that's the textbook definition of an inferiority complex, but that's what these depictions of dorky Asian sidekick characters instilled in me.

I suppose we didn't have a lot of role models for romance—on-screen or off.

SIMU: Well, I think as children of immigrants, you don't always have parents who are touchy-feely, or open about physical affection, with each other or with you. I'd sometimes look at my friends' families, and I'd look at white families on TV and think, *Damn it, why isn't my family more like that? Why isn't my house just full of physical affection being given in abundance?* And maybe that's why we're seeing this recent Asian American rom-com renaissance. We're telling these stories as a kind of proxy for that abundance.

ALICE: I guess for me, the lack of romantic models has led me to make movies that all ask the same question: Is it even possible to have romantic love and love for your family, and have them coexist peacefully? Because as an Asian lesbian, that did not seem possible in, you know, the year 2000. Now it seems possible, but not then. And maybe that's why I don't really make romantic comedies in the traditional sense, where "getting the girl" is the most important thing. For me, the key relationship is not actually the romantic couple, but two other people. Like, *Saving Face* is really a "romance" between a mother and a daughter. And *The Half of It* is really a "romance" between two friends. The romantic plot acts as a red herring that makes you consider the impact of romance on others.

People tend to think of romance as just fluff, trivial stuff. But it has ripple effects on everything around us.

SIMU: There's a reason why most Hollywood stories revolve around love and romance, to some degree! Which, of course, is part of the reason why Asian men have not had so many chances to be leading men—it's directly linked to the fact that nobody sees us as romantically viable. In most Hollywood movies, romance is an intrinsic part of being a cinematic protagonist. You can't just be funny or interesting or competent; you can't just fix problems or defeat the villain. Audiences also expect you to "get the girl"— or guy—at the narrative's end. And if the powers that be can't imagine you doing that, you're probably not getting cast as the lead.

ALICE: But the rising tide of romantic comedy lifts all boats! I loved that in *Crazy Rich Asians*, the Asian men were all very sexy and hot. I loved it even though I'm not attracted to men, because I love that Asian people can be seen as attractive or sexy, no matter their gender. And that Hollywood looked at the results and said, "Oh, that movie made money! Let's make more Asian stories!"—the fact that that's what it took to finally break the dam still seems a bit ridiculous to me, but I'm grateful it happened.

At the end of the day, what do you think romance means to you?

SIMU: Well, honestly, it's something I've had to relearn over time. Growing up in the Western world, there's this expectation that men need to take charge, be extroverted, and have these aggressive traits in romantic situations. And I look at Tony Leung, who played my father in *Shang-Chi*. He's been the biggest male lead in Asia for decades, and he has this incredible ability to evoke romance with stillness and nuance. Part of it is just that there's a different sense of what it means to be masculine in Asia, but part of it is also him being in a film industry where there was an abundance of opportunities to play romantic leads. For a lot of Asian Americans, we are only now getting our chance at bat, and the learning curve is high. As someone who grew up thinking the be-all and end-all of masculinity was the high school jock, one of the joys of getting older and attaining a degree of self-awareness has been learning that yeah, I don't need to be that guy.

ALICE: The learning journey is so important. Part of what romance means to me is coming to the realization that things can never truly be perfect, but standing your ground, sticking with it, and trying to make it work anyway. That's true about movies too. Maybe that explains why I've only made two movies! I'm just a very monogamous filmmaker.

Afterword

I remember when I first discovered the power of cinema. It wasn't in the movie theater—although I loved movies and thrilled to the experience of seeing them along with others.

No, the moment I realized the power of movies, the power to move hearts and minds, was when I first picked up a video camera, turned it to face other human beings, and saw their faces light up when they realized that for the very first time, they were *being seen*.

And it wasn't even a real camera. I was in middle school, and I'd made a fake camera out of a tissue box. Even though it was a prop, it gave me permission to go around "interviewing" people at lunch. Fame overnight, every group wanted me around, including ones who'd ignored me in the past. I could ask any question. I could express myself however I wanted. All because I had this device that made people feel like they were the center of attention, if only for a few minutes at a time.

Because that's something we hunger for as humans. We instinctively want to know that we cast a reflection; that we matter to others, and that we'll be remembered by lingering images we've left behind after we're gone. And that's not even considering the creativity involved in turning those images into full-fledged stories. When you bring the impact of being seen and the power of storytelling together, you get a unique kind of magic—one that can make people laugh and cry and scream, that can turn back time, and erase the divides of geography, language, and culture, that can speak truth into the world or bring the fantastical into existence.

That's the magic of movies. And for us, a community that has been invisible for so long, *movies matter*. I still remember the day I saw *The Joy Luck Club*. It was a big moment for us. My dad had organized the outing and even he didn't quite know what to expect; he only knew that this was the first time a family like ours was being shown on screen in a big Hollywood movie. So he decided to bring everyone—my mother, me, and my four siblings—to go see it on a Sunday morning together at this little theater near our house in Cupertino. Seeing the aunties talk like my aunties, the uncles talk like my uncles, getting the inside jokes and crying at stories that sounded like some of the ones in our own family tree, it was incredible.

Afterward we went to dim sum and talked about it for hours. And for years later, we'd drop quotes from the movie—*best quality!*—into our conversations with one another. Because it allowed us to see our own reflection and gave us a common language to talk about things that we often didn't talk about.

But as powerful and as important as *The Joy Luck Club* was for Asian Americans, it didn't do the kind of numbers Hollywood expected. It made about $33 million, more than three times its budget; that still wasn't nearly enough to drag the studios out of their nearly century-long rut of dismissing, erasing, and stereotyping Asians. They went right back to making mass-market entertainment for an audience that was never as white as they imagined.

It took two decades more for the tide to finally turn, two decades during which Asian America tripled in size from 7 million to 21 million, and became the most educated, most professional, most technologically savvy part of the US population. Two decades during which the pop culture powerhouses of Japan, Hong Kong, India, and Korea cranked out some of the most influential work and biggest stars in global entertainment. Two decades in which the Internet exploded, and a generation of creators—many of them Asian American—demonstrated that it was possible to build audiences of millions without the resources and star power of the studios.

All this magic was happening around me, and yet I almost missed it. I'd spent a decade making movies, and, other than my student thesis project at USC, had never made a film that was anchored in my own cultural identity. Though it won acclaim and awards, that first attempt to tell a story about being Asian American ultimately felt so distant and shallow to me that I vowed not to try again until both I and the world had matured enough to do it right.

In 2016, the Coalition of Asian Pacifics in Entertainment (CAPE) had a twenty-fifth anniversary gala—I was shocked that an organization like CAPE had even been around for a quarter century!—and it was at that event that I realized the world, at least, might just be ready. The cast of the hit Asian American family sitcom *Fresh Off the Boat* was there. YouTube influencers and creators with millions of followers were there. Directors and studio executives

and actors like Steven Yeun and Daniel Dae Kim and yes, the stunning ladies of *The Joy Luck Club* were there. They all were dynamic and glamorous and, for the first time, it felt like we didn't just have stars, but a whole constellation.

It was a magic moment. And into that moment a book came into my life, a brilliantly dishy bestseller that took a satirical look at Singapore's super-rich through the eyes of a very familiar protagonist: A Chinese American woman named Rachel Chu with roots in Cupertino, whose cousin, according to the book, was a movie director.

Her last name was *Chu?* She had roots in *Cupertino?* And her cousin was a *filmmaker?* It was like the book had been written with me in mind to direct. And when I met its author, Kevin Kwan, it turned out that in a sense, it had—he was, in fact, friends with my cousin, and my cousin had told him about me and my family, and now I was being asked to turn it into a movie.

That's what finally helped me decide it was time to make an Asian American movie—one that would invite everyone in and be a fun, joyful ride that people would want to go on again and again. For me, that's the essence of movies: the community they create and the shared imagination they spur in those who watch them.

This book felt destined to be that movie. The title alone was evocative; it would create debate. And the Rachel Chu character was an Asian American striver from a blue-collar background who visits Asia for the first time and faces the supercilious judgment of a condescending upper class. I knew what that felt like. I knew that people would be attracted to that trope, and to the glorious color and energy of what we could show them through the fashion, music, pop culture, and architecture of Asia. And it was a rom-com, which would let us show off the ability of Asian Americans to be sexy and loving and debonair but also human and funny and vulnerable.

And if you took all those actors I saw at the CAPE event, all those stars just beginning to sparkle, that's the untapped energy source we needed to make this happen. Michelle Yeoh—as soon as I thought of Eleanor, I thought instantly of her. Who else could pull it off the way she could? Awkwafina. Constance Wu. Ronny Chieng. Jimmy O. Yang. All of them were in my pitch for the movie before we even started casting. We were assembling the Asian Avengers to reverse generations of invisibility, with the goal of making us the center of attention, if only for 121 minutes.

Turning *Crazy Rich Asians* from a movie into a movement took more than just an amazing cast, an incredible script, and big-studio belief and support: It took a concerted effort by an entire nation of Asian Americans, from the group of tech entrepreneurs and Hollywood icons who gathered in my family's restaurant and pledged to buy out whole theaters on opening weekend, to the activists, cultural critics, and community organizers who highlighted Asian America's need for representation, explained the deeper context behind the story and used the movie to bring generations together.

In the process, we proved something: That our stories were worth telling—and watching. That we could pull together and remake the rules of Hollywood. That all we ever deserved was the same chance everyone else has had for a hundred years—to point the magic eye of the camera at ourselves rather than serve as the blank screen of someone else's imagination. If *Crazy Rich Asians* opened doors, it was only because so many people before us spent their lives trying to push them ajar. We've always had the people and the passion and the purpose; we just never had the permission.

Now we have the green light. We're ready. The screen is ours. And the future is gold.

—JON M. CHU

Acknowledgments

This book is built on and dedicated to the incredible work of generations of Asian American performers, filmmakers, and critics, many of whom toiled with little recognition or reward, and who might never have seen or benefited from the changes that their contributions have manifested in our society and community. Thanks to them for laying the foundations.

Special thanks to the many dozens of people who shared with me their memories and experiences of the movies in this volume—friends, mentors, inspirations, past and future collaborators—and the wonderful creators and artists who spoke with me for this book's wonderfully insightful conversations: Janet Yang, Bao Nguyen, Daniel Kwan, Diane Paragas, Ronny Chieng, Daniel Wu, Daniel Dae Kim, Kelly Marie Tran, Justin Chon, Renee Tajima-Peña, Ken Jeong, John Cho, Nisha Ganatra, Kal Penn, Simu Liu, and Alice Wu, you've lit the way with your work and wisdom, both here and across the culture.

Thanks particularly to Michelle Yeoh and Jon M. Chu for bracketing this book with your brilliance. And to the talented illustrators who've brought a text about an inherently visual medium to life: Jun Cen, Cliff Chiang, Cryssy Cheung, Yu-Ming Huang, Jiyeun Kang, Ashraf Omar, Zi Xu, barbarian flower, and our amazing cover and chapter heading artist, Toma Nguyen; and to my book assistant Brandon Liao for keeping the trains running.

Thanks to the keepers of past legacies (in particular Arthur Dong and Shannon Lee); curators of the present (Asian American museums, film festival programmers and media arts organizations across the nation, #AsianFilmTwitter and my *Rise* coauthors Phil Yu and Philip Wang), and those laying a path to the future (the good folks at East West Players, Coalition of Asian Pacifics in Entertainment, Gold House, and other institutions and organizations engaged in training, advocacy, and funding of the next generation of talent).

This book wouldn't have been possible without the patience, love, and support of my family—YeWon Min, Hudson Yang, Skyler Yang, and my parents David and Bailing Yang—and all the close friends and colleagues with whom I've seen and enjoyed so many hundreds of these films in the course of my life. Thank you also to my agent Rachel Vogel at Dunow Carlson & Lerner, and to Becky Koh and her terrific team at Black Dog & Leventhal and Hachette Book Group.

But most of all, endless thanks are due to my editor Zander Kim, whose vision and passion sparked this project, for reaching out to me to bring it to life, and for the endless patience, persistence, hard work, and humor throughout the process of building it from blank pages to book. Stay gold, Zander.

Artists and Contributors

Artists

barbarian flower is an illustrator based in Malaysia. Favorite movie memory: "The movie that influenced me the most is Pixar's *Soul* because of the character Joe. I have been thinking about life after death and what life is. *Soul* reminds me to go after our dreams and that life only comes once. Be brave while you're alive or you won't have a chance."

Jun Cen is a New York–based illustrator from China. Jun's favorite movie from this book is *The Last Emperor* because of its spectacular depiction of the Forbidden City and the film's memorable soundtrack.

Cryssy Cheung is a Chinese American from New York City. She is a freelance art director, illustrator, and designer. Her favorite movies and TV shows growing up were anything *Journey to the West* because of the adventure.

Cliff Chiang is a Taiwanese American comic book artist from New Jersey. An Eisner Award winner and the co-creator of *Paper Girls*, his most recent book is *Catwoman: Lonely City* from DC Comics. Favorite movie memory: He has always had a soft spot for Egg Shen (*Big Trouble in Little China*).

Yu-Ming Huang is from Taiwan, R.O.C. Currently, he is a freelance illustrator serving mainstream brands in the United States. Favorite movie memory: "Any movie directed by Stephen Chow, a legend in most Chinese people's minds."

Jiyeun Kang is from South Korea. She is an illustrator of the Anna Goodson illustration agency. Favorite movie memory: I love *The Scent of Green Papaya*'s simple beauty, peaceful moods, and heart-rending stories of growth and discovery like its lovely movie poster.

Toma Nguyen is an illustrator from Vietnam with the agency IllustrationX. Favorite movie memories: "*Searching* and *Everything, Everywhere, All at Once*—I love the theme of Asian family movies, they are culturally rich and deeply associated with my childhood."

Ashraf Omar is an illustrator hailing from Malaysia, whose passion for the Star Wars franchise has greatly influenced his art. Luke Skywalker, in particular, serves as a constant source of inspiration for him, shaping his imaginative and creative style.

Zi Xu is from Hainan, China, but she immigrated to the US at a young age and now lives in California. An illustrator and poster artist who loves classic films, she enjoys incorporating historical styles and influences in her work. She's also passionate about Asian representation in American media, and had been wanting an excuse to paint Anna May Wong professionally for some time before finally getting this job!

Contributors

Tanzila "Taz" Ahmed is a political strategist, storyteller, and artist living in Los Angeles known for being the host of the award-winning podcast *Good Muslim Bad Muslim*. Favorite movie memory: "When Dominic Rain's character is playing the azaan on his bass guitar while standing on the roof of a punk house in *The Taqwacores*."

Eric Byler is the director of *Charlotte Sometimes, Tre, Americanese* and a co-director of the documentary *9500 Liberty*. Favorite movie memory: "Watching the impromptu piano recital scene in *Yellow*—for the audience reaction (it was the world premiere at NAATA) as much as the performances and filmmaking."

Momo Chang is a journalist who covers arts, culture, health, and community and the former content manager at the Center for Asian American Media. Favorite movie memory: "The in-person screenings I've attended at CAAMFest and the LA Asian Pacific Film Festival have all been special."

Walter Chaw is a senior film critic for FilmFreakCentral.net and author of *Miracle Mile* and *A Walter Hill Film*. Favorite movie memory: "When Short Round puts a torch in Indiana Jones's side, waking him from his trance in *Temple of Doom*."

Laura Mariko Cheifetz is a queer multiracial Asian American of Japanese and white Jewish descent, an ordained Presbyterian Church (USA) minister, theological education professional, occasional writer, and rescue dog mom. Favorite movie moment: "When the humpback whales are beamed onto the *Enterprise* in *Star Trek IV*."

Bing Chen is an impact founder and investor as CEO of AU Holdings, cofounder and chairman of Gold House, and a principal architect of YouTube's global digital creator ecosystem. Favorite movie memory: "When the last petal fell in *Beauty and the Beast*, I learned what love was."

Lynn Chen is an actress, filmmaker, and creator of *The Yellow Pages* newsletter and *The Actor's Diet* blog and podcast. Favorite movie memory: "The moment where Tamlyn Tomita puts her hair down before kissing Daniel in *Karate Kid II*."

Preeti Chhibber is an author living the dream of writing her favorite characters, including her latest *Spider-Man's Bad Connection*. Favorite movie memory: "Kal Penn struggling to tell his dad he didn't want to be a doctor in *Harold & Kumar* was perfectly and painfully familiar."

Curtis Chin is a documentary film-maker and the author of a memoir, *Everything I Learned, I Learned in a Chinese Restaurant*. Favorite movie memory: "After my dad died, I couldn't cry, except in the theater while watching *Brokeback Mountain*, which I ended up doing almost a dozen times."

Tanuj Chopra is showrunner/director of the Emmy Award–winning *Delhi Crime* on Netflix and directed such films as *Punching at the Sun*, *Chee and T*, and *Staycation*. Favorite movie memory: "Really hard to beat the time when Optimus Prime tells Megatron, "One shall stand, and one shall fall," in *Transformers: The Movie*."

Eileen Cheng-yin Chow was often a kid extra because she lived next door to the Central Motion Pictures studio lot in Taipei; now she teaches film, literature, and storytelling at Duke University. Favorite movie memory: "Walking out of *Amélie* at 14 and feeling very childlike/delighted and cultured/grown-up at the same time."

Keith Chow is the creator of The Nerds of Color and host of the podcasts *Hard NOC Life* and *Southern Fried Asian*. *Vanity Fair* calls him an "incisive interviewer and chummy conversationalist." Favorite movie memory: "Watching *Batman* approximately 152 times in the summer of 1989, then getting the VHS for my birthday that fall and watching it 150 times more."

Philip W. Chung is a Los Angeles–based writer and producer. Favorite movie memory: "With the rise in anti-Asian violence, watching the final shot of hapa filmmaker Beth de Araújo's *Soft & Quiet*—a powerful reminder that they can't keep us all down...literally."

Sujata Day is a 2023 NAACP Image Award–nominated director for her Netflix feature film, *Definition Please*, which she also wrote, produced, and stars in. She is a native of Pittsburgh. Favorite movie memory: "When the kids chase the train in *Pather Panchali*, I'm overwhelmed with Bengali pride and emotion."

Stephanie Foo wrote the book *What My Bones Know: A Memoir of Healing from Complex Trauma* and is a journalist and radio producer for shows like *Snap Judgment*, *This American Life*, and *Invisibilia*. Favorite movie memory: Walking out of *Amélie* at 14 and feeling very childlike/delighted and cultured/grown-up at the same time.

Jamie Ford is the bestselling author of *The Many Daughters of Afong Moy* and *Hotel at the Corner of Bitter and Sweet*. Favorite movie memory: "Seeing my grandfather on film in *Secret Agent X-9* (1945) with Key Luke and Benson Fong."

Linde Ge is a screenwriter whose most recent credits include the CW's *Kung Fu* and Peacock's *Vampire Academy*. Favorite movie memory: "Wearing out our family's copy of *Speed* on VHS by watching it at least once a day after school."

Thao Ha is a writer, philanthropist, and professor of sociology at MiraCosta College. Favorite movie memory: "Seeing so much of myself in *Bend It like Beckham*!"

Brian Hu is the artistic director of the San Diego Asian Film Festival and associate professor in film at San Diego State University. Favorite movie memory: "Till sickness and DEATH!," from *The Wedding Banquet*.

Frankie Huang is a culture writer and illustrator, and the co-editor of Asian American feminist outlet *Reappropriate*. Favorite movie memory: "When, in *Eternal Sunshine of the Spotless Mind*, Joel's dream version of Clementine tells a deeply regretful Joel to try his best to remember her, as his memories of their relationship are erased."

Anna John is the Los Angeles–based cofounder of the seminal Desi group blog *Sepia Mutiny*. Favorite movie memory: Getting a DVD of *The Sound of Music* for Christmas after she broke her VHS copy from overuse. She has seen the movie over 150 times.

Michael Kang is a filmmaker based in Los Angeles, known for *The Motel* and *West 32nd*. Favorite movie memory: "The opening tea house shootout in John Woo's *Hardboiled*."

Albert Kim is a TV writer and producer, best known for creating and executive producing Netflix's live-action adaptation of *Avatar: The Last Airbender*. Favorite movie memory: "Watching *Enter the Dragon*, the first time I saw someone who looked like me as the hero of the story...a hero who could kick James Bond's ass."

Anthony Y. Kim is a multimedia storyteller based in Los Angeles. Favorite movie memory: Tony Leung whispering his secret into a hole in the wall of a temple at Angkor Wat in *In the Mood for Love*.

Lee Ann Kim is the founder of the San Diego Asian Film Festival and a former news anchor/reporter for KGTV. Favorite movie memory: "Seeing a woman of Korean descent in a leading role for the first time: Sandra Oh in Mina Shum's *Double Happiness*. I thought to myself, 'Damn, she's a pretty good actor (for a Korean), *and* she can run!'"

Nic Cha Kim is an Emmy-winning journalist and producer of the documentary series Artbound on KCET and PBS SoCal. Favorite movie memory: "Watching *Indiana Jones and the Temple of Doom* at the age of nine at Grauman's Chinese Theatre."

Michelle Krusiec is an actor, writer, and director whose favorite roles include Wil Pang in *Saving Face* and Anna May Wong in *Hollywood*. Favorite movie memory: "Trying to show my Mom *The Joy Luck Club* as an attempt to express some of my feelings around being her daughter, while she kept running off to cook in the kitchen. My plan ultimately failed."

Scott Kurashige is author of *The Shifting Grounds of Race* and co-author with Grace Lee Boggs of *The Next American Revolution*. Favorite movie memory: "Watching the scene with my aunt in *Snow Falling on Cedars* where Japanese Americans are being shipped off to camp and hearing her say, 'There I am!'"

Anderson Le is the artistic director of the Hawai'i International Film Festival and co-founder of EAST Films. Favorite movie memory: "My refugee parents mistakenly taking me to see *Flesh Gordon* instead of *Flash Gordon*. Eye opening!"

Brook Lee was the first Miss Universe of Korean and Hawaiian ancestry. Favorite movie memory: "Reef Rash Brah! Scar fo' life," from *North Shore*.

Jennifer 8. Lee is co-founder of Plympton, Inc., producer of the documentaries *The Search for General Tso* and *The Emoji Story*, and author of *The Fortune Cookie Chronicles*. Favorite movie moment: "The watermelon-slicing scene in *The Joy Luck Club*—and then many years later meeting Russell Wong in person at an Asian American gala in San Francisco!"

Stacey Lee is the *New York Times* best-selling author of *The Downstairs Girl* and her most recent novel, *Luck of the Titanic*. Favorite movie memory: "Seeing Jason Scott Lee's butt in *Map of the Human Heart*."

Traci G. Lee is a Los Angeles–based, award-winning producer and the former editorial manager of NBC Asian America. Favorite movie memory: "Watching *Mulan* in theaters and being in awe of finally seeing an Asian Disney heroine."

Judy Lei is an actor, writer, filmmaker, and community organizer, born and raised in NYC's Brooklyn and Chinatown. Favorite movie memory: "When Elaine tells Raymond and Tina she will not keep their red envelope money. <broken heart emoji>"

Michelle Li is the co-founder of the Very Asian Foundation, a children's author, transracial adoptee, and news anchor in St. Louis. Favorite movie memory: "When Jo Koy says in *Easter Sunday* that he's already doing a 'half-Filipino accent' when he's asked about doing an accent for a TV role. My new favorite movie moment!"

Shirley Li is a staff writer at *The Atlantic*. She covers Hollywood and the shifting culture of the American entertainment industry. Favorite movie memory: "What does Ponyo love? Ham. Who loved Ponyo instantly, at our first moviegoing experience sans parents? My sister and me."

Ashley Liao is a Los Angeles–based actress known for the film *Loveboat, Taipei* and *The Ballad of Songbirds and Snakes*. Favorite movie memory: Watching *Everything, Everywhere, All at Once* on Thanksgiving with family in the living room, and again on New Year's Eve with friends!

Dennis Liu is a writer and filmmaker best known for *Raising Dion* and *Ling*. Favorite movie memory: Meeting my wife Marie at an NYU Asian American film class in 2003, the same year *Better Luck Tomorrow* was taking over Sundance.

Theresa Loong is an artist and interactive media professional and the director of the documentary *Every Day Is a Holiday*. Favorite movie memory: "As a child, watching an age-inappropriate slasher movie with my father at the Music Palace in NYC's Chinatown."

Lori Lopez is a professor of communication arts and the director of Asian American Studies at the University of Wisconsin-Madison. Favorite movie memory: "Crying at the end of *The Joy Luck Club* every single time, no matter how many times I watch it."

Dave Lu is the managing partner of Hyphen Capital, organizer of Stand With Asian Americans, and was the executive producer of *38 at the Garden*. Favorite movie memory: As a kid, seeing another Asian kid, Ke Huy Quan, stealing every scene he was in throughout *Indiana Jones and the Temple of Doom*.

Grace Hwang Lynch is the communications and engagement director for the Center for Asian American Media and an essayist writing about Taiwanese food and family. Favorite movie memory: "'Best quality heart,' from *The Joy Luck Club*."

Dan Matthews is a creative producer and indie rapper (under the name DANakaDAN), a subject and producer of the documentary *aka DAN*, about his personal story as a Korean adoptee. Favorite movie memory: "Hearing Randall Park rap 'I Punched Keanu Reeves' in the ending credits of *Always Be My Maybe*. Beautiful."

Kristen Meinzer is a culture critic, podcaster, and author. She hosts *By The Book* and *Movie Therapy with Rafer & Kristen* podcasts. Favorite movie memory: "Seeing my family nonchalantly depicted in *Sideways*—Stephanie is Asian, her mother is white, her child is Black—it just is what it is. No explanation necessary."

Tze Ming Mok is a writer, activist, and race sociologist based in Auckland, New Zealand. Favorite movie memory: *"Hold on to your potatoes."*

Bao Nguyen is an Emmy-nominated filmmaker best known for his documentaries on Bruce Lee (*Be Water*), and Saturday Night Live (*Live From New York!*). Favorite movie memory: Seeing Jason Scott Lee's butt in *Map of the Human Heart*.

Hanh Nguyen is the senior editor for culture at Salon Media Group. Favorite movie memory: Juzo Itami's *Tampopo* made young me hungry for more: satires, food-centric films, art, and of course, noodles!

Rick Noguchi is a poet and children's book author and chief operating officer of programs and external relations at the Japanese American National Museum. Favorite movie memory: "The 'cat takes' during the sequence when Bruce Lee kicks Chuck Norris's ass in *The Way of the Dragon*."

Joy Osmanski is an actor, award-winning audiobook narrator, and educator. Favorite movie memory: "Watching my dear friend Lynn Chen's film *I Will Make You Mine* and knowing she was all of the reasons it was made."

Greg Pak is a comic book writer and filmmaker best known for *Robot Stories*, *Mech Cadet Yu*, and *Planet Hulk*. Favorite movie memory: "Seeing *A Great Wall* in 1986 and realizing anything was possible."

Jennifer Paz is an actor/singer known for *Steven Universe*, *Miss Saigon*, and is a writer/producer who is a 2023 National Alliance for Musical Theatre Writers Residency Grant recipient. Favorite movie memory: "When Abigail (Dolly De Leon) asked, "Who am I?" in *Triangle of Sadness*. Then she later gets down-and-naughty with Carl (Harris Dickenson); it was such an unexpected dalliance that made me cackle so hard!"

Bao Phi has been a performance poet since 1991. He has written two poetry collections, *Sông I Sing* and *Thousand Star Hotel*, and two children's books, *A Different Pond* and *My Footprints*. Favorite movie memory: Seeing the trailer for *Ong Bak: Thai Warrior* in a movie theater for the first time.

Pornsak Pichetshote is a multi-award-winning writer of comics and TV, best known for his comics *Infidel* and *The Good Asian*. Favorite movie memory: "Seeing *Rumble in the Bronx* and realizing Hong Kong's perception of New York is as skewed as New York's perspective of Hong Kong."

A. J. Rafael is a singer/songwriter known for his videos on YouTube, amassing over 1 million subscribers worldwide. Favorite movie memory:

"Watching *The Debut* as a kid and seeing a Filipino house, a Filipino cast, and all these Filipino traditions in a movie. I asked my mom to buy the DVD at Costco, not even realizing that the lead character Ben was also Rufio from *Hook*. Now I'm friends with Dante Basco. Would you look at that?"

Dino-Ray Ramos is a Los Angeles–based journalist who founded DIASPORA and has written for *Deadline Hollywood*, *Entertainment Tonight*, *Vogue*, and others. Favorite movie memory: "When Roger Ebert defended *Better Luck Tomorrow* at its Sundance premiere in 2002 against an ignorant critic."

Arune Singh is an entertainment marketing executive, comic book and prose writer, and a *Publishers Weekly* 2022 Star Watch honoree. Favorite movie memory: "I've never seen myself or my life reflected in a movie, but when I do, it'll be my favorite movie memory."

Simran Jeet Singh is the national bestselling author of *The Light We Give: How Sikh Wisdom Can Transform Your Life*. Favorite movie memory: "The discussion and outrage in Spike Lee's film *Inside Man* after police presume the Sikh character to be a criminal and take his turban."

Valerie Soe is a professor in the Asian American Studies department at San Francisco State University and is a writer and documentary filmmaker known for *Love Boat: Taiwan*. Favorite movie memory: "Sitting next to a Cantonese speaker during a Stephen Chow movie and realizing that I was only getting one-third of the jokes because they were untranslatable in English."

Aisha Sultan is a syndicated columnist, features writer, and independent filmmaker based in St. Louis, Missouri. Favorite movie memory: Watching the Bollywood smash hit *Dilwale Dulhania Le Jayegne* in a theater in Texas.

Renee Tajima-Peña is a documentary filmmaker best known for co-directing the Academy Award–nominated *Who Killed Vincent Chin*, and for directing *My*

America: Honk If You Love Buddha. She was showrunner of the groundbreaking PBS docuseries Asian Americans. Favorite movie memory: "Gorgeous Asian Americans dancing to 'Chop Suey' across a Technicolor dreamscape in *Flower Drum Song*."

Timothy Tau is an award-winning writer, director, and producer known for *Keye Luke, Nathan Jung v. Bruce Lee*, and the forthcoming *Russell Wong: Pioneer*. Favorite movie memory: "Realizing the true power of genre upon witnessing Bong Joon-ho's *Memories of Murder*, which seamlessly combined and integrated horror, drama, comedy, crime / procedural, and historical period piece, all in one film."

Jeremy Tran is the executive director, COO, and a co-founder of Gold House, the leading Asian Pacific changemaker community. Favorite movie memory: "All two hours and twenty minutes of *Everything Everywhere All at Once*."

Ada Tseng is the co-host of *Saturday School* podcast, creator of the Haikus With Hotties calendar, and an editor at the *Los Angeles Times*. Favorite movie memory: "The scene in *Colma: The Musical* when Rodel (H.P. Mendoza) jumps on top of the car and does a drunken duet with the car alarm."

Arun Venugopal is a senior reporter in the Race and Justice Unit at New York's flagship public radio station, WNYC. Favorite movie memory: "After mom proudly took ten-year-old me to a Malayalam movie and discovered that instead of scenes of pure village simplicity the characters had loud, grunty sex, in true Asian deflection mode, she held up a leaflet right in front of my eyes and started reading from it. Out loud!"

Kulap Vilaysack is a Los Angeles–based writer, director, producer, and podcaster. Favorite movie memory: "Watching *The Raid* in a theater and being amazed at its relentless artistry of brutality."

Cynthia Wang is a freelance pop culture writer, editor, and radio commentator based in Sydney, Australia. Favorite movie memory: "In *The Farewell*, whenever Awkwafina's Billi has to make small talk in American-accented Mandarin? I feel so seen!"

Oliver Wang is a Los Angeles–based culture writer and a professor of sociology at California State University Long Beach. Favorite movie memory: "Patrick Adiarte's doing his 'square, strictly' eyeroll at his dad in *Flower Drum Song*."

Philip Wang is a filmmaker (*Everything Before Us*, *Single by 30*, *Yappie*), co-founder of Wong Fu Productions, and co-author of the *New York Times* bestselling *Rise: A Pop History of Asian America from the Nineties to Now*. Favorite movie moment: "The end of *Armageddon*, when the crazy mechanic character is trying to get the rockets to turn on, slamming the panels and screaming, 'Russian components, American components—*all made in Taiwan!*' I remember as a kid feeling very seen at that moment."

Abigail Hing Wen is the *New York Times* bestselling author of the *Loveboat, Taipei* series of novels and executive producer of *Loveboat, Taipei*'s film adaptation. Favorite movie memory: "Lea Salonga was my hero in musicals, and I loved her voice in films—Jasmine in *Aladdin*, and *Mulan!*"

Alice Wong is a disabled activist based in San Francisco and author of *Year of the Tiger: An Activist's Life*. Favorite movie memory: "When Auntie Suyuan picked the crab and said, 'Best quality!' in *The Joy Luck Club*."

Kristina Wong is the first Asian American woman to be named Pulitzer Prize Finalist in Drama for her solo show *Kristina Wong, Sweatshop Overlord*. Favorite movie memory: "Remembering Deedee Magno in *The Mickey Mouse Club* and wanting to be her."

Dan Wu was a contestant on season 5 of MasterChef and is the founder of the restaurant Atomic Ramen. In 2022 he was elected as Lexington, Kentucky's first Asian American vice mayor. Favorite movie memory: "Seeing the promo picture for *Star Wars: Rogue One* almost a year before it came out and getting so hyped to see Donnie Yen, Jiang Wen, Riz Ahmed, and all the diversity of the cast...and immediately starting to work on my Baz Balbus cosplay for Comic-Con!"

Jen Yamato is a film reporter for the *Los Angeles Times* and co-host of the podcast *Asian Enough*. Favorite movie memory: "Watching the classics—*Aliens*, *Terminator 2: Judgment Day*—with my dad, who'd tape them onto VHS tapes off the TV."

Kelvin Han Yee is an actor whose career spans forty years of stage, film, and TV. He was a pioneer of the Asian American theater movement, originating characters in plays like *Yankee Dawg You Die* and in early Asian American films like *A Great Wall*. Kelvin is frequently seen as a guest star on television shows like *Hawaii Five-0*, *9-1-1*, *S.W.A.T.*, *Magnum P.I.*, *Kung Fu*, *Partner Track*, *The Brothers Sun*, and *Beef*.

Paula Yoo is an award-winning children's book and young adult author and a TV writer-producer whose credits range from NBC's *The West Wing* to the CW's *Supergirl*. Favorite movie moment: "When *They Call Me Bruce?* came out, I was a Korean American eighth grader living in a mostly white, conservative small town in Connecticut. It was the first time I had ever seen someone who not only resembled my dad but also shared his same corny 'dad joke' sense of humor. The movie always makes me smile and think of my dad, who died in 2016. Thank you, Johnny Yune, for representing corny Korean dads everywhere."

Phil Yu is the Peabody Award–winning creator of the blog *Angry Asian Man*, co-host of the podcast *They Call Us Bruce* and co-author of the *New York Times* bestselling *RISE*. Favorite movie memory: "Seeing *Crouching Tiger, Hidden Dragon*, opening night. When Michelle Yeoh is about to fight Zhang Ziyi, I swear I heard every single butt in the sold-out theater shifting forward in their seats."

William Yu is a Korean American screenwriter and creator of the viral phenomenon #StarringJohnCho. He is based in Los Angeles. Favorite movie memory: "'Asian August,' a succession of Asian movies in 2018 that proved every ignorant, close-minded assumption about our community wrong."

Nancy Wang Yuen is a sociologist and author of *Reel Inequality: Hollywood Actors and Racism*. Favorite movie memory: "Seeing Tamlyn Tomita as Waverly say, 'You don't know the power you have over me,' to Tsai Chin in *The Joy Luck Club* and realizing that I'd never seen my trauma so authentically represented before on-screen."

Helen Zia is an author and activist whose previous work, *Last Boat out of Shanghai*, was an NPR best book and shortlisted for a national PEN America award. Favorite movie memory: "Watching the film *Yi Yi* with Taiwan-born scientist Wen Ho Lee: how he laughed at the scene about the false spy accusations!"

Photo Credits

Index